# LEAD US NOT INTO TEMPTATION

Previously published as:

Balm in Gilead (Hardcover)

No Fall Too Far (Paperback)

# LEAD US NOT INTO TEMPTATION

A Baptist Minister's Personal Journey Through Drug Addiction

---

## DON JEFFRIES

Lake Wylie, SC

Published in Lake Wylie, SC

Jeffries, Don.
  Lead us not into temptation /don jeffries.

ISBN 10:  1-4662-9642-9 (softcover)
ISBN 13: 978-1-4662-9642-8 (softcover)

Printed in the United States of America
10 9 8 7 6 5 4 3 2 1
**FIRST EDITION**

*To my sons, Sean and Scott, from whom I got more than I ever gave; to my parents, for the loving environment they provided; and most especially to Joann, wife, lover, friend.*

## ACKNOWLEDGMENTS

The overwhelming majority of the information in this book comes from the mind and memory of Gordon Weekley. Providing that information was a remarkable achievement on his part, considering the fact that he was under the influence of drugs or alcohol for eighteen years, and considering, too, that he suffered periods of blackouts and bouts of deep depression. He told the story bravely, providing details that most of us, in the same position, would hide deep in our own personal closets.

There were many others who also helped, people who were there at Providence Baptist Church, like Jarvis Warren, Arthur Smith, Al Edwards, Howard Byrum, and Harry Bacon—good people, all.

Thanks also to the Rev. Henry Crouch, the pastor who replaced Gordon at Providence, and to Bonnie Adams, his administrative assistant, who went out of her way to get pertinent historical information for me. Tackie Vosburgh gave me newspaper accounts of the bank robbery; Gordon's favorite psychiatrist, Dr. Bill Griffin, helped me get a better picture of Gordon's stay at Appalachian Hall; and pharmacists Dan Lemelin and Al Simmons gave me valuable information about drugs and their effects. My thanks to them, and to author Sara Pitzer, for opening the door to August House, the original publisher, for me.

Gordon's sons were helpful, too, digging up memories that had to be painful for them.

Pat LeNeave, who for years worked closely with Gordon as director of operations for Rebound Christian Rehabilitation Center, shared with me her knowledge of his life and helped fill in many blanks.

Finally, thanks to my wife, Joann, who offered continual encouragement and trod softly those many mornings I sat behind the computer trying to find the right words to say about this remarkable man and his remarkable life.

*Lead us not Into Temptation*

# One

Dogwood, more than anything else, heralds the arrival of spring in North Carolina. It dominates the landscape from the mountains in the west to the Piedmont and down through the coastal plain. So beautiful, so abundant, it is not surprisingly the state flower.

To devout Christians, particularly those in the Bible Belt, dogwood is accorded a far higher honor than any state legislature could bestow. It is Christ's flower, resurrecting itself every spring as a reminder of the great sacrifice and the Great Promise, the promise that brings worshipers to the church doors on Sunday, and especially on the Sunday called Easter.

It is Easter, 1972. The dogwoods are in bloom. Worshipers in great numbers are arriving at the church on Randolph Road in South Charlotte. They move across the parking lot, drawn by the organ's call to worship. Wives and husbands exchange greetings with other wives and husbands. Little boys, looking uncomfortable in sport coats and ties, go forth reluctantly. Little girls in Peaches 'n Cream dresses and Mary Janes giggle secrets to each other.

It is a glorious day, a day of bright sun and the smell of new- mown grass, with the aura of peace and love about it. It is especially fine in South Charlotte, because South Charlotte is the American Dream come true: two cars, two kids, riding lawnmower, Pawley's Island hammock in the backyard. And dogwoods. It is a nice place, inhabited for the most part by nice people. It is home to Providence Baptist Church.

Providence Baptist is the church that Gordon Weekley built with the help of his dedicated parishioners. As they move now through the doors and into the beautiful sanctuary, they see the man in the high-back chair who will deliver the message of the Great Promise—but the man they see there is not Gordon Weekley, who once held such great promise of his own.

Gordon Weekley is spending this Easter Sunday in another part of Charlotte, in a small one-bedroom apartment near uptown. And he is on his knees, but he is not praying. He is throwing up the fifth of Four Roses he drank the night before, without ice, without mixer, and without company. He is an addict, alone in his misery. He cannot hear the strains of "Amazing Grace" from the organ in the sanctuary of the church that he built in South Charlotte.

When he was pulled from the Baptismal pool at age ten Gordon Weekley didn't know for a fact that he would one day be a minister, but it was almost preordained.

He might not have been born with a Bible in his hand, but his mother gave him a New Testament on the day he arrived. He arrived, not coincidentally, in a Baptist hospital in Atlanta.

Love of church ran strong in the Weekley family, at least as far back as Gordon's great-grandfather. George Washington Weekley, ordained a minister in 1863, was destined to spend his life presiding over the church of human suffering, first as a chaplain in the 17th Georgia Regiment during the War Between the States and later as a minister to the homeless and destitute. Gordon would think of this man often because of the parallel paths they traveled in their autumn years.

Gordon had five parents, counting his paternal grandmother and grandfather and Katie, the black housekeeper who was with the Weekley family from the day Gordon came home from the hospital until she went on to meet her beloved Maker nineteen years later. They were five people, all under one roof, all with authority over the young boy, and they all exercised it lovingly, constantly, protectively.

Until he was ten and his sister, Mary, was born, Gordon was an only child. Until he was eight and the family moved to another neighborhood, he had been the only child on the entire block. With no playmates nearby, he lived a grown-up childhood that centered on the church and the work ethic instilled in him by his hard-working, middle-class family.

He participated in every church-sponsored organization for young people from Sunbeams to Royal Ambassadors. At fourteen, he was the second Royal Ambassador Plenipotentiary in the state of Georgia, a rank as difficult to achieve as Eagle Scout.

He even excelled at delivering newspapers. After only three months on the job for the *Atlanta Journal*, he was promoted from carrier to district manager of carriers. He was in the eighth grade.

He approached school with the same zeal. When he graduated from Boys High, he didn't make valedictorian as his father had—he did better than that. Of all the awards handed out at graduation, the most prestigious was the H.O. Smith scholarship. Each year, it was given to a boy who not only performed well academically but who also demonstrated a deep and abiding thirst for knowledge and lived an exemplary life. With credentials like that, he could look forward to a brilliant career in the ministry, a career that would begin in Masonboro, North Carolina.

---

The small wooden boat sat at anchor in the middle of the Inland Waterway. To his left, on the mainland, Gordon Weekley could see many of the homes that made up the tiny fishing community of Masonboro, south of Wilmington, North Carolina. To his right lay Masonboro Island, and beyond that, the Atlantic.

If he had stood up in the boat, he'd have stood to just under six feet tall. It is also likely he would have tumbled into the water—he was not an athlete, nor did he look like one. Even in his jeans and slicker, he looked like the scholarly minister of the Gospel that he was. At twenty-eight, he had coal black hair that was already receding and kind brown eyes that peered out through horn-rimmed glasses.

"Got another one," said Annie Beasley, jerking smartly on her rod and cranking the reel expertly. She was a small, white-haired woman in her late fifties, and she was catching fish with almost every cast.

Gordon was not having nearly as much luck, but he enjoyed watching the virtuoso performance of his new-found friend. He had never seen anyone, man or woman, handle a boat or a rod with such skill.

"What is it?" he asked as she dropped her catch into the live well at the bottom of the boat.

"Croaker," she answered. "That's about all that's running right now, croaker and pig fish."

He marveled at the names, and with the inquisitive mind that had earned him *cum laude* honors at Furman, he searched for the Latin translations of the names of the fish swimming aimlessly in the well at his feet.

Finally, perplexed, he asked her, "Why are they called pig fish and croaker, Mrs. Beasley?"

"Because one grunts and the other one croaks," she answered matter-of-factly as yet another croaker tugged sharply at her line.

When they docked a short time later, Gordon thanked the lady for the fishing trip and accepted her invitation for another one the following week. Then he made his way on foot through a stand of pines toward the churchyard a few hundred feet away.

He stopped at the road, took off his glasses, and wiped the salt film from them with a handkerchief. He put them back on and took in the scene. In front of him was the little brick house of God that had served this fishing community for two hundred years, and behind it, the white frame parsonage, home to who-knows-how-many ministers.

North of the church about 150 yards, and across a depression in the earth, a valley of sorts, was the cemetery, fronted by a twenty-five-foot-high wooden cross outlined in clam shells. She was waiting for him there by the cross.

*How pretty she is,* he thought. *And how wonderful she was to come here with me without question, almost a thousand miles from Indiana and the good life her parents have given her.* He put his arm around her, and they walked together to the house.

They had been married a year now. They had taken their vows on May 9, 1948, two days after he had graduated from Southern Baptist Seminary in Louisville.

Gordon had met Norma Lou during his seminary internship in Indiana, not at the church he was assigned to, which was in the town of Sardinia, but at another church fifteen miles away in Columbus. He was filling in for a fellow preacher one Sunday in June, and he was filling in completely alone. Somehow, no one had gone over the order of worship with him before the service. He had only the church bulletin to go by.

The going was good for the first few moments, until he failed to notice just after the offering that the choir was scheduled to sing. After receiving the gifts from the congregation, the young intern stepped forward toward the podium to deliver his sermon. Before he could open his mouth, something caught his eye. It was a hand, attached to the arm of a pretty girl in the choir, and the hand was telling him to sit down.

He sat down, embarrassed a little, but grateful to the girl in the choir.

It was the beginning of a beautiful friendship, a friendship that brought him up the road from Louisville, some ninety miles south, every chance he got.

He fell in love with Norma Lou Atkinson, and love and lack of money led him to the decision to withdraw from seminary for a year to accept a job as a schoolteacher in a community near Sardinia. Now he was seeing her every day. On July 4, 1947, he slipped an engagement ring on her finger. Norma Lou accepted the offering, but when they announced the news to her widowed mother and grandmother, they got mixed reviews. Gordon felt that the eldest Atkinson, the matriarch, was less than thrilled. He attributed it to his Southernness. The Atkinsons were an educated, upper-middle-class, Midwestern clan. Gordon was a Georgia boy and a Southern Baptist, and neither of those fit grandmother Atkinson's picture of a husband for her granddaughter. The Georgia boy, for example, greeted people with hugs and verbal displays of genuine warmth, something the Atkinsons would never allow themselves to do except among members of their own family, and then only on special occasions.

Norma Lou's mother, on the other hand, had always treated Gordon kindly, if not affectionately. She accepted the announcement graciously, though she was fearful that a marriage would ultimately take her beloved daughter away from Indiana.

Having cleared the Atkinson family hurdles and his hiatus from seminary, Gordon returned to school, graduated with honors, and married Norma Lou.

He figured then it was time to look for a pastorate. What he didn't figure on was Norma Lou's mother convincing him to stick around and go for his doctorate, but she did. He likely would have gone through with it if his side of the family hadn't stepped in with an agenda of their own.

"Gordon," his mother said, "we're moving to California. We want you and Norma Lou to come with us. Dad will be more comfortable there."

Gordon's father was afflicted with neurocirculatory asthenia. Cold weather, even mildly cold Georgia weather, caused him great misery. California would be better. Gordon couldn't believe that his parents would abandon their Georgia roots, even though his father was suffering.

It was not his father's first illness. Some years earlier, he had been afflicted with an abscess in the neck that had gone undiagnosed for months and made him weak and lethargic. When it was finally discovered and treated, he recovered almost immediately—but not soon enough for his employer. *Southern Banker* magazine let him go, let go an editor who in his eighteen years there had taken the magazine to new heights.

Gordon Weekley's father was crushed. All those hours hunched over a typewriter, all those years of dedication, all gone.

That had happened at the beginning of Gordon's college studies at Furman, and he became one of the few students who, instead of getting money from home, was sending money to his parents. It was money he earned as a part-time English teacher in nearby high schools.

He was not surprised then to find himself, after four years of college, three years of seminary, and a lifetime of preparation for the ministry, going to Inglewood, California, with his parents, and leaving behind a very unhappy Mrs. Atkinson who watched her dream of keeping Norma Lou close to home vanish over the western horizon.

He got a job in Inglewood with a surgical supply company. Norma Lou found work, too, and together they supported the Weekley family while Gordon's father tried to find work of his own.

The young couple joined the First Baptist Church. After a few months, Hermon Ray, the pastor, offered Gordon a position as associate minister. Gordon jumped at it. Now he was doing what he was trained to do, what he was born to do.

He immersed himself in his work and met many new people. It wasn't long before he and Norma Lou felt they had found a home in California, and not long after that, his parents announced they were going back to Atlanta. Gordon's mother and younger sister were homesick. Gordon's dad was unable to find anything. And so that was that. Gordon's family returned to the South, and the younger Weekleys went back home to Indiana until the call came from Masonboro.

Now they were here, Gordon and Norma Lou, on a finger of sandy earth, in the summer of 1949. They were together alone for the first time, in his first real pastorate. But they weren't quite alone. Norma Lou's mother and younger brother were just up the road in Wilmington. If the daughter and son-in-law wouldn't stay in Indiana, then the mother wouldn't either.

For generations, Masonboro Baptist had been a part-time church, sharing a pastor every second Sunday with another church in the community. In 1947, they had hired Dr. James Blackmore full time, and although he stayed only a couple of years before deciding to move on, the congregation had gotten used to and liked the idea of a full-time minister.

They liked Gordon Weekley too, almost from the moment they met him. Masonboro was a quiet village, inhabited mostly by fishermen and their families, and Gordon learned immediately that "quiet" did not necessarily mean "slow." Addison Hewlett, Jr., was head of the search committee, and he and his fellow committee members wasted no time making their pitch for Gordon Weekley.

Gordon had arrived by train on a Friday afternoon. By Sunday morning, he had met half the congregation, been treated to three seafood dinners, and been given a history of the church from the day of its inception.

The history lessons came from Addison Hewlett, Sr. The elder Hewlett lived in a mansion overlooking Masonboro Sound. The mansion was 150 years old, and the view of the sound from the porch was timeless. So too, it appeared, were the Hewletts. It seemed to Gordon that they were a part of the land itself. Addison Sr. had lived in the great house all his life and was a powerful man not just in the community but in the southeastern section of the state. At the time Gordon met him, he was in his thirty-fifth year as chairman of the New Hanover County Commission. Grandfather Elijah was founder of the Masonboro Baptist Church. Son Addison would later go on to be Speaker of the State House of Representatives.

Addison Jr. asked Gordon to preach two sermons, one on Sunday morning, another in the evening. After the second service, Gordon would either be asked to stay or to be on his way. He was asked to stay after the first service. Gordon didn't say yes—Dallas Orrell said it for him.

Dallas Orrell owned a fleet of tugboats and was the wealthiest man in the church. He was as impressed with Gordon as the committee members, and he made an offer that Gordon couldn't refuse.

"Reverend," Addison Hewlett, Jr., said, "Dallas thinks your wife needs to be here to help you in this decision, and he's willing to pay for a round-trip plane ticket to get her down here for a look-see. What do you say?"

At that moment, Gordon couldn't have turned down the call to the Masonboro ministry if he had wanted to. These were considerate people, kind people, the sort of people Gordon Weekley wanted to be around. He stayed for three years.

There were two hundred members in the Masonboro church when he came, and he was minister to each and every one of them. He visited every person in the hospital. He visited every home. He married. He buried. He counseled. He sought out new members. It was a full-time job, and he earned every nickel of his $56 a week. He never thought of it as a job, though, and never thought much about the money. This was what he was born to do, and he loved it. He particularly loved these people of Masonboro, and their easy, gentle way of life. He got caught up in it, and in the love of the land and the sea.

He planted a garden and waited for months for something to come from it. Nothing did, so he decided to raise chickens. Dallas Orrell gave him a hundred chicks to get started, but by the time they had grown, Gordon could not kill them.

He had to eat, though. After all, that was what he was raising them for. He fretted over this dilemma for several weeks, until he at last devised a plan. Mrs. Beasley, his neighbor, raised chickens, too, so every time Gordon and Norma Lou wanted a chicken for dinner, they took one of theirs to her, and Mrs. Beasley gave the Weekleys one of hers. It was less personal that way.

The arrangement worked well, until suddenly his beloved feathered friends came down with limber-neck disease, a throat infection that caused their necks to flap and flop. Gordon and Norma Lou agonized over the plight of their pets, and were at a loss about what to do.

One night, long after they had gone to bed, Gordon remembered his mother's treatment for throat ailments.

"Norma Lou, wake up. I've got it."

"Got what?" she muttered sleepily.

"Vicks Salve," he said, standing over her with a jar of it in his hand.

At two o'clock in the morning, a hundred chickens woke in their roost to the sight of a man and a woman in night clothes with globs of Vicks Salve on their fingers. For the next two hours, the chickens ran, and Gordon and Norma Lou ran them down. Once caught, the birds were forced to accept the offering the minister and his wife gave them—a fingerful of Vicks stuffed down their limber-necked throats.

It was an act of love, though an act the chickens likely would just as soon have done without.

After they all died from limber-neck disease, Gordon decided to stick to preaching. And fishing.

At least twice a week, old Mrs. Beasley would motor out into Masonboro sound, and now, often, Gordon and sometimes Norma Lou would go with her. No man or woman on the peninsula could match Mrs. Beasley's success with the rod and reel. She almost never came home empty, and frequently returned with a filled cooler.

She was a kindly and generous woman. Nearly every Saturday, she and her husband Roy would have Gordon and Norma Lou over for lunch, always the same lunch: vegetable soup and rat cheese.

"Your vegetable garden is beautiful this year," Gordon said to Mr. Beasley one day while they were eating.

"Would have been beautiful last year, too," said Roy, looking up from his soup and cutting his twinkling eyes over to Mrs. Beasley's rods and reels in the corner, "but the fish ate it all up."

It was here at Masonboro that Gordon Weekley was beginning to feel the depths of himself as a minister. He had preached many sermons before this pastorate, in Indiana and South Carolina, and he had been an associate pastor for a few months in California, but Masonboro was different. Now he was living among the people he served, getting to know them, sharing their joys and sorrows, their problems large and small. He was at the center, the hub, of the human experience.

When he prayed for a Mrs. Williams or a Mrs. Jones or a Mrs. Smith in the hospital, that lady, whoever she was, was much more than a name on the Sunday bulletin. She was a friend who, perhaps, grew roses in her backyard like nobody could, a woman who had raised her sons or daughters more carefully than her flowers, and watched them turn into fine young men and women with good families of their own. She might be a woman who had sat by her husband's bedside through the long nights and days of his dying, and then finally said goodbye to a companionship of forty or more years with a kiss on his cold cheek.

Gordon loved the Mrs. Williamses, loved all the members of his little church. Seeing now from a close perspective the laughing and crying, the dying and living, his sermons took on greater meaning. He wrote them more carefully, preached them with more empathy. And no one escaped the reach of his compassion. If someone needed sitting up with, Gordon sat up with them through the night. If someone needed an ear, Gordon gave it.

He was becoming the preacher he was meant to be—not the man in the high pulpit, but the man who, like Christ, walked among the people and washed their feet. He was one of them.

He was one of them that day in June when the phone rang and he listened with terror in his heart as a mother frantically told him that her child, her beautiful sixteen-year-old child, had been burned in Charlotte.

The girl had been visiting her grandmother who lived in an old house near the Catawba River. The woman had been unable to start her wood-burning stove and had poured gasoline on it from an open bucket. The gasoline exploded into flame, and the startled grandmother let fly the bucket, splashing herself and her granddaughter with the deadly liquid. In a flash they were both in flames.

Within moments of the call, Gordon had the mother and the father in the car, racing toward Charlotte. It didn't matter how fast they drove; it was a race they could not win. They could not change the outcome of what had happened. The three of them, Gordon, the mother, and the father, sat vigil outside the rooms of the girl and the grandmother. For two days and two nights, Gordon didn't set foot off the hall, staying, and praying, and feeling a depth of grief he had never experienced before. It was as if his own grandmother and his own daughter were dying. When he finally did leave, he left with a grieving man and woman who had lost in one fell stroke two branches of the family tree: the mother who was and the mother who was to be.

The people in the little community were a long time getting over that loss, but life went on in Masonboro, as it had before Gordon Weekley came, before the beautiful sixteen-year-old girl died.

People were born, people died, and the church under Gordon Weekley continued to grow. He received many members, but perhaps none better remembered than the dead man.

The dead man was alive when Gordon met him—very much alive. And loud. And profane. He had been a sea captain and had retired to Masonboro. Gordon befriended the wiry, feisty little man and countered his bluster with gentleness, canceled his profanity with scripture. They would talk for hours, Gordon about God, the captain about Godlessness.

Finally, after many months of knowing each other, the old man sent for Gordon to come to his death bed.

"Do you think preacher, after all these years I've been away, that God might have a room for me?"

"God does have a room for you," answered Gordon. "All you have to do is accept it."

The old man died with God in his heart, and the following Sunday, Gordon Weekley mounted the pulpit and asked the congregation to please signify by raised hands their acceptance of the old sea captain as a member of the Masonboro Baptist Church.

The captain passed with flying colors.

And so it went at Masonboro, a good life if there ever was one, for both the shepherd and the flock. When Gordon left to go to another pastorate, he took with him memories for a lifetime. He would likely never again watch the sea turtles lay their eggs on Masonboro Beach under the first full moon in June; he would likely never again go to Masonboro Island with a band of professional fishermen and camp with them and scan the sea with them, nets at the ready, waiting for the great schools of Virginia mullet.

The memories were etched, and in the years that followed, he would play them over and over in his mind. He would play, too, the memory of the day the deacons came to see him.

"Preacher," one of them said, "we love Norma Lou. She's friendly—she's kind—but we're just wondering if there's any way we can help her."

"With what?" asked Gordon, already knowing the answer.

"Help her, well, you know..." he was hesitating now, "...help her get more involved."

Gordon felt a pain in his stomach. He had known this was coming, had known almost from the first day in Masonboro that Norma Lou Weekley was not going to be the typical Southern Baptist minister's wife. She was not going to be choir leader. She was not going to be president of the Women's Missionary Union. And she was not going to sit down front on Sunday morning gazing in admiration at her husband in the high chair behind the pulpit. None of this bothered Gordon Weekley, the man. All of it bothered Gordon Weekley, the preacher.

Had she been anyone but a minister's wife, she would have been considered a very active participant. She didn't lead the choir, but she sang in it. She helped with the young people's programs. And when Gordon was unavailable, she listened sympathetically to church members who brought their personal problems to the parsonage.

Gordon could have told the deacons all that, but he didn't. Nor did he tell them Norma Lou had married the man, not the minister, that he was being paid, not her. He did not tell them because he was loved by these people, and he would do nothing to jeopardize that love. So he thanked the men for coming and told them it was something he could work out alone with Norma Lou.

He wished Norma Lou would go along with the deacons' request not for her sake, but for his. He asked her to, but she resisted. A baby would be born soon, and she had a house to look after. She saw no need and had no desire to be what amounted to an associate minister. He didn't blame her. He did blame her. He wanted everything concerning his ministry to be perfect. And it wasn't.

# TWO

On October 7, 1780, a force of 1100 loyalists, under the command of Major Patrick Ferguson came face to face with 900 backwoodsmen at a place called Kings Mountain. The mountain really doesn't belong there. It's in the Piedmont section of the Carolinas, some forty miles east of true mountain territory. Major Ferguson undoubtedly came to the realization that he didn't belong there either, but he is still there today, buried along with his hopes for an America under British rule.

On August 17,1952, a contingent from the town of Kings Mountain came to the Masonboro Baptist Church to scout out Gordon Weekley. He didn't know where they were from when he spotted them from the pulpit that Sunday morning, but he knew they were a search committee. He knew it by the way they scattered themselves among the congregation in an attempt to be inconspicuous, and he knew, too, because no one had told him of their arrival. Gordon was almost always told that a friend or a relative would be visiting. This time he had heard nothing, and five unannounced visitors was certainly unusual.

The search committee liked what they saw that Sunday morning, and Gordon liked what he saw a few days later when he received, along with a letter from the committee, a picture of the huge First Baptist Church of Kings Mountain.

He couldn't believe a church of that size would want him, a first-pastorate preacher in a community church with fewer than four hundred members.

This was something he at least had to look into. If it worked out, it would be a major career move, and it was coming years earlier than he would have expected.

A few weeks later, he preached a trial sermon in the sanctuary, and that very afternoon, he was invited to be the new pastor.

When he told his friends in Masonboro the following day that he had accepted the call from Kings Mountain, his dear friend Addison Hewlitt put his arm around the young preacher's shoulders and said, "We hate to lose you, but we will yield to God's will."

Gordon assumed he was doing God's will—he had, of course, prayed about his decision—but his mind kept going back to the picture the committee had sent him. He was honest enough with himself to realize that the size of the church had swayed him. And the salary. And most of all, the need to be needed.

He smiled to himself as he remembered the old joke pastors told among themselves. It was about the pastor who, upon hearing the job offer from a visiting search committee, got up from his chair, excused himself, and went into his study to pray about his decision.

"I'll keep this short, Lord," he said from his knees in the study. "I've got packing to do."

And so he went to Kings Mountain, he and Norma Lou and mother Atkinson and Norma Lou's brother Marvin. Mrs. Atkinson was apparently still not ready to let her daughter out of her sight, and so she settled in a small home not far from the parsonage.

Kings Mountain, though small by city standards, was much larger, much faster-paced than the fishing community of Masonboro. It was largely textile-mill supported, and the parishioners were blue-collar, with the exception of three or four mill or textile machinery executives and a few doctors and other professionals.

For all its contrasts with Masonboro, Kings Mountain still had charming small-town qualities. This was affirmed one day early in his pastorate when Gordon left the church office without telling his secretary and went to visit Griffin's Drug Store.

The store was a few doors down from the church, just past the post office and the Southern Bell telephone office, where operators, in this era before dial phones were available to the community, spent eight hours a day saying, "Number, please."

Gordon swung open the door of the drugstore, walked to the counter and saw Mr. Griffin standing with a telephone receiver in his hand.

"It's for you," Griffin said.

"How could anybody know I'm here?" Gordon asked.

The answer would come Sunday, when Louise Early, a parishioner and telephone operator, said she had seen him walking to the store from her perch in the Southern Bell building and had simply transferred a call that had come through the switchboard for him.

Gordon easily adapted himself to the ways of the small town and to the demands of a larger church. He simply did as he had done in Masonboro, which was to immerse himself totally in the lives of his congregation. Though he had a staff now, he believed it was his responsibility to be present at every birth, to visit all the infirm, to preside over every wedding and funeral. That's what he was called for. That's what he enjoyed doing.

The more time he spent with others, the less time he spent with Norma Lou. And it was not just her now, but son Steve, born just before the couple left Masonboro. Gordon loved them dearly, but he was a man with a mission—a man who genuinely wanted to help others, and who enjoyed deep down, too, the heroic stature accorded him by the people he served.

It didn't help matters that Norma Lou once again was not fully involving herself in the church in the role that custom dictated. Gordon didn't know it then, but the seeds of a strained marriage were in the ground and would one day blossom.

Meanwhile, he went about the business of responding personally to every need of everyone, except maybe his family.

When a church couple asked Gordon to intercede on behalf of their son who was imprisoned in West Virginia, Gordon put his whole heart into it and eventually was instrumental in obtaining the boy's early release. He did it not by letter or phone but by driving to West Virginia and spending hours with the warden, the prison chaplain, and the probation officers.

He drove to New York, too, a twelve-hundred-mile round trip to pick up and deliver to Kings Mountain a family whose immigration he had arranged. He had heard of their desire to get out of post-war Germany and into America, and he had charged his congregation with helping them make that dream come true. The Piel family came to Kings Mountain, North Carolina, thanks largely to Gordon Weekley and thanks also to the members of the First Baptist Church who, perhaps because of the proximity of the famous revolutionary war mountain, knew just how much the desire for freedom and opportunity meant to a man and his family.

They knew, too, how much their pastor meant to them. He seemed to be everywhere at once, doing everything—and there was much to do.

Like Masonboro, this was a church with an old membership. It seemed to Gordon that he spent as much time burying old members as he did visiting prospective ones. He knew, as all ministers do, that a church's survival depends on new blood. He went after new members with zeal, particularly families with young children.

Doors were opened to him partly because of his kind and humble personality, and partly because of the German family he had brought to Kings Mountain. That event was big news in this small town. Gordon Weekley's name was a household word.

He became even more familiar when his Sunday sermons began being broadcast throughout Cleveland County by a local radio station. In little more than a year, the sizable First Baptist church got bigger and younger.

Gordon Weekley had found a home. When his second son, Dan, arrived, he envisioned his two boys growing up in this splendid small community. He envisioned, too, a new and larger church to handle the now overflowing crowds. Meetings were held. Sites were suggested. Plans were beginning to be drawn up. First Baptist Church was on its way.

# THREE

In 1953, the land south of Sharon Amity Road was still largely undeveloped, almost rural, but changes were coming. Charlotte, North Carolina, was growing. Two of the best roads for residential development were Providence and Randolph, primarily because of their direct access to uptown, some five miles away. The roads ran perpendicular to Sharon Amity and parallel to each other, scarcely a half-mile apart.

For the Baptists who already lived in this area, getting to church wasn't always easy. Only one was within a fifteen-minute drive of the site on which Providence Baptist now stands. And so it came to pass that a handful of decent, dedicated, energetic families decided Southeast Charlotte needed a church.

They began with Sunday afternoon meetings in each other's homes, and before many months had passed, they were meeting and worshiping in a recreational hut at the home of Dr. and Mrs. Franklin Bumgardner. The hut soon proved too small for the growing flock, and services were moved to the auditorium of Eastover School. In those early months, the small congregation had no sense of place, but they were imbued with a deep sense of purpose. They spent many hours in each other's homes, discussing the kind of church they were going to be. They decided in the end that their church would be what they were themselves: moderate, tolerant, loving, and nonjudgmental.

These were special people, and by now the Mecklenburg (County) Baptist Association was sufficiently impressed with the group's intentions that it offered them a four-acre tract on Providence Road. This was prime land even then, before the residential explosion, but the congregation took only the name Providence and turned down the land. Four acres weren't enough for what these farsighted people had in mind. They wanted eight acres on Randolph Road. With the help of the Baptist Association and the personal signatures of several families on a mortgage note, they got it.

It was a bold act of faith for those mostly middle-class families to take on a $35,000 debt, but they were not to be denied. Somehow they knew they would have a great church. There was no doubting it. As their signatures were still drying on the mortgage, they set about putting up a building, a fellowship hall.

All they needed now was a preacher. They didn't want just any preacher. They wanted a great one. This was a confident group of people, unafraid to search out some of the finest ministers in the state, and convince one of them to give up his successful pastorate and come to eight acres of uninhabited ground and a congregation numbering fifty-six. They knew they would find just the right man, and when they did, they would have their preacher.

---

For some reason, Gordon did not stand in the doorway of First Baptist Church in Kings Mountain this particular Sunday morning and therefore did not bid good day to his parishioners as they filed out into the autumn sunshine. Had he done so, he would have shaken hands with five people from Charlotte—and he would have assumed that either a startling coincidence had taken place, or those five people were a pulpit committee.

It was no coincidence. Billie Logan, one of his lay leaders, had seen them scattered throughout the sanctuary during the service and later had seen them gather in a small bunch on the front lawn. The people at First Baptist liked this tall, gentle man from Atlanta—many of them loved him, and he loved them— but the strangers in the congregation this day liked him, too.

A few days later, he had a visit from the committee, and they told him how much they liked him. A few days after that, he was intercepted on the front steps of the First Baptist Church of Charlotte. He was there for a meeting of the State Baptist Convention, and so was Clyde Griffin of the pulpit committee. Clyde was also there to see Gordon and let him know the committee was seriously considering him.

They were serious all right, so serious Gordon couldn't have gotten away from them if he had wanted to. While Gordon and his fellow hunters were calling geese at Mattamuskeet near the Carolina coast, Clyde Griffin was calling Gordon on the telephone.

Gordon left the blind and took the call. Providence Baptist was hunting for a preacher, and Gordon got the distinct sense that he was their prime target.

He was intrigued by the tenacity and the confidence of this group of people. They were few in number. They had a piece of land with no building on it, although a small one was under construction. And they were in debt to the tune of $35,000.

*Why,* thought Gordon Weekley, *should I leave a six-hundred-member congregation, a church that offers me a secure and promising future? Why should I even consider such a thing?*

He talked to other ministers, respected ministers, ministers on the way up. He found out that one or two of them were also being considered by Providence, and they were excited about the prospect of being invited.

He went to Charlotte and the site of the new church. With committeeman Amos Bumgardner as his guide, he drove some three miles out from the site and encircled the entire area. Other than Providence, there were no Baptist churches within the circle, but several on the perimeter.

He knew then that the location was good, but even as he drove he was asking himself why he was going through this exercise. *Maybe,* he thought, *it's ego fulfillment.*

Whatever it was, the following week he accepted an invitation to preach a Friday night trial sermon to the Providence people at St. John's Baptist near uptown Charlotte.

If Gordon had any doubts that Providence Baptist would succeed, they were dispelled after the service. It was then that he had a chance to mingle with and meet the congregation, and he realized that the people on the pulpit committee weren't the only ones with something on the ball. These were successful, energetic people who were going to have the kind of church they wanted, with Gordon Weekley or without him. Gordon was impressed with them all, and as he drove back to Kings Mountain that night, their names filed themselves in his mind: Al and Bill Edwards, brothers with prominent positions in the local power company; Bill Barksdale, owner of Durable Wood; Clyde Griffin, owner of a brokerage firm; Henry Keziah, regional manager for American Cyanamid; Russ Tucker, zone manager for Sealtest; Harry Moss, owner of a window company; Don Jeffries and John Doyle, executives with Celanese; Howard Pike, zone manager for Chevrolet; architect Jim Benton; CPA Hanson Dunbar; Gus Vinroot of Vinroot Construction; Bomar Lowrance of the NBC network; and Dr.Grady Wilson, one of the most valuable players on the Billy Graham team.

The women impressed him, too, particularly Martha Lowrance, the friendly, feisty Texan, wife of Bomar. She, perhaps more than anyone, epitomized the energy and spirit of Providence. She was a doer, and an outspoken one at that. No challenge was too great for her, and no person was a stranger. Although she had only known Gordon a couple of weeks, since their first meeting at Kings Mountain, she knew him well enough to tell him that his St. John's sermon was great but his choice of ties was terrible.

Gordon was overwhelmed by the praise that he, if not his tie, got that night, particularly because it came from so many impressive people. If the praise set him up for the job, it was a simple statement of fact that closed the deal. Charlie Helms, a big, genial man, was the last person in the receiving line. As he shook Gordon's hand, he looked him in the eye and said, "You're the one."

And Gordon Weekley knew he was.

The people of Providence had a dream of not just a church but a church campus, and not just on four acres but on eight, and not just with any preacher but with a truly good one. They had signed their names on the note for the land. They had signed their names on the note for the pastorium in the upper-middle-class neighborhood called Sherwood Forest. They had begun putting up a building. Come spring, they intended to hire a summer youth director. Gordon had never seen such people. There was no stopping them.

When Gordon got back to Kings Mountain, the night was just beginning for him. Norma Lou's grandmother had died the day before his St. John's sermon, and so they stopped at Kings Mountain only long enough to pick up the children before beginning the long trek to Indiana.

By the time they had gotten deep into the western North Carolina mountains, everyone except Gordon was asleep. His was often the only car on the road, and as the headlights guided him along the twisting way through the majestic Blue Ridge, he thought about the possibility of becoming the first pastor of what promised to be a great church.

He had no trouble projecting himself into the pastoring part. He had always been a people person: that was his great strength. And he knew that he preached good sermons, sometimes great ones. It was administration that scared him. He had a small staff in Kings Mountain. Providence would one day have a very large one. Could he handle it?

Could he be a fund raiser? This church was going to need a lot more money in order to fulfill its dreams. Save for his annual tithe sermons, Gordon had never attempted to raise large sums of money.

And what about the politics within his denomination? A pastor in a large and influential church would be expected to involve himself in statewide Baptist organizations. Gordon had never aspired to that role, had never aspired to anything beyond serving the people around him.

He wondered if he could do it. Then he began to realize that on a small scale he already had. He had been a member of the board of trustees at Gardner Webb and Wingate colleges, and he had been president of the Kings Mountain Baptist Pastors Conference.

Gordon was taking inventory. He thought of his education and was satisfied with the fact that he was well schooled. He had graduated with honors from Boys High in Atlanta, winning the coveted H.O. Smith scholarship. He had done exceedingly well at Furman, too, majoring in Greek and graduating as a member of the Hand and Torch, Furman's equivalent to Phi Beta Kappa. At seminary, he had maintained a 92.5 average, good enough to qualify him for doctoral studies.

He reasoned too that he had come out of a great church in Atlanta, a church he had participated fully in, winning more honors there than perhaps any other young man ever had. Certainly that experience would serve him well in this new, large church-to-be.

As he drove on, he thought of his father: valedictorian at Boys High, a brilliant journalist. *Surely*, thought Gordon, *I inherited some of his brain power. Surely I can do this job.*

He thought of Harold Miller, the man who perhaps more than any other had fueled his desire for knowledge and excellence. The picture was still clear in Gordon's mind. He saw himself as a tentative freshman, entering Dr. Miller's Greek class for the first time. In that one short lecture hour, he found himself falling in love with not only the language but with the charming, charismatic, energetic man who taught it. Gordon would later go on to become Dr. Miller's graduate assistant and best friend.

He considered stopping the car to call Harold, but he realized there was no need to.

By the time the sun rose over Kentucky that morning, Gordon knew that if the call came, he would answer it. And he would do the very best he could.

*God help me,* he prayed.

## FOUR

On January 2, 1955, Gordon Weekley stepped into the pulpit at the Eastover school auditorium and delivered the first sermon by the first official minister of Providence Baptist Church. It was entitled "The *raison d'etre* for Providence Baptist Church." He gave the rest of the sermon in plain, strong English. The words, coupled with the deep resonance and Southern warmth in his voice, made for a very effective sermon indeed. He had impressed them with his heart despite his youthfully exuberant attempt to impress them first with his knowledge.

The next Sunday, Gordon laid down the goals for himself and the little congregation. Had an outsider been there that day, a person unfamiliar with the group and its young minister, he or she surely would have smiled at the loftiness of their dreams.

Here they were, a handful of people meeting in an elementary school auditorium, listening to a young man with only six years of ministerial experience paint a picture of what would someday be one of the great churches in North Carolina—not just in size but also in spirit. It would be a church that would influence not only its own members but also the larger community.

With that group, whose own first small permanent building was six weeks away from completion, Gordon Weekley envisioned that Providence Baptist would one day become a church from which other churches would spring forth. He envisioned a church environment so powerfully loving and giving that some, perhaps many, of its children would grow up to become ministers and missionaries.

He challenged the congregation to double in size the first year. He challenged them to give fifty cents of every dollar to missions.

The feisty, friendly, energetic congregation shared his visions that day and accepted his challenges. Everything they envisioned on that Sunday in January eventually came to pass. The dream came true—for everyone except the pastor. For him, it became a nightmare.

---

These were heady times for the Weekleys. They had moved into their new house, the pastorium, in an upper-middle-class neighborhood called Sherwood Forest, and it was a far cry from their little home in Masonboro or their modest dwelling in Kings Mountain. The pace of activity for Gordon was different, too. The people at Providence were in a hurry, eager to get on with the business of building a great church. So was he. In the first few weeks, he visited the home of every Providence member, held uncounted committee meetings, courted a host of prospects, and spent long hours writing and refining his sermons.

Norma Lou seldom saw him except at bedtime and at church functions. There was simply no time for the young man in a hurry to spend with his family, although he loved them dearly and deeply.

It seemed as if Gordon and the entire congregation were perpetually energized. No one held back. Everyone participated. They gave their time, their money, even their possessions. They donated curtains, desks, typewriters, and chairs to the building that was nearing completion. On weekends, the men busied themselves landscaping the grounds, making ready for the big day when the people of Providence would move into their new home.

The day came February 13, 1955. Eastover School became part of church history. Now the cars were rolling into the gravel parking lot and stopping in front of the little brick multi-purpose building on Randolph Road. It sat among the pines on the back corner of the eight acres. It was small: the auditorium held little more than a hundred people, and the door behind the podium led to a few classrooms and the pastor's office. Nevertheless, it was home, and it is doubtful that anyone that morning paid much attention to the cinderblock walls of the sanctuary or the vinyl tile floor or the folding chairs. For now, for the moment, it was their cathedral, filled to overflowing, standing room only.

The next week was no different, nor the next. Even Wednesday night prayer meetings drew large crowds. It seemed that something was going on every evening at the church. Baptist Training Union was in full swing. A Royal Ambassadors group was formed. The choir was growing, and youth choirs were being created. People liked being at the little church and being with each other. When they weren't at church, many of them were getting together in homes for bridge or cook-outs. Acquaintances were becoming friends. Friends were becoming family.

Nothing could stop this little church, not even Howard Byrum's fire later that year. Howard, an adult youth leader, burned most of the eight Providence acres to a crisp one autumn afternoon when he and some teenagers from the church were clearing the property of weeds.

"Why don't we just burn it off?" someone said, laughing. With that, easy-going Howard struck a match and dropped it in the dry high grass in front of him. He lifted his foot to stomp out the small blaze, but before his shoe leather touched ground, the fire was off to the races. Howard and the kids frantically beat at it with rakes and hoes, but they couldn't slow it down. In seconds, it was ten feet wide, then twenty, then fifty. As Howard and the kids ran after it, he noticed a solitary man standing in his yard adjoining the church property, with a garden hose in his hand. If the situation hadn't been so serious, Howard would have laughed at that lonesome figure with a little green garden hose facing what was now six or seven burning acres.

Fortunately, the volunteer fire department arrived and put out the blaze in minutes. When the fire chief wanted to know what happened, Howard 'fessed up to what he had done. The chief looked at him sternly and made him promise never to play with matches again.

Several weeks later, at the Providence Christmas party, Frances Bumgardner presented Howard with a bucket full of candy. The bucket was red, and painted in white letters on the side was the word FIRE.

Days after that first February service in the fellowship hall, the deacons gathered in Gordon's office to discuss expansion of the building. There weren't enough classrooms to keep up with the growing church population. The meeting was brief and the action decisive. A wing would be added immediately. By June, it was complete.

Every Sunday brought new faces, and on one Sunday in May, thirty-three of them came to stay. Thirty-three people rose up out of their folding chairs at the hymn of invitation and came forward. It was a sight no one at Providence had ever seen before, not even at the extraordinarily large churches some of them had come from.

With the growing Providence population, there was almost always baptizing to do, but without a baptistry, it had to be done at neighboring churches. Baptisms are unforgettable experiences for those who submerge for a brief moment and emerge forever changed. Saved. Reborn. Washed in the blood of the Lamb.

Preachers perform so many Baptismal ceremonies that, though gratifying, they are hardly memorable. But there was one evening of baptisms destined to burn in Gordon Weekley's memory all his days. It happened on a spring Sunday evening that first year, at St. John's. As he and Claude Broach, minister of this fine, old church, were about to enter the water, Broach cautioned him.

"Gordon, something's gone wrong with the water mixer. This water is inordinately warm."

If Gordon didn't know the meaning of *inordinately* then, he knew it a few seconds later when he stepped into the near-scalding water without the benefit of Baptismal boots, which he did not then own. There was a long line of people ready to accept Christ, and some of them must have wondered why Gordon had such a pained look on his face at this most joyous of experiences. Moments later, dunked in the cauldron, they must have wondered if they had truly died and gone to Hell itself. Each of them was in and out in seconds, but Gordon was in for the duration.

"I baptize you in the name of the Father, Son, and Holy Ghost," he said again and again, as he moved them through with assembly-line speed. Finally, after what seemed like Eternity itself, it was over. As the people filed out of St. John's, Richie Funderburk, a charter member and registered nurse, moved to where Gordon was standing alongside the Baptismal pool.

"You're burned,"she said.

"A little," he answered.

"A lot," she retorted, and she popped him in her car and drove him to the hospital where he was treated and released with second-degree leg burns.

The next day, he was back on the job, back to the business of building a church. He had put the Baptist World Alliance meeting out of his mind. It was scheduled for the summer of '55. While he was still pastor at Kings Mountain, he had planned to attend. Now, as the meeting date approached, he was thinking about it again.

He wondered what the deacons would say if after only six months in the pulpit, he asked for a leave of absence in order to attend.

*All they can say is no*, he thought.

But they said yes. Emphatically. They wanted Gordon to participate in events of that stature, to expand his own knowledge and experience and to let those he would encounter know about Providence Baptist. They were excited for him.

He went to London with his good friend Milton Boone, who had succeeded him at Masonboro. They went on the SS *United States*, the fastest and one of the finest luxury liners of its day.

They arrived in England several days before the start of the Alliance, so they used their time to see some of the English and Scottish countryside, darting about in a little rented Austin. Up the east side of England they went, past Roman ruins and centuries-old stone sheep fences that stretched for miles, on up to Edinburgh and the Firth of Forth, to Glasgow, and Loch Lomond, and back south to Stratford on Avon, Shakespeare's home.

Finally they came to the thatched-roof cottage in London owned by the Foote family, pen pals of a member of the Providence congregation. This picture-postcard kind of place—just as Gordon imagined English cottages to be—was Gordon's and Milton's temporary home. The Footes were generous and gracious hosts, welcoming the wayfarers as if they were returning prodigals.

The Sunday before the Alliance began, Gordon, through arrangements made by Grady Wilson, found himself in the heart of London, preaching from the pulpit of the Leighton Stone Baptist Church. It was an awesome moment for the young man from Atlanta, but he spoke well and was warmly received in the grand old church. His awe was matched by his surprise at looking out over the congregation and spotting the chairman of his board of deacons at Kings Mountain. It was a small world.

After the Alliance, Gordon and Milton, in keeping with their plans, set out to see a little more of the world. They turned in their rental car and rode the train to Dover and the ferry across the English Channel to France.

It was there that Gordon bought his car. A few weeks before the trip abroad, he had visited with a man who lived next door to Providence Baptist. Another man, the national sales representative for Renault, was there too.

"How are you going to travel in France?" asked the sales rep.

"I'll probably rent a car," answered Gordon.

"I can work it out so you can buy a car for almost the same amount you could rent one for," the man said.

"I'm all ears," answered Gordon.

The man explained that he could have a car waiting for Gordon in Paris. Gordon would pick it up, pay for it, use it to tour France, and then return it to the Riviera, preferably to Nice. There he would tell the manager of whatever hotel he stayed in that he had a car for sale. He would sell the car, and when he returned to the United States, there would be another one just like it waiting for him in New York. So Gordon bought the Renault in Paris, toured France, drove to Nice, checked into a hotel, and told the manager he had a car to sell.

The manager took one look at the shiny new Renault and said he could have a buyer there in a few minutes. Sure enough, according to the script, a buyer showed up. Gordon sold the car for almost exactly what he had paid for it. He took the money, $900, to the nearest American Express office.

'I just sold my car," he announced to the clerk, "and I don't want to carry this much cash home with me. Could you convert it to a traveler's check please?"

"Sir," the clerk replied, "if I do that, the French government will be down on me before nightfall. What you did was illegal."

"What in the world is illegal about selling a car?"

"Selling something and taking that many American dollars out of the country amounts to black-marketeering," she replied.

Gordon was thunderstruck. Here was a man who had never so much as snitched a cookie from a jar caught up in the black market and international money laundering, and *Lord knows,* he thought, *what else.*

He left the American Express office and walked quickly to his hotel—but not too quickly. He didn't want to attract the attention of the gendarmes. It seemed to him at that moment they were everywhere. One was directing traffic at an intersection, and two more were across the street, paralleling Gordon's path. He wondered if he should just approach them, confess his crime, and throw himself on the mercy of the French courts, or if he should go on the interminable two blocks to his hotel, hoping they hadn't spotted him.

He went on, and after what seemed like hours, arrived at the hotel entrance. He glanced around. No gendarmes in sight. He dashed inside, strode rapidly across the lobby, and caught the elevator to his floor.

He closed the door to his room and leaned his back up against it. Safe. At least for the moment. But what to do with the money? He decided he had to carry it with him at all times—but not in his billfold. If a gendarme for some reason stopped him and asked for identification, he would surely see the money. And what about robbers? He could be mugged, and the billfold taken, and he wouldn't even be able to report it. He imagined the repercussions of going to a police station and announcing that some criminal had hit him over the head and taken his black-market money. He removed the forty-five $20 bills from his bulging wallet, stuffed them in a hotel envelope, and pinned the package to his inside suit coat pocket.

He spent two more days in Nice, and nobody knocked on his door with a warrant for his arrest. Still, it was not until he got off the ship in New York and cleared customs that he felt he could breathe normally again.

*I would have made a lousy criminal,* he thought to himself.

---

Back home, Gordon picked up where he left off—visitations, meetings, plans for yet another annex to the fellowship hall, preparation of the 1956 budget, development of the Thanksgiving and Christmas programs, and in the middle of it all, a month-long stint as guest pastor of a television program called "Vespers." It aired five nights a week on what was then Charlotte's only television station, WBTV. His selection so early in his Providence career signified the impact the young minister was making on the Charlotte community.

He was not alone in his energy and ambition. He was surrounded by talented people, church members, to whom excellence was an everyday word, and nobody typified that more than the music director, Martha Iley. She amazed Gordon. She was a housewife, a mother, a Sunday school teacher, holder of two masters degrees and a doctorate in music. It seemed to him she spent every waking minute of her life in some positive endeavor. She had much to do with Providence's having not one robed choir but four by the end of Gordon's first year. But it was her Christmas music that winter of '55 that amazed him most. In that tiny fellowship hall on Christmas Eve, an organist, a string ensemble, and the sanctuary choir performed a cantata so magnificent that Grady Wilson was moved to say he had never heard anything like it in any of the great churches around the world.

Gordon did some singing of his own that season. He gathered up a flock of young people and adults and night after night took them caroling to the homes of Providence members.

It was a joyous time in a joyous season, and the young preacher looked forward with great enthusiasm to many, many more. He couldn't wait to get started on the next year, to continue in his drive to make this great little church a great big church.

His days began early and ran late. He was a whirlwind, always on the run, but Norma Lou was not running alongside him. As in their days at Masonboro and Kings Mountain, she chose not to be the classic minister's wife. Although she attended every service and served on a few committees, it seemed to Gordon that home was really where her heart was.

Norma Lou seemed content with raising the children, now three with the arrival of David in 1956. He loved her for that, but he anguished over her lack of church involvement and secretly hoped that the deacons would not come to him as they had done in Masonboro and ask what they could do to get her more involved. It was a pressure he did not need in an already pressure-packed environment.

Although these were happy times for the minister and his congregation, he knew that much of that happiness was attributable to the electrically charged environment of growth. Gordon couldn't slow down, couldn't stop if he wanted to—and he didn't want to. It was fun being the leader of this merry band of young achievers. So what if he didn't get enough sleep every night? So what if he felt a little pressure? Many men thrived on pressure. He would, too. He was sowing the seeds for what would someday grow into a great church. He was also, without knowing it, sowing the seeds for the near destruction of his own soul.

FIVE

"You need a doctor," said Bob Hollingsworth one afternoon.

"I'm feeling fine," answered Gordon.

"Yes, but you and your family are going to need one. Everybody needs a family doctor. And I've got just the one for you."

Bob Hollingsworth was a pharmaceutical salesman and a Providence member. He knew every doctor in Charlotte. "His name is John Doe," said Bob. "You'll love him."

Gordon did come to love him. They were friends almost from the moment they met. Dr. Doe was not much caught up in Christianity, but he and the young minister were on an intellectual and educational par with each other, and both enjoyed good conversation.

They began having lunches together at a cafeteria near Dr. Doe's office, discussing the political and social issues of the day, along with philosophy and religion. They found in each other a respite from the daily pressures their respective careers imposed upon them—and from the pressures, too, they imposed upon themselves. Each could escape in the other's company.

Dr. Doe was a pilot, and before long, he and Gordon were winging their way around the Piedmont, high above and far away from their everyday cares.

Their wives came to know each other too, which resulted in occasional dinners involving the four of them. The families even vacationed together once for a week at nearby Myrtle Beach.

It was a friendship Gordon valued and trusted, and one he would live to regret.

If he needed a friend like Dr. Doe, he also needed and thrived on the joy and excitement of the growing Providence pastorate. The 1956 budget doubled to $60,000. By 1958, it was $85,000. People kept coming, and the little fellowship hall, with its additional wing and adjacent prefabricated annex, could take no more. A sanctuary had to be built, one large enough to hold five hundred worshipers, a church office, and Sunday School classes.

It would be a sanctuary building most congregations would contentedly call home for ages to come, but true to the optimistic nature of the preacher and his people, this building would only be a step along the way toward another.

It would look and feel like a permanent sanctuary, with altar and baptistry and pews, but it was designed so that one day it could be converted into another fellowship hall and a second floor could be added for even more classrooms. The final sanctuary was yet to come.

On February 15, 1958, the architects presented the plans to the building committee, and on March 9, the building committee presented the plans to the congregation. The project would cost the staggering sum of $402,000.

No problem. They'd simply raise the money.

They broke ground on May 25. Al Edwards, co-chairman of the building committee, thought everyone should participate. Everyone did. Al found an old hand plow, painted it gold, and attached three long ropes to it. The members took their place in front of the plow and pulled the ropes taut. Gordon and Al's brother Bill each hung on to a handle, and at Gordon's signal, the congregation pulled, opening a furrow of earth from which a mighty church would grow.

---

Nineteen Fifty-eight was a benchmark year for the shepherd and his flock. Gordon and Norma Lou now had three sons. Although he was proud of them, Gordon was not much around them. There were so many things he had to do, not the least of which was finding a replacement for Wendell Sloan, the young, affable minister of education, who had accepted a call to First Baptist in Augusta, Georgia. Martha Hey was resigning from her unpaid post too, and so a choirmaster had to be found.

It was a hectic time, and Gordon, though reveling in it, found his nights a little more restless, a little more sleepless. There was a twinge of nervousness in his demeanor. In moments of great fatigue, he wondered if he was up to the task of taking this church where it wanted to go. Those moments would pass, and he would reassure himself that he was indeed that man. After all, he wanted to go there, too.

The pressure might have clamped down on him more quickly if it hadn't been for the genuine good nature of the congregation. They were mostly Southerners, with a smattering of long-since-converted Yankees. They were open and good-humored with each other. They were ambitious, but their ambition was wrapped in a cocoon of kindness and caring. God was Gordon

Weekley's strength, but so were they. The love he poured out on them from the pulpit was returned a hundredfold to the tall, gentle man from Atlanta.

They had fun with him too, taking advantage of his warm, self-effacing nature. Gordon was not a fire-and-brimstone preacher. He was a thoughtful, quietly persuasive purveyor of the truth as he saw it.

So it was not without plenty of persuasion that on a certain fun night in the fellowship hall, a long-haired, guitar-toting, gaudily attired rock-and-roll singer appeared on stage and, to peals of side-splitting laughter, lip-synced his way through his first and only Elvis Presley imitation.

There was much joy in this congregation, much energy, and many years to look forward to. With the exception of a few members, old age had not yet found its way into their midst. But death did. It came not for the husband in his forties, or the young wife, or the newly married— it came instead for the children.

It came for Becky Byrum, age nine, daughter of Howard and Billie. One moment she was a happy, healthy, contented little girl watching evening television with her mother. The next moment she was telling her mother that she couldn't move her legs and arms. Then came the frantic flight down Randolph Road to the hospital, the phone call to Gordon, his own frantic dash to be at the family's side, and finally, the scene that lay before him in the emergency room.

Howard and Billie Byrum, two of the loveliest people Gordon had ever known, were huddled in the corner being consoled by Dr. Tom Burnett, a neighbor and friend who had accompanied Billie in her race to save her beloved child. On the table between Gordon and his two friends lay Becky. A cerebral hemorrhage had snatched her from the Byrums. One moment she was with them. The next moment she was with God.

It was an iron-fisted blow to the Providence congregation, bringing them to their knees. Rather than weakening them, though, this sad loss strengthened their faith in an Almighty Being and increased their resolve to close ranks even tighter and go on. They did go on, even in the face of the deaths of three more Providence children in the next three years.

Tiny Pam Oxendine died two years after Becky. A balloon, an innocent-looking balloon, caught in her windpipe. And little Susan Jordan, assumed by her mother, Pat, to be inside the house, was instead playing in the driveway just behind the car when her mother backed up and ran over her own child. Recognizing what had happened must have been as terrible a moment as any mother has ever known.

A car killed Ann Helms, too. She was a teenager, a junior high school student, happy and popular. She was out on her first date, and in an all too familiar scene, the car she was riding in spun out of control in a curve, and a life filled with promise was gone. Almost the entire student body turned out for Ann's funeral. Gordon's message was sent by loudspeaker out onto the funeral home grounds. So poignantly did he speak of Ann Helms and so earnestly did he plead with her assembled friends to guard their own precious lives that the governor of North Carolina sent him a letter of thanks and encouraged him to keep speaking out whenever he was in the presence of teenagers with drivers' licenses.

Gordon had a way of reaching people, of healing hurt, of showing how sorrow could renew faith and not destroy it, could strengthen and not weaken man's ties with God. To many who knew him, he seemed to have knowledge and depth of understanding beyond his years.

At Pam Oxendine's funeral, he said this: "As a proclaimer of the Gospel, as a student of the vicissitudes and sufferings of human life, and, most of all, as a searching student of the deep meaning of life, I have come to the conclusion that no life on this earth finds the real, deep springs of eternal communion with the Almighty until, in some form, it has met adversity and, by that adversity, has been forced into contrition, to a point that it was utterly helpless before God, utterly dependent on him, utterly broken."

He did not know it, but those words would soon and fully apply to his own life.

---

By October 1958, the church had two morning services to handle the ever-increasing crowds. Providence was no longer a neighborhood church. People were coming from all over Charlotte, drawn by the energy and drawn, too, by the man who seemed to have genuine affection for everyone he met. And that affection extended beyond the boundaries of the Providence property, beyond even the boundaries of this country.

When Gordon was small, he had dreamed of going to Africa and preaching there for a year or so, telling a people he loved but never met that God loved them, too.

He had tried to go once in seminary when he heard of the need for an English teacher at a Christian mission. The mission's board turned him down, explaining that they wanted their seminary students to graduate before taking on assignments.

The people in the Providence congregation who knew him best were not surprised when he suggested the church pay the costs of educating "a few" Nigerian ministers-to-be at the Ogbomosho Baptist Seminary. Everyone *was* surprised when he announced how many those few were.

"Twenty-four," said Gordon Weekley.

"Amen," the congregation said, or might just as well have said, and twenty-four students got full scholarships, as simply as that.

It seemed then that everything Gordon wanted he got, and everything his church wanted to do, it did.

"Really, things couldn't be better," he said to his friend Dr. Doe as they lunched at their favorite cafeteria in South Charlotte on an afternoon in August 1958, "except that I've been feeling a little jittery lately."

"Jittery?" asked Dr. Doe.

"Jittery, jumpy, I don't know. Maybe a bit edgy. You know my days are pretty full, and, well, something's just not right. What makes it worse is that I'm having a hard time getting to sleep at night. I just lie there and look at the ceiling and think about all the things I have to do tomorrow and all the things I didn't get done today. But really I'm not worried about anything in particular. I love what I'm doing. I'm just... jittery."

"That, we can handle," said Dr. Doe. "After we finish eating, walk over to my office with me. I'll write you a couple of prescriptions."

At his office, Dr. Doe quickly scratched out the two prescriptions and handed them to Gordon.

"The first one is a Miltown. Take it in the mornings, and it should relieve the jitteriness."

"This one," he said, handing him the second prescription, "is a new wonder drug. It's called Doriden. It's safe and non-addictive. Take it about a half-hour before bedtime, and it'll help you get the sleep you've been missing."

Doriden, generic name *glutethimide,* is a sedative-hypnotic that was used as a sleeping pill and also prescribed by some doctors for daytime use to relieve anxiety. Although considered safe, its possible side effects included slurred speech and a staggering gait, not unlike the symptoms of alcohol intoxication.

Gordon stopped at the Eckerd Drug Store on Providence Road and had the two prescriptions filled. He drove back to the church in light early-afternoon traffic, thinking about all he had left to do that afternoon and about the sermon he had to work on that evening and about hospital visitation the next morning. He gave no thought at all to the little bottles in the paper bag beside him.

At ten o'clock that evening, Gordon Weekley got up from his easy chair at his home on Addison Drive, walked to the kitchen, unscrewed the top of a prescription bottle, shook out a pill called Doriden, placed it on his tongue, and swallowed it with a sip of water.

He went back to the den and sat down in front of the television set, but he wasn't much interested in television that night. He was thinking of the sermon he had begun writing that day. He hoped it would be a good one. He desperately wanted it to be, but he was not quite satisfied with its wording. He prided himself on his ability to preach, to reach across the chasm between pulpit and pew with a message that knifed to the very hearts of his listeners. To do that, the content and the phrasing had to be just right.

He did not believe in burdening his parishioners with guilt and fear; he chose instead to preach a Gospel of hope and love and the need for an ever-strengthening relationship with God. Sometimes he felt a twinge of guilt, though, wondering whether the sermons were written for the glory of God or for the glory of Gordon.

The television program was almost over, and he was sleepy now. The sermon, which only a few moments before had been troubling him, seemed not to be a problem anymore. He felt, in fact, quite happy with it. He glanced around the room. *How lucky I am,* he thought, *to live in this nice home, to be part of such a wonderful church, to be blessed with my fine family.*

For weeks, he had been concerned about Norma Lou, worried about her less than total involvement in church activities, worried the deacons might come again, as they had done in Masonboro, asking Gordon for more from her. Now, alone in the den except for the faces on the television, he was not worried at all.

He was feeling better than he had ever felt in his entire life, enveloped in a sense of total well-being. He was happy. He was filled with peace. He was, because of a little pill called Doriden, high as a kite.

He slept that night better than he could ever remember and awoke refreshed, ready to go to work. He took a Miltown to ward off any jitteriness that might come calling.

It didn't work. Not long after he settled behind his desk in the church office, he began to feel anxious. As usual, it was mixed with the excitement of what was happening with Providence and with him, and he pushed on as he always did. He knew now that come nightfall, come ten o'clock or so, he would find respite. He would sleep. And before sleep, he might even get that feeling again, that incredible feeling.

He got it. And he got it the next night and the next and the next.

After about a week, the euphoria began to diminish. Peace did not come as readily or to as great a depth as it had in the beginning, and Gordon craved that peace, even at this early stage of addiction.

"Maybe," he thought, "instead of one, I'll take one and a half. Maybe that will do it."

It did.

It didn't seem to affect his work. He performed eagerly and diligently each day, trying to be the preacher he wanted to be: the giver of great sermons, the visitor to prospective members, the patroller of hospital halls, the meeting attender, the man who before he left on vacations would call on almost every church member personally and explain where he was going and how he could be reached.

No matter how busy he was, he always had time for Dr. Doe. From Gordon's standpoint, the relationship was deepening, strengthening. He profoundly appreciated what the good doctor had done for him, and he looked for ways to show that appreciation.

The opportunity came a few weeks after he began taking the medication. Dr. Doe called and told him of a strange occurrence. He had been on his way to the hospital the evening before to check on his patients.

"I was driving down Randolph Road," he said, "and the next thing I knew, I was sitting in the Charlotte Coliseum at the Billy Graham Crusade. So help me, Gordon, I don't know how I got there or why I got there. I just ended up there. I don't remember a thing between Randolph Road and the Coliseum. For God's sake, can you explain this to me?"

"No, no, I can't," Gordon stammered. "Maybe, subconsciously, you just wanted to go there."

"Gordon, you know I'm not a particularly religious man."

"Maybe," said Gordon, searching his mind for an answer, "maybe you're more religious than you think."

"He's going to be here four more nights," Doe said.

"I know. I have a small part in the Crusade myself."

"I'm really impressed by Billy Graham. I want to hear him again, every night. You don't suppose there's any way you could get me tickets close to the front do you?"

Gordon was thrilled. Dr. Doe wanted a favor, a favor Gordon could likely grant.

He wasted no time contacting Grady Wilson and had the tickets in hand the next day.

For the next several nights, Gordon and Dr. Doe shared each other's company at the Crusade. Doe seemed deeply appreciative of Gordon's gesture, but Gordon felt he hadn't done nearly enough for this man who was his friend.

A few weeks later, he visited the Baptist Book Store and bought the finest Bible he could find. The Graham team was by this time in Hawaii, but Gordon couldn't wait for them to get back. He sent the book airmail to Grady, along with a note asking Billy to write a personal message to Dr. Doe on the flyleaf.

Doe again seemed touched and appreciative, and Gordon still felt he hadn't done enough to return his doctor's kindness. He would keep looking for more ways to do just that.

---

The months rolled by, and 1958 became 1959. People kept coming, making their decisions to become a part of Providence Baptist Church. Gordon Weekley made a decision, too. He decided that one-and-a-half pills every evening weren't enough. Two would be better, he thought, and they were. Not long after that, he reached the conclusion that if the pills worked well on a full stomach, they would work better on an empty one—and they did. He stopped eating supper and started losing weight.

People noticed, but when they talked to each other about it, they attributed it to hard work. They wished he would slow down a little and eat, but they weren't really worried about it.

On May 17, 1959, the Providence congregation moved into the beautiful new sanctuary and its adjacent classrooms. At eleven that morning, looking over the multitude in front of him, Gordon knew this building, like the fellowship hall before it, would not hold the burgeoning church for long.

In the weeks and months that followed, membership mushroomed. Sunday School enrollment rose forty-three percent from the previous year. A kindergarten was started. The budget for calendar year 1959 was up to $102,000.

Providence had come a long way in a short time, and Gordon Weekley had, too. He was becoming well known throughout Charlotte and throughout the state Baptist Convention. In the fall of that year, he received an invitation to accompany Billy Graham's crusade team on its tour of Africa in early 1960.

It was a dream come true. It was Africa. The very mention of it brought out the missionary zeal in him. He was so excited he could barely think of anything else. He pictured himself wandering the continent, bringing the news of Jesus to ears that had never heard the Word. He saw people coming forth, accepting Christ as their Savior. He heard them singing the old hymns. He heard them speaking the Lord's Prayer.

And finally he heard himself saying to Grady Wilson, "Thank you, but no." He couldn't afford it. Neither could Providence, not with a new building and a $400,000 mortgage. Some luxuries were unaffordable, even for this band of doers.

Enter Arthur Ross, bricklayer, a man of no great financial means, but of a very great heart. He stopped Gordon in the parking lot one day after church.

"Gordon, why aren't you going to Africa?"

"M-O-N-E-Y, Arthur," answered Gordon.

"I want you to go. I'll pay your way," he said, dropping his eyes. Gordon was moved.

"Arthur, you'll never know how much I appreciate your offer, but I can't accept it."

"I think it's important that you go. You've always wanted to. And you've done a lot for me personally and for our church. You have to go." It was an offer Gordon couldn't refuse and it was later enhanced by Tom Pfaff. Mr. Pfaff owned an equipment company, and he and the company came forth with a contribution that made it possible for Gordon to go not for just a few days but for several weeks. Gordon Weekley was on his way.

But he wasn't going anywhere without his pills. Some time later, when he went to Dr. Doe to get his required shots for the trip, he asked if he also might have extra pills to take along. He explained that the crusade would be moving from place to place throughout Africa on a tight schedule, and he would need all the sleep he could get.

"Sure," said Dr. Doe, without even batting an eye.

Within minutes, Gordon Weekley was walking out of Eckerd Drug Store on a cloud, with a hundred extra of his beloved Doriden for the trip.

As consumed as he was beginning to be with his pharmaceutical crutches, he never once during this period failed in his efforts to be the shepherd of his flock. Early on Christmas morning, 1959, with his own three children still sleeping soundly in their beds, Gordon Weekley slipped out the back door and drove to Hunter Lane. It was Billie and Howard Byrum's first Christmas without Becky, and when Billie opened the door to the gentle knock, she came face to face with the man who bore their burden with them. He stayed until after lunch.

SIX

In February 1960, the Billy Graham Crusade set out to shed light on the Dark Continent. There were at that time about 275 million Africans, and only 30 million of them were Christians. There was much work to be done, and not much time to do it. The Crusade would last only ten weeks, with some of the schedule being allocated to Israel and Lebanon.

Aside from Dr. Graham's nightly messages to vast audiences, there were missionary schools and hospitals to visit, pulpits to preach from, and meetings and social gatherings with local dignitaries.

Gordon was to catch up with the Crusade in Nairobi at the conclusion of the East African campaign. That plan suited Gordon perfectly. He would arrive in Africa early and see people he wanted to see. Go places he wanted to go.

He had many missionary friends there, and now as the plane touched down in Lagos, Nigeria, it was for Gordon like the beginning of old home week, in a home he had never been to before. He thought about Iwo College at Ogbomosho, some 150 miles north of Lagos, the school he had volunteered to teach in while he was at seminary and the school of the twenty-four Providence scholarship students. Now, at last, he would get to see the campus he almost came to and meet the young men the people of Providence were sponsoring.

Seeing it with him would be Dr. Harold Miller, his best friend and former Greek professor at Furman. Dr. Miller was on sabbatical and joining the Crusade along with Gordon.

It was a delightful several days in Nigeria. Gordon and Dr. Miller first visited with missionary friends John and Doris McGee in the village of Igede in Ekiti country 150 miles northeast of Lagos. On the way there, Gordon saw the Africa he had pictured in his mind. He saw miles and miles of red dirt roads knifing through hilly, dense jungle, interrupted only by an occasional small village inhabited by men, women, and children dressed in brightly colored tunics and headpieces.

Many were not townspeople but had come in from the countryside to sell their farm products at the village market. As the Land Rover inched its way through a crowded marketplace, Gordon saw sides of beef lying on white sheets on the red dirt, surrounded by customers competing with clouds of large flies for an opportunity to view the merchandise. Some of the yams, perhaps Nigeria's most famous foodstuff, were every bit of two feet long.

After a week in Igede, the two travelers moved on to Ogbomosho, to the beautiful Baptist mission that was both a seminary and a hospital. They visited there with Dr. Martha and Prof. Mack Gilliland. Martha ran the hospital, and Mack taught in the seminary. This was where Gordon Weekley had wanted to work years earlier. Now, for a moment, he had his wish. He was invited to speak at both the seminary and the hospital, and he did, complimenting the students and the hospital employees for choosing to dedicate their lives to the betterment of their fellow man.

Gordon and Harold left Nigeria on March 10 and traveled to Accra, Ghana, where they caught a flight to Johannesburg. There they would change planes and fly on to Salisbury, Rhodesia (now Zimbabwe). Their itinerary called for them to visit a mission in Gatooma near Salisbury, then go to other missions near Dar es Salaam, Tanganyika (now Tanzania), before catching up with the Graham team in Nairobi.

If Gordon Weekley had not already feared God, he would have begun to on the flight to Johannesburg. The plane encountered a ferocious thunderstorm. As it bounced from one altitude to another, Gordon hoped his place in heaven was secure. Finally the storm passed, and Gordon saw two other sights he had seen only in his dreams and in National Geographic. One was Victoria Falls and the other was great herds of wildebeest and giraffe and impala on the wide plains of southern Africa.

Gordon was enjoying himself immensely. The trip offered everything a man of his nature could ask for. It was a chance to serve God as part of one of the great evangelical crusades in history, and it also gave him the opportunity to satisfy his continuing curiosity about the world and the people in it.

His mind was always working, and it was working as he and Harold Miller entered their hotel room in Gatooma. No sooner had Gordon set his bags down than he was drawing water in the basin. When it reached a level that satisfied him, he abruptly pulled the plug and stared intently at the drain.

"What in the world are you doing?" asked a bewildered Harold Miller.

"It works," said Gordon Weekley, "just like he said it would."

"What works? Who's 'he'?"

"My eighth-grade science teacher. He told me water drains clockwise south of the equator, and by gosh, he was right," Gordon said, citing a myth widely believed to be fact. Something *was* going down the drain, though, and that something was Gordon's life.

Harold Miller smiled at Gordon. He had seen that kind of curiosity in him often before. He had noticed it almost from the first day Gordon had walked into his Greek 101 classroom many years before.

Harold was only eleven years older than Gordon, but from the time they became friends, he had fretted and fussed over him like a father. He even on occasion called Gordon "son."

He had called him that some days earlier in Ekiti Country, as they were preparing to go to bed. Harold had noticed changes in Gordon's demeanor before bedtimes. Gordon seemed drowsier than a man ought to be, and less lucid.

"Son," Harold Miller said, "you know you're out of it every night, don't you?"

Harold didn't know Gordon was addicted. Gordon didn't know Gordon was addicted. There in a hotel room in Africa, the older man had passed a message, a warning. The young man had not received it.

It was a missed moment for Gordon Weekley. Here, seated across from him, was the friend he loved and respected most in the world, a friend Gordon would lay down his life for. If Gordon Weekley were going to listen to anyone, this would be the one man he would listen to. But he didn't listen. He didn't really hear the message that Harold didn't really know he was delivering.

Had Gordon Weekley suddenly sat up straight on his bed and said, "My God, I'm an addict," what happened a few days later might not have happened. And what happened a few days later made matters much, much worse.

---

Gordon Weekley had been to many Billy Graham Crusades before, but what he saw now as he made his way into the large outdoor stadium in Nairobi, amazed him. Billy Graham was a long way from home, in a land of relatively few Christians, and yet as Gordon watched, the stadium seats changed from institutional gray to red, green, purple, a profusion of colors created by thousands upon thousands of black Africans clad in traditional attire. They had come to hear the farm boy from red-clay country in North Carolina, the farm boy who with grace, authority, and assuredness would deliver to them the Great Promise.

Not all who came were from Nairobi. Many had journeyed on foot from as far as one hundred miles away. Such was the power of the man and the message. The message not easily delivered: every sentence Dr. Graham uttered had to be translated twice, once into Luo, once into Swahili.

Nonetheless, when the call to invitation came, so did the Africans. Old men and women, young people, mothers with babies strapped to their backs flowed down the long aisles of the stadium floor, drawn by the message and the music and the magnificent singing voice of Cliff Barrows.

*Just as I am, without one plea,*
*O Lamb of God, I come! I come!*

The scene was repeated every night for seven nights, and Gordon Weekley was moved by it, and humbled, and proud to be part of such a soul-saving endeavor. Gordon was making valid contributions of his own, receiving converts as they came forward at the Crusade, meeting with missionaries hungry for news from home, preaching at a Baptist church in Nairobi.

His only problem, his only concern on the entire trip, was supper and how to avoid it. So far, he had been doing well by spreading his food around on the plate, making it look as if he'd eaten more than he had, or simply by skipping supper, making an excuse, saying he had to be somewhere and would eat later. Supper ruined the high of the Doriden. Gordon needed the high, the euphoria, the release it offered him. He needed, too, the deep, dreamless sleep that gave him strength for another day, and allowed him to be the hard-working, dedicated preacher he had always wanted to be.

It was not all work in Nairobi. Like everyone on the team, Gordon got a day off. When he was told that Grady Wilson had planned a hunt for him, he was thrilled, because in a world of many wildernesses, there were few places better to hunt than where they were headed. They were going to the north slopes of Mt. Kilimanjaro.

The idea of the hunt may have thrilled him, but the idea of the drive didn't. They would leave in a station wagon late at night and travel until just before dawn. He knew he would have to deny himself a pill that night because he would be asked to share in the driving. And even though he had trouble falling asleep without pills, he was afraid he would do just that when he was behind the wheel of the car.

At the last minute, Grady had to bow out, so the hunting party was made up of Gordon, missionary friend Andrew Lozier, Andrew's teenage son, and a guide. Guides were required on all hunts in East Africa, and all guides in this part of the continent were white. This one was also, not surprisingly, British.

Just before the hunters left, Gordon voiced his concern about falling asleep to a medical missionary friend.

"Don't worry about it," the missionary said, "I've got a capsule that will keep you awake."

Gordon thanked him and stuffed it in his pocket. He knew nothing about the nature of the capsule and cared nothing about it. It was simply some kind of medication that would keep him from falling asleep at the wheel. It was Dexamyl.

Dexamyl was a popular time-release diet pill that while suppressing appetite also gave the user a great rush of energy that manifested itself in excitability and talkativeness. Dexedrine was the main ingredient, but the capsule also contained a barbiturate intended to offset the jumpy side effects. Gordon did not know this, and if he had, he likely wouldn't have given it a second thought. All that occupied his mind now was his big chance to hunt big game in Africa.

They pulled out of Nairobi after nightfall and headed south toward Tanzania. When the lights of the city faded in the rear view mirror, Gordon found himself again in an Africa of old, different from the thickly jungled territory around Lagos but in its own way just as untamed. This was bush country, land of low scrub, grassy plains, flattop trees, and dirt roads little more than trails. The Masai lived here, a nomadic band of cattle herders who wore cow dung in their hair, mixed with red, green, and gold dye, and drank milk mixed with blood drained from a cow's jugular. As they moved on toward Kilimanjaro, Gordon could see scattered silhouettes of these herders, standing watch over their precious commodity.

Halfway to their destination, Gordon began to feel drowsy. He took the green and white capsule from his pocket and washed it down his throat with water from his canteen. In fifteen minutes, Gordon was feeling a euphoria much like he felt with Doriden, but with Doriden, he would get sleepy. Now, he was incredibly alert, filled with energy. Ready to drive. Ready to hunt. Ready for anything. His companions, at this time of night, were subdued. Gordon couldn't understand it. This was Africa! Magnificent Africa, with her deep jungles, vast deserts, beautiful plains. Mother of the Nile. Home of the lion, the elephant, the zebra, the Zulus, Bushmen, Hottentots. Home now, at least for a time, of Gordon Weekley, Billy Graham, the Crusade, Harold Miller, the safari. This was life at its fullest. The Great Adventure. The dream come true.

*Why,* thought Gordon, *is everyone so quiet?*

He tried conversation but got only short responses. They had been traveling now for hours. Weariness was setting in for everyone except Gordon—but then he was the only one in the car who was wired.

They arrived at the hunting grounds two hours before dawn. Gordon opened the car door, stepped out, and stared in wonder at the magnificent 19,000 foot Mt. Kilimanjaro. It was almost flat on top, except for a depression in the middle as if some giant had licked the peak off an ice cream cone.

Gordon's companions wanted to sleep until dawn since hunting couldn't begin before then anyway, but sleep was the last thing on Gordon's mind. He wanted to talk. Or walk. His pulse was racing. His mind was more alert than he could ever remember. He was feeling good. The world was wonderful. The mountain was wonderful. The station wagon was wonderful.

Wonderful as it all was, his friends persuaded him to rest. They did not know about the amphetamine and, except for Gordon's unusual alertness, did not notice anything different about him.

His friends quickly fell asleep in the car. Gordon climbed back in and tried to do the same, but he couldn't. So it was he who first felt the ground shake. The station wagon shook, and the people in it shook, and the sound that accompanied the shaking was like a freight train out of control and passing close.

It was a freight train, of sorts. It was two tons of angry rhinoceros headed straight for the frightened hunters in the station wagon. It was too late to move, to jump, to do anything except pray a very short prayer.

At the last possible moment, the rhino decided it had better things to do than fight a car. It turned and went on its way.

Gordon's friends decided they had had enough sleep. They stood by the car talking, waiting for dawn, and listening for the sound of freight trains.

Dawn came, followed a few minutes later by a herd of impala. They were a hundred yards away and moving on a trail that would bring them within thirty yards of the hunters.

The guide handed Gordon a rifle, stationed him in front of the car, and suggested a kneeling position for firing.

"The does come first," the guide said. "Put the scope on them, hold the rifle steady, and let them walk through your site line. When the good buck appears, aim above and behind the right foreleg and fire."

"I'll try," said Gordon, "but I'm not a very good shot."

The scope was attached to a .375 magnum rifle, a weapon Gordon had never fired before. He soon would, because the impala were here now, moving slowly in a straight line. Through the scope, Gordon saw one doe, two, a dozen or more, until at last the horned head of a buck appeared. Gordon took a breath, held it, and gently as he could, squeezed the trigger. *Blam.* The blast broke the morning silence like a bomb. The rifle kicked violently. The herd leapt forward, and Gordon fell back, flat on his rear end.

"I told you I wasn't a good shot," Gordon said, as he picked himself up off the ground.

"Good enough," said the guide.

The impala lay dead, a bullet square in its heart.

Back with the Crusade team the following evening, Gordon looked up from his dinner plate and into the eyes of a concerned Billy Graham.

"Gordon, are you feeling all right?" he asked. You haven't touched your food."

"I'm fine, Billy. Just a little tired from the hunt, I guess."

SEVEN

Gordon came home filled with the zeal of the missionaries he had met in Africa. It had been good for him to get away from the demands of a growing church, from meetings filled with building plans, budgets, membership goals, visitation lists. In Africa, he had seen missionaries doing what they believed God had asked them to do: *Preach the Gospel. Spread the Good News.* They too had buildings and budgets and memberships to deal with, but there was something different about it there. Perhaps it was the excitement of bringing the Word to people who had never heard it before.

Whatever it was, it refreshed and refilled Gordon—at least for a little while.

*I am a preacher. First and foremost, I am a preacher,* he said to himself. *My duty is simply to serve God, whether I am in the pulpit at Providence or Masonboro or in a mud hut in Africa.* He wanted desperately to believe that. He did not want to believe that he was also a young man on the way up who enjoyed the adulation of his followers and the success of Providence, who sometimes enjoyed them as much as he enjoyed his humble serving of God.

To compound the situation, not all the baggage Gordon brought home with him was suitcases. He also brought back a deep fondness for Dexamyl.

"Gordon," the voice on the other end of the line said, "this is Frank Caldwell. I know this is short notice, but I was wondering if you could possibly come down this Thursday and speak to the men."

"Well, I..."

"I realize you were just here six weeks ago, but Al Harwick has a funeral out of town and had to cancel. I thought of you first because the men seem to enjoy your sermons."

Gordon had spoken many times at the Charlotte Rescue Mission, a downtown refuge for wayfarers, mostly alcoholics. Three hots and a cot and the Word of God. It was a thankless job that Frank Caldwell did well. Gordon often wondered what kind of a man it took to stand every day in a pulpit and look over a sea of brain-dead, unshaven, stony-eyed, hollow-cheeked faces. They were there for two reasons: food and bed. God was something they had to listen to before they got either.

Gordon admired Frank, but knew he could never be like him. Gordon needed feedback, needed to see response in the faces of his congregation, needed people moving down the aisles to accept Christ. Needed choirs singing. Frank brought a fair share forward to the altar and over the years got hundreds to swear off booze, but whether they stayed in the fold and off the sauce, no one knew. They were there one day and gone the next, and those that did come back were back for the same reasons: three hots and a cot. Gordon often thought that if he had to work there, he'd find another profession.

But he could preach there once in a while to help Frank, and maybe, just maybe, to reach the ears of one of those lost and lonely souls.

"Of course I'll come," said Gordon.

The mission was on Church Street then, on the west side of town, the industrial side. The building was a small, dingy, one-story storefront of no more than three or four thousand square feet. The inside was as dark as the street. A smattering of hand-me-down chairs and sofas and an old television set filled the front section. Beyond the first partition was the makeshift chapel, really no more than a bare room with folding chairs and a beat-up piano. The kitchen was in the back, across the hall from the sleeping area with its old Army cots.

It was dark when Gordon pulled his car up to the sidewalk in front of the mission, and he wasted no time locking his door and walking the several steps to the front entrance. This area was no place to be at night, and as he stepped inside, he felt a sense of refuge and a sense of empathy for those thousands who had come before him in tattered clothes and worn-out shoes, seeking that same security from the night that he had sought in those few steps between his car and the door.

He shook hands with Frank and went with him into the chapel. The men shuffled in from the sleeping area and the front lounge and quietly took their seats. Frank settled in at the piano and ran through a less than professional rendition of "The Old Rugged Cross." Gordon scarcely heard the voices in front of him, voices whose vocal chords had been chronically assaulted by alcohol and cigarettes and whose souls had been scarred by life.

Nevertheless, he preached with passion, reaching out with his heart and his intellect, hoping that somehow the words would reach across that infinite chasm, which seemed to be only a few feet wide, and touch the hearts of these broken and beaten men. It appeared that indeed the words did reach one man, because he shuffled forth at the hymn of invitation, took Gordon's hand, and announced in quiet tones that he was accepting Jesus Christ as his personal Saviour. He was about sixty, toothless, stubble-chinned, with blue eyes that seemed to Gordon to have been permanently frightened by some terror once seen.

The young minister drove home that night pleased and praying. He prayed that the man truly had found Christ, and he was pleased that his words had struck a chord.

He also drove home relieved that he would not have to go down there again for some little time.

---

"By the way," said Gordon Weekley to Dr. Doe at one of their Wednesday lunches, "a doctor in Africa gave me some medication called Dexamyl. It seemed to make me feel a little more energetic, a little peppier during the day. Do you think I might get some of those?"

"No problem," said Doe. "Let's go by the office after lunch, and I'll write you a prescription."

Once again, Gordon Weekley stopped by the drugstore on the way back to the church. Once again, he got a prescription filled. Now he was set. Energy tinged with euphoria in the day. Drowsiness tinged with euphoria in the evening. The circle was complete. There were no gaps, no escape holes to crawl through. He was on his way to destruction.

---

To some of the Providence members, Gordon's hiatus to Africa seemed to have given him a renewed energy, an even greater enthusiasm than he had had before—not that he had been lacking in either. But now he was a whirlwind. He never seemed to tire, and his speech and body language were more animated than ever. If anyone thought there might be something wrong, nobody mentioned it.

The church continued to grow, and Gordon's reputation grew along with it, not just with his public but with his peers. In 1960, he was elected president of the North Carolina Baptist Pastors' Conference. It was a high point in his life, but then, at this stage of the game, he was high all the time.

The year before, Norma Lou had been elected corresponding secretary of the Conference of Ministers' Wives of the Convention. Gordon was pleased that she agreed to run and relieved that she won. He didn't think she cared anything about the office but had let her name be placed in nomination because their dear friend and the president of the organization, Elsie Davis, had asked her to.

*Anyway,* thought Gordon, *the office looks good on paper, and maybe it will keep the deacons from my door.*

Only one deacon came to the door, and he came on his own accord, not as a representative of the others. One was all it took to cause concern in Gordon. He didn't want anyone to be discontented with anything having to do with his pastorate.

Gordon was a diplomat. Partly because of his position as a minister, partly because of his personality, he liked arguments and discussions to end with all parties feeling reasonably good about themselves. In this case, the party of the third part, Norma Lou, was not present, and although Gordon felt in his heart that she was wrong for her lack of involvement, he made excuses for her, talking about her dedication to the children, talking about her dedication to him. He believed the part about the children but, down inside, questioned the part about her concern for him. She was, after all, making overtures about going back to college to get her degree.

But Gordon agreed with the deacon, too. He had a point. Gordon would speak to her. He did. It did no good.

They argued. He told her she could damage his career. He told her that her lack of involvement was adding undue pressure to an already stressful situation.

She countered that the church was enormously successful and he was loved and respected by virtually everyone.

"It's not enough," he answered. "This is a church of achievers. They're not going to be content to reach a certain point and then suddenly put the brakes on. They want to go wherever their energy takes them. And I have to go with them."

As he was saying the words, he knew they weren't entirely true. Certainly the church wanted to climb to great heights. Certainly the members placed enormous demands on his time, albeit in a friendly and loving way—but Gordon wanted everything the church wanted. Most of all, he wanted to be the man out front, the man leading the way. Providence Baptist was big, but not nearly as big as the ego of the man behind the pulpit.

Yet ego's counterweight was compassion. Gordon truly wanted to be at the hospital to witness every birth, truly cared about everyone in a sickbed, truly loved every man, woman, and child in his pastorate.

He struggled with his inner conflicts constantly. *Am I doing this, whatever good deed it was, out of love or a desire to be loved? Am I spending too little time with my family? Too much time with my family? Am I working too hard? Am I not working hard enough? Am I relying too much on the Doriden and the Dexamyl? No. No, I'm not. They help me. That's why the doctor prescribed them.*

Martha Lowrance was no doctor, but she knew trouble when she saw it. The outspoken Texan who never met a stranger waited patiently that Sunday morning until the crowd had said their goodbyes to the preacher and left.

"Gordon," she said, as he stood by the pulpit, gathering his notes, "are you okay?"

"Sure, I'm okay," he said, surprised. "What makes you think I'm not?"

"Your sermon."

"Didn't you like it?"

"I liked it a lot," she said, "but you delivered it so fast, I had to hang on for dear life just to keep up."

"Really? I didn't realize I was doing that."

"You've been doing everything at super speed lately. It's almost like you have a case of hyperactivity. And besides that, you're all skin and bones. Maybe you need to slow down a little."

That was the second reference Gordon had heard about his weight in a week. For most of his adult life, he had weighed around 165 pounds. Now he was closer to 130.

He knew what was causing the weight loss. Dexamyl curbed his appetite, and supper was the meal he most wanted to miss. After the supper hour, late in the evening while he was still on the high from the Dexamyl, he would take the Doriden. Together, the two produced a high that far exceeded the one he got from Doriden alone.

But the hyperactivity was a revelation to him. He didn't realize he had been acting that way. No one had mentioned it before. *Maybe,* he thought, *Norma Lou has said something about my behavior.* But if she had, he couldn't remember, at least not in the context of "hyperactivity." Norma had certainly mentioned the pills to him. She'd said he seemed to be taking an awful lot of them.

"Maybe I do need to slow down a bit," he said to Martha. "Maybe I'm working too hard."

"I think that would be a real good idea," she said. Then she hugged him and left, leaving him to wonder whether his behavior was the result of drugs or hard work or both.

He didn't have to wait long to find out. A few weeks later his phone rang. It was Dr. Doe.

"Gordon, could you drop by my office this afternoon? I have to talk to you about something."

"Can it keep until evening?" Gordon asked. "I have some appointments this afternoon."

"It won't keep, Gordon," Doe said firmly.

When he arrived at the doctor's office, he found a grim John Doe.

"My nurse brought this to my attention," said Doe, holding up a chart. "It seems we've been okaying too many of your prescriptions. Far too many."

"Well, I..." Gordon stammered.

"Gordon," Doe interrupted, "I want you to check into Presbyterian."

---

"Gordon's in the hospital."

The word couldn't have spread much faster through the Providence congregation if it had been announced on the nightly news. Tongues wagged on Randolph Road, on Sharon Amity, on Providence, in living rooms and backyards and porches.

"He's overworked."

"I know. At least, I hope that's all it is. He's lost so much weight, it could be cancer."

"Well, whatever it is, I'm sure he'll be all right. He just hasn't been the same since he got back from Africa."

"I don't know. I think it goes back before, before he went to Africa. He used to act groggy sometimes, like he was tired all the time. Then, after Africa, it was like he had to get everything done today. I've never seen anybody so busy."

"Too busy to eat, that's his problem."

"What do I tell them?" Gordon asked Dr. Doe. "Do I say you think I'm addicted to the medications you put me on? Do I tell them I'm some kind of a dope fiend."

"Of course not," Doe responded.

"Well, I hope not, because I'm not dependent on those medications. I can stop taking them any time I feel like it. I've done it. Several times."

---

"Gordon, if you're not going to lie on the bed, at least sit on it. You're wearing a path in the floor. Norma Lou, tell your husband to sit."

Gordon sat, but sitting didn't mitigate his anxiety. He was in room 353 of Presbyterian Hospital. He had come willingly, if not enthusiastically, from Dr. Doe's office. Now, faced with the reality of hospitalization for drug abuse, he was not so sure he was willing to stay.

"If this gets out, I'll never preach again, anywhere. Everything I've worked for, everything I've prayed for will be gone. Preachers aren't drug addicts. Alcoholics, maybe, once in a blue moon, but not drug addicts. And *I'm* certainly not one. I can't go through with this."

"Have you ever heard of anorexia?" Doe asked.

"No. No, I haven't."

"Well, it's a disorder related to weight loss and lack of desire for food. It's often attributed to stress, to overwork. Anyway, for the record, that's what you are. You're anorexic. You're also dependent on Doriden and Dexamyl, but nobody but us will ever know that."

Gordon realized reluctantly that there was no winning this argument—with somebody else, maybe, but not with his wife and his doctor. He decided, finally, that since he was not truly addicted, withdrawal could not be that bad. He didn't know better until the second day.

He awoke early to the sounds of clanging and banging above him. Plumbers, working almost directly overhead. The sounds of the pipes and wrenches slammed against his eardrums and the two membranes tom-tommed the decibels into every corner of his brain. He punched the call button by his bed, covered his ears, and pushed his face in the pillow.

A few minutes later, a nurse entered.

"Tell them to stop," he said, almost screaming to make himself heard about the racket.

"Stop what?" she asked.

"Can't you hear them, the plumbers?" he said, voice full of anger and frustration.

"They're working on the floor above. What's wrong?"

"Loud, loud, they're too damn loud."

"They don't seem very loud to me."

"Then you need to get your ears checked," he said icily.

She left, but the noise didn't. All morning long, it went on. Gordon did everything he could to take his mind off the sound. He tried reading. He paced. He studied the vial of insulin and the syringe Doe had left with him, along with instructions for injection. Why insulin, he didn't know. Why self-injections, he didn't know. And didn't care. He wanted Doriden or Dexamyl.

*Maybe insulin will turn down the volume,* he thought. *Anyway, it's worth a try.*

He stuck the needle in the vial and slowly withdrew the fluid. Pointing the syringe skyward, he pushed the plunger, ejecting some of the insulin and any air that might be trapped. He dabbed his leg with an alcohol saturated cotton ball and, gritting his teeth, jabbed the needle into his flesh. He waited. Waited for the sound to diminish. Waited for his longing for Doriden and Dexamyl to cease. Nothing happened. For the next few hours, he thought he was going crazy. At noon, the clanging stopped. He let out a sigh and laid back on his pillow.

And then he heard it, clearly, obtrusively, the sound of a car's tires turning in the circular driveway three floors below.

*My God,* he thought, *what's wrong with me? What's wrong with my ears? I can't stand it anymore.* He was in a frenzy now, and he circled the room again and again, hands clasped over his ears.

"Please Lord, help me, help me," he said.

"What do you want me to do?" the voice asked.

He looked up, startled, and saw the face of Norma Lou.

"Get me a doctor. I've got to have something, anything. I'm going mad, Norma Lou. I'm losing my mind."

A doctor arrived and, seeing Gordon's condition, gave him a sedative. He lay back down on the bed. The clanging resumed, but less loudly now, as if it were somewhere far off.

He awoke the next morning to marching feet in the hall, breakfast trays being raked off carts, a phone ringing at the nurse's station a hundred feet away. He was back where he had started yesterday. By the third day, his hearing became less acute and his desire for drugs less demanding. Still, he was miserable. Agitated. Resentful. He resented Doe. He resented Norma Lou. He resented the fact that he had been hospitalized for no good reason. And he vowed he would never again let himself be subjected to this kind of treatment.

Late in the afternoon of the fourth day, Doe arrived.

"How are you feeling, Gordon?"

"I'd feel a lot better if I were out of here."

"Well, do you think you can get by now without the medications ?"

"I know I can. I could before you put me in here."

"Gordon, you went through withdrawal. There's no denying that. You were in agony."

"All right, John, I'm too tired to argue. Certainly my body reacted to the absence of something it was used to. But John...I am not an addict."

"I never said you were, Gordon. I said you were too dependent on those things. You're better off without them."

"I probably am," he said.

"Good. Then let's get you out of here."

The following Sunday, he was back in the pulpit, warmly welcomed by the Providence congregation and admonished by many to stop working so hard.

"Put some meat on your bones," said one of the more matronly women.

And that's exactly what he did. For the next several weeks, he stayed away from the medications and gained back ten pounds.

Although he performed his job masterly, putting in fourteen- and sixteen-hour days, he seemed to tire easily. At night, he would lie in bed sleepless for hours, tossing and turning, not getting the rest he needed. He worried about so-and-so in the hospital, worried about a couple with marital problems, worried about getting next week's sermon just right. He worried about getting to sleep.

After about a month, he decided that he and he alone should be the judge of what was good for him and what wasn't. The medications, he decided, were not harmful. Doe and Norma Lou had been measuring his tolerance level by their standards, not his. His tolerance level was higher.

He had heard of a young doctor just starting his practice in a township only minutes from Charlotte. He decided to give him a try. The doctor readily bought the story of a hard-working preacher who sometime before had used a medication called Doriden to help him sleep at night and another called Dexamyl that gave him a little pick-up in the morning. That hard-working preacher would like to try them again now, because they seemed to help a little. He would only use them occasionally.

The first occasion was that night when he walked into his bathroom, fished the prescription bottles from his pocket, and downed a Doriden. Then he hid the evidence.

The next morning he took a Dexamyl, and that night, another Doriden. He was back on the beam and feeling fine.

The young doctor became the Weekley family physician. Gordon would go to him periodically for drugs, but not too often. He knew now that he had to spread himself out to avoid suspicion. He visited a medical complex near uptown Charlotte, and standing in the lobby, he ran his finger down the building's directory until he found a throat specialist. Being a public speaker with an occasional tendency toward hoarseness made him a legitimate candidate for a visit. While he was there, he said, "By the way, could you possibly do me a favor? My prescriptions have expired on a couple of medications I'm taking, and you could save me a visit to my general practitioner if you could write them for me. On my schedule, it's difficult to get to my doctor's."

A Charlotte dermatologist got the same story after he looked at a minor skin ailment Gordon felt he "needed to have checked out." And then there was the oral surgeon he happened to know.

Doctors weren't his only prey; he went after pharmacists, too. When a prescription would expire at a particular pharmacy, Gordon would go there anyway and act surprised when the person behind the counter told him he had no more refills. Somehow, some way, he would talk the pharmacist into one more.

# EIGHT

In the winter of 1961, Jarvis Warren, chairman of the deacons, told Gordon about another Billy Graham Crusade.

"It's in South America, Venezuela, and Grady suggested that you come along. I think it's a good idea. You've been working hard. You need to get away."

Gordon agreed. In the spring of 1962, he and Grady Wilson boarded a plane in Charlotte and headed south.

The first stop was Miami, for an overnight layover. They arrived in the early afternoon and checked into a hotel. Grady had some business to take care of with some other Graham people in the city. Gordon was left with time on his hands, which gave him the opportunity to do a little shopping. He picked up the phone and dialed the number of a nearby pharmacy.

"I'm Gordon Weekley, Reverend Gordon Weekley. I'm calling from the Holiday Hotel. I'm from out of town, on my way to South America with the Billy Graham Crusade, and I'm afraid I've done something foolish."

"What's that, Rev?" the friendly pharmacist asked.

"I left my medication at home, something my doctor had prescribed for me, and I was wondering if possibly I might get some from you."

"What do you need?"

"I'm taking something called Dexamyl and another one called Doriden."

"No problem," the druggist said. "We've got to keep that team rolling. Would you like to come pick it up or would you rather I sent it over?"

*My Lord,* thought Gordon, *they're willing to deliver the stuff to my door.* Gordon declined the delivery and picked it up himself. The next morning, he and Grady were flying to Venezuela.

They arrived in Caracas, stayed the night, and flew on to Maracaibo, one of the many cities on the Graham itinerary. An ancient city in the northwest of the country, having been established in 1529, it now had 800,000 residents.

The Crusade team was quartered in the magnificent Del Lago Hotel overlooking the 6,300-square-mile Lake Maracaibo. The city is bordered to the north by the Gulf of Venezuela which opens to the Caribbean Sea. The other three directions out from the city formed a great horseshoe of mountains, but Maracaibo itself was lowland country.

Gordon was awed by the natural beauty of the lake but put off by the oil rigs that sprang from the waters like so many Loch Ness monsters. They stretched as far as he could see from the balcony of his hotel room. There were too many to count.

It was a typical Graham Crusade, with Grady and Gordon and many other pastors preaching in the various churches and missions and Billy drawing the large crowds to the huge stadium.

One of the missionaries stationed in Venezuela was Charles Clark, an old seminary classmate of Gordon. After reuniting and filling each other in on news of mutual friends and former classmates, their talk turned to missionary work.

In the course of the conversation, the famed old Catholic mission, El Tucuco, came up. While most missions are created to save souls, El Tucuco was created to save lives. It was deep in the jungle, at the base of the Sierra de Perija range. Its only neighbors were the Yukpa and Motoloni Indians, tribes that disposed of unwanted children and old people by abandoning them in the jungle to die of starvation or be eaten by predators.

The mission was their only salvation, and it saved many.

"I've never seen it," said Charles, "and I'd like to."

"So would I," said Gordon. "Let's go."

They took Charles's car on the eighty-mile journey. In a few minutes, the city gave way to delta farmland. While Charles drove, Gordon soaked in the pastoral beauty of the farmers at work in their fields. The warm glow he felt that morning was partly from the scenes he saw in front of him and partly from the Dexamyl he had taken earlier.

The farmlands ended abruptly and the jungle began. As they went deeper, the land began to rise up toward the mountains in front of them.

For the better part of the next hour, they saw no cars and no people. They did see a thirty-foot anaconda in a tree beside the narrow road, and the incredibly beautiful foliage of this South American jungle. And soon, they saw the militia bearing down on them in a jeep.

A young officer hopped out, strode quickly to the driver's side of the car, and in anxious tones and near-perfect English said, "Where do you think you are going?"

"To the mission," answered Charles. "To El Tucuco."

"Gentlemen," said the officer, "you are in great danger. This is Indian country, and the Indians are not friendly. Being here now is like being in your own old wild West a hundred years ago. I strongly suggest that you turn your car around and get back to Maracaibo. Fast."

The two out-of-place preachers looked at each other.

"What do you think?" Charles asked Gordon.

"I don't know. How far to the mission?"

"How far to the mission?" Charles asked the officer.

"About ten miles."

Charles looked at Gordon. "We've come this far," he said.

"Might as well," Gordon answered.

"We're going on to the mission," Charles said to the officer. "Thank you, and we'll be careful."

"Being careful won't help you much," said the soldier. "Two weeks ago, a man was killed not far from here."

"How?" asked Gordon, not wanting to know.

"Spear," he replied.

The jeep turned around and headed east toward Maracaibo. The two ministers watched it until it disappeared around a curve. They were alone again, and Gordon felt suddenly not as brave as he had when the militia man was there.

They drove on. The jungle they had been driving through before was the same as this, and the road was too, but now it all seemed different. The road seemed narrower to Gordon, the trees on either side taller and more dense. Every movement in the brush brought a stab of anxiety.

A mile passed. Two. There was no indication that they were getting any closer to El Tucuco.

What they saw next made Gordon's heart sink. It was a small sign with the words El Tucuco and an arrow painted on it. The arrow pointed up a dirt road that was little more than a trail. They turned. The road was winding and bumpy and so narrow that tree limbs on either side brushed the car. The sky had virtually disappeared. Gordon wondered how far it was to the mission and silently prayed that it would only be a few yards ahead.

The car had slowed now to less than ten miles an hour. Jungle sounds were all around them. Gordon was convinced there was an Indian behind every tree.

He looked at Charles, but Charles was staring straight ahead, jaw set, both hands on the wheel. It was not a time for talking.

They rounded a curve and climbed a long hill toward a plateau. As they reached the crest, Charles grabbed Gordon's arm with his right hand.

"Look," he shouted.

Gordon looked, and there in front of him was a clearing, and in the clearing, a complex of old Spanish-styled stucco buildings: El Tucuco.

The compound was surrounded by a high fence that obviously wasn't there to keep people in. Charles stopped the car in front of the large iron gate, and Gordon jumped out to open it. Just as his hand touched the latch, he was frozen by a sound he had only heard before in the movies. It was the loud, fearsome yipping and whooping sound of Indians—and they were close, as close as the woods were to the compound, a distance of only a few yards.

Gordon lifted the latch, pulled open the double gate, and frantically waved Charles forward. Charles didn't need a second invitation. The car zipped into the compound, Gordon right behind it slamming the gate.

They walked briskly to the administration building and were greeted by a smiling priest. He closed the door behind them, and the environment immediately changed. The sounds of the Indians were gone, in their place were soft words of greeting from the priest and the hollow footsteps of a nun coming up a hallway toward them.

They stayed about two hours, touring the compound and talking to the priest about the work being done there. He was pleased to see them; the mission had few visitors. Neither Gordon nor Charles needed to ask why.

They saw the dormitories where the old Indians cast out by their communities would live the rest of their lives. They visited the small school where the young people were being educated and trained to enter the outside world of Maracaibo or beyond.

Gordon was impressed by the dedication and selflessness of the priests and the nuns who labored here in a jungle filled with hostile people. He was very aware that the people the priests and nuns were trying to save belonged to the two tribes outside the wall.

*Love thine enemies,* Gordon thought. *Do good to those who persecute you.* Rarely had Jesus' words spoken to him as clearly as they did here at El Tucuco.

Finally it came time for the travelers to leave.

"Hang on," said Charles to his passenger.

They zipped out the gate the priest had opened for them and down the winding jungle road at a speed that would have been considered unsafe except that slower, in this case, would have been less safe.

After a few harrowing minutes, their car hit the hard-surface road and careened left toward Maracaibo. If the Indians were going to get these gentlemen, they were going to have to be very fast.

They arrived at the hotel in record time and found an anxious Grady Wilson waiting for them in the lobby.

"Do you know where you've just been?" asked Grady.

"We know," said Gordon, sheepishly.

From then on, Gordon stayed in the city. He spent the rest of the week assisting with the Graham Crusade and preaching in various churches throughout Maracaibo. He even spoke one afternoon to a large group of prisoners at the local penitentiary. Standing in the courtyard of the fortresslike structure, speaking through a translator, he told a hundred men about the love and forgiveness of Jesus Christ. He felt particularly eloquent that day, and he was holding his audience's attention well. He felt even more eloquent when he looked up from his sermon notes and noticed several monkeys in the courtyard trees hanging on every word.

The Crusade was going well. Dr. Graham filled the huge outdoor stadium every night, and thousands came forward to accept Christ or to renew their faith.

What little free time Gordon had, he spent walking the streets, visiting the shops, watching the people, soaking up the culture.

Late one afternoon, he entered a pharmacy and browsed around the hundreds of products on the shelves. Many of them bore familiar names and labels: aspirin, Bufferin, milk of magnesia, Doriden.

Doriden! He couldn't believe his eyes. Bottles and bottles of it. On the shelf. An over-the-counter product.

Gingerly, almost lovingly, he gathered up every Doriden bottle in sight and carried them in his arms to the cash register. The pharmacist looked down at the array in front of him, then up at Gordon, but he said nothing. He took the money, filled a paper bag with the bottles, and handed it to the wild-eyed man across the counter from him.

Back in his hotel room, Gordon dumped the bottles on his bed. He was ecstatic—but only momentarily.

*How am I going to get these out of the country? What if there's a law against it? What if I get caught?*

He was torn between fear and desire. Desire won. He left, went to a nearby store, and came back moments later with a four-foot length of plastic, about three inches wide. He fashioned a belt out of the plastic, folding it lengthwise to make a tube. He filled the tube with Doriden and wrapped it around his waist. He would wear the Doriden out of South America under his shirt.

Gordon had planned to stay for only the first half of the Crusade. He was booked to leave the following morning. By tomorrow night, he would either be home free with his Doriden or he would be in jail in Miami.

The phone rang. It was Cliff Barrows, Billy Graham's music director.

"Gordon, can you come to my room?" Gordon went.

"We have a problem," Barrows said. "Chicago's snowed in, and we can't fly the 'Hour of Decision' tape there."

The "Hour of Decision" was the weekly Billy Graham sermon broadcast from Chicago to radio stations around the nation.

"We've arranged to do the national hook-up from a Miami station. If you'll take the tape with you, someone from the team will pick it up from you at the Miami airport."

Gordon took the tape, went back to his room, and packed.

The following morning, he nervously boarded the plane, Doriden wrapped around his waist, a Billy Graham sermon in his hand.

The flight was uneventful, though the flights of fantasy in Gordon's mind weren't. At last the plane landed at Miami International and taxied toward the gate.

*Well,* said Gordon to himself, *this is it. I'm either going home or going to jail.*

The stewardess spoke over the plane's intercom. "Would everyone please remain seated for just a moment after we stop." What could this be? Gordon asked himself.

The plane stopped, the door opened, and an airline representative stepped into the plane's interior.

"If there's a Reverend Gordon Weekley on board, would he please identify himself?"

Fear struck Gordon's gut like a knife. He was had. It was over, his career, his freedom, his life. He could see the headlines in the *Charlotte Observer*. LOCAL PASTOR INDICTED FOR DRUG SMUGGLING.

He raised his hand and waited for the cold steel of the cuffs to be snapped around his wrist.

"Reverend Weekley, please come with me," the man said.

He got up and reluctantly went forward. The man placed his arm on Gordon's back, and together they walked down the steps from the plane.

"What's this all about?"asked Gordon.

"Dr. Lane Adams is waiting here for you. He's come to pick up the 'Hour of Decision' tape."

Gordon's spirits soared. There at the foot of the steps was Dr. Lane Adams.

"Here it is," said Gordon, waving the tape over his head.

"Excellent," said Dr. Adams. The three men turned and walked toward the terminal.

"Is this your final destination?" the airline rep asked.

"No, I'm catching a plane to Charlotte in about an hour."

"Fine," said the attendant, "after we clear customs, I'll take you to your gate."

*My Lord,* thought Gordon, *customs. I still have to go through customs.*

They stopped by the baggage pick-up, retrieved Gordon's luggage, then entered the customs area and walked toward an inspection table. It was the longest walk of Gordon's life.

As they neared the table, Gordon saw that the uniformed agent standing behind it was looking straight at him.

*What does he see? Does he see the bulge around my waist?*

"Hi, Bill," said the airline representative to the customs agent.

"Hi, Tom," said the agent, smiling. The three men kept on walking, past the table, past the agent, past customs.

Gordon Weekley was home free.

- 74 -

Not long after his return to Charlotte, Jarvis Warren told him Providence was getting out of the residential real estate business. "It's your home now, Gordon, to do with what you want."

Gordon was stunned. He was being handed the house on Addison Drive. The mortgage payments would be his to keep up, but Providence was giving him a housing allowance, too, $125 a month. The house, though lovely and in a fine neighborhood, was too small. With the birth of son John, there were four Weekley children now.

Gordon decided almost immediately to sell it and build his own home, farther out, in an area of South Charlotte more sparsely developed. By now, his neighborhood, which was less than a mile from the church, was growing up and filling in. He wanted a place where he could watch the squirrels and hear the birds, and he wanted a creek through his property.

He wanted a fine home, too, a large one. Although he would not admit it to himself, deep down, he wanted that house to be a symbol of all he had achieved at Providence.

To the people who knew him, he was a humble man. That was how he thought of himself. But there was a battle going on inside Gordon Weekley, a battle between humility and pride. Pride was winning.

He searched weeks for just the right piece of land, going out to look almost every day. Finally he found it on Country Lane, a short distance from Providence Road. Country Lane wound its unpaved way through the wooded, rolling terrain of South Charlotte. There were only a few widely scattered houses there then. His would sit on sixteen acres of land fronted by a creek. It was perfect, and it was only five miles from the church. He wasted no time in contracting for the construction of a two-story colonial, using the pastorium as a down payment to the builder.

Before anything could happen, a bridge had to be built over the creek. Gordon wanted to build the bridge himself, and he didn't know exactly why. Building it became almost an obsession for him.

Construction engineering was not among his talents. He sought out an engineer in his congregation and spent hours talking to him about the bridge, soaking up his ideas and knowledge. Nights, he drew plans, and he did it with a clear head. There was no Doriden, no Dexamyl to cloud his thinking. His preoccupation with the house and the bridge gave him a reason to quit taking drugs for a while and prove to himself he could do without them if he wanted to. He figured his abstinence would also deflect any suspicions Norma Lou might be harboring. If he didn't do them all the time, he reasoned, she wouldn't know he was doing them some of the time.

He felt the nagging emptiness of withdrawal but fought it off with his attention to the bridge and to the house he would have built. Even now, after his hospitalization and his ultimate return to drugs, he did not acknowledge his addiction, admitting only that he occasionally relied too heavily on his bottled friends. He knew, he told himself, that they were crutches and that he could not walk on them forever.

His days had always been full, and they were fuller now. He spent every free moment at the property clearing brush from the creek banks, reluctantly marking a few trees for removal, visualizing the layout of the house, and finally, building his beloved bridge.

As bridges go, it was nothing special. It was not covered. It was not railed. It was just a bridge, but it was *his* bridge. He built four forms for the abutments, two on each side of the creek, and filled them with concrete. With the help of strong-armed parishioners and some heavy equipment, he placed two steel I-beams over the expanse and secured two large concrete slabs to the beams.

"You could drive a train over this bridge," his engineer friend said to a beaming Gordon Weekley.

Gordon felt good—tired, but good. Construction of his dream house could now begin. He was filled with a sense of accomplishment that last day at the bridge. He climbed into his car and headed for his home on Addison Drive. As he drove down to Providence, sadness began to creep in. The bridge was finished. The bridge he had worked on so hard and with such joy no longer needed his attention. He turned right on Sardis Road, left on Randolph, and pulled into the parking lot of the church. He sat there for a few minutes, staring straight ahead. Then got out, went to his office, unlocked his top desk drawer, and took out a small bottle marked DEXAMYL.

# NINE

On the evening of January 6, 1963, Gordon Weekley stepped into the pulpit and looked out over the people before him. Evening services always brought good crowds, but this was unusual. Every seat was taken. Elbow room was at a premium.

Gordon announced the opening hymn, and while the organist banged it out with gusto, the members of the congregation sang as if they were being lifted up to heaven.

When the last noted faded, Gordon bowed his head in prayer, and then lifted his eyes and saw a smiling Oscar Whitescarver, his minister of education, walking up the aisle toward him. He mounted the pulpit and eased into the podium beside the bewildered pastor.

Gordon was stunned. He didn't know what was coming next.

"Excuse me, Mr. Weekley," Whitescarver said, "but there is an interruption that needs to be made in this worship service. This type of interruption takes a particularly special kind of individual to do it. So with your permission and the consent of the congregation, I'd like to recognize Mr. Oscar 'Sonny' Smith at this time. Please take this chair."

With that, he pulled a chair forward from in front of the choir loft, and a speechless Gordon Weekley sat in it. Now it was Smith's turn. Positioning himself beside Gordon's chair, he opened a dark green scrapbook and began to read: "August 1, 1921, was the hottest day on record at Atlanta's Baptist Tabernacle Infirmary, when a little six-pound two-ounce baby boy was born to proud parents Louise Thrash and Henry Gordon Weekley. The little boy had lots of black hair and great big brown eyes. Everybody said he was a beautiful baby. This is your life, Henry Gordon Weekley, Junior."

Thus began an hour-long tribute to the tall, bespectacled preacher on the eighth anniversary of his Providence pastorate.

Turning a page in the scrapbook, Smith read a long, loving letter from Gordon's mother, one that revealed the depth of his religious upbringing: When Gordon was ten years old, he joined First Baptist Church. Dr. Ellis Fuller was the pastor. His influence and counseling played a very great part in

Gordon's life. On Dr. Fuller's last Sunday as pastor, he ordained Gordon and three other young men to the ministry.

During the service, our family kept noticing that Gordon was holding something in his left hand... We learned that it was the little black New Testament, the very first gift from his daddy and mother when he was born.

Gordon spent many, many hours studying and working on his ranks in R.A. It was due to this study and work that he became the second Royal Ambassador Plenipotentiary in Georgia.

After finishing grade school he attended Boys High. He realized by this time the importance of real study and really went to work, studying some nights all night long.

He finished the seminary on May 7, 1948. On May 9th, he was married to Miss Norma Lou Atkinson of Columbus, Indiana. Dr. Fuller performed the ceremony. Dr. Fuller had baptized Gordon, was instrumental in his going to Fur-man, ordained him to the ministry, presented to him his degree from the seminary, and performed the wedding ceremony.

When Sonny Smith finished reading the letter, a voice leapt from the loudspeaker system. It was a tape-recorded congratulatory message from Harold Miller, Gordon's former Greek professor at Furman, his mentor, his traveling companion on the African crusade, his best friend.

And then the calls were coming down AT&T's wires, into the Southern Bell system, and out through the public address speakers: One came from a pastor friend in Indiana for whom Gordon was substituting the Sunday he first saw Norma Lou in the choir. One came from Inglewood, California, from the pastor for whom Gordon had worked as an assistant during his brief stay there. One came from Masonboro, from Annie Mae Beasley, his former fishing companion.

Arnold Kincaid spoke from the pulpit. The deacon and church leader from Gordon's Kings Mountain pastorate had driven over to personally express his love and appreciation. He did not miss the opportunity to chide the congregation, or more specifically, the search committee, for interrupting a perfectly fine goose hunt at Mattamuskeet some years before with a phone call for Gordon Weekley.

On and on it went, letters, telegrams, speeches, an outpouring of affection. A love feast. Near the end, Norma Lou joined him at the pulpit, and as he stood there, wife at his side, friends all around, he was deeply moved.

Love was what life was all about for Gordon Weekley. He had given it out in full measure all his life. Tonight he was getting it back.

He thought of the winter night eight years before and the long, dark drive through the Blue Ridge and the Great Smokies. He remembered his uncertainty about being able to handle the Providence pastorate that he knew would be offered him on his return from the funeral in Indiana.

Tonight, in the Providence pulpit, looking out at four hundred adoring faces, he thought he was handling it pretty well.

He profusely thanked the planners, the participants, and the congregation for the love and kindness that created this very special night. Tucking the green covered scrapbook under his arm, he stepped down from the pulpit and waded into the eight hundred arms outstretched to him.

He was on cloud nine—partly because of his congregation's outpouring of affection and partly because of the Dexamyl he'd taken earlier.

---

The eyes of Texas were on Gordon Weekley. His reputation had spread throughout the denomination, and in mid-1963, the Texas Baptist Convention asked him to participate in the New Life Crusade, a four-wave Christian invasion of Japan. Gordon was to be in the first wave. His destination: Tokyo.

By the time his plans were formulated, there were many more destinations. It became an around-the-world trip, thanks partly to airline scheduling that permitted Gordon to travel west from Japan on his return trip. Theo Patnaik, a young Providence member originally from India, wanted Gordon to meet his brother, Zachariah, in Calcutta. Theo would ultimately go on to become head of youth work for the Baptist World Alliance, but now he was a ministry student.

"Go there," said Theo. "Stay with him a few days. I will write him and tell him you are coming, and he will arrange a great tiger hunt in your honor."

*This,* Gordon thought, *is going to be one wonderful trip.* It wasn't.

The flights from Charlotte to Atlanta to Dallas and on up to Seattle had been uneventful. Gordon had felt good, excited to be at the threshold of an around-the-world journey.

But now, sitting in a plastic chair at the gate, a magazine in his hand, waiting for the boarding call to the Tokyo flight, fear slapped him on the back as unexpectedly as might an old acquaintance.

But this was no acquaintance. Certainly he had known fear before, but not like this. This was terror. He sat bolt upright, eyes wide, head turning right and left as if searching for the source of his terror. His rational mind ran quickly down a list of possible culprits. *A phobia, a nervous breakdown, a heart attack, what in God's name is happening to me?* The intellect broke down, and he decided he was going to die. Die here, three thousand miles from home, from Norma Lou and the kids, from all the friends at Providence.

*I'm too young, I'm too young, I'm too young,* he screamed silently.

He heard a voice: "Flight 337, now boarding for Anchorage and Tokyo."

He stood up and walked like a zombie toward it—through a door, down steps, across the tarmac, up steps, and into a seat on a 727. He wondered if he would die on the plane, sitting up. He imagined being dead in his seat while passengers all around him ate, drank, and made small talk. Maybe they'd talk about him, sitting there, staring straight ahead. Dead.

The more he thought, the sadder he became. Now he was not just terror stricken but depressed as well. He ate nothing, drank nothing. He tried to read but couldn't concentrate.

He walked the aisle, looking at the faces of his fellow travelers. He wished he could be like them: happy, or at least content. Some were even sleeping.

*What am I afraid of?* he anguished.

When the plane landed in Anchorage, he got off for a few moments, but the change of scenery didn't change the way he was feeling. He was a basket case and he stayed that way until the plane touched down in Tokyo.

He managed to pull himself together on the cab ride to the hotel. He stayed relatively calm through a meeting of the New Life group in the hotel ballroom, but the rest of the night was hell for him.

He was sharing a room with an affable Texan who professed to be a sound sleeper. All night, Gordon paced back and forth from the window to the bed.

Sometimes he paused and lay down, but only for a few moments, and then he would be up again. Pacing. Pacing.

*God, please help me,* he prayed, *or at least tell me what's wrong. I'm frightened, Lord, and I don't know why.*

The night passed as slowly as any Gordon had ever known. The ordeal didn't end with the night.

*God, I need a Doriden,* he thought.

He had none, nor any Dexamyl. This was to be a clean trip. No matter what Dr. Doe or Norma Lou had said, he wasn't drug dependent. He would prove it by going all the way around the world without an upper or a downer in his body.

The sun rose, and the Texan along with it.

"What's wrong, partner?" he said. "You didn't get hardly a wink of sleep, did you?"

"I think I was just too exhausted to sleep," said Gordon, fully clothed and on his way out the door. "I'll be all right."

Down the elevator, through the lobby, and out into the busy Tokyo streets he went. He passed store after store, studying the signs on each and understanding almost nothing. Finally, he found what he was looking for and in a few minutes emerged with a small bag containing a small bottle of Doriden.

Back in his room, the Texan gone now, he studied the pills in his hand, wanting to take them. He knew if he did, they would knock him out and he would miss the first day of activities. Someone would come looking for him.

*But that would be all right. I could just tell them I'm ill.*

He poured a glass of water and put the pills up to his mouth, but went no further.

*My God, I'm afraid to take them. Why?*

He put the pills back in the bottle and sat on the edge of his bed for several moments.

Whatever this is, whatever's wrong, it will surely kill me. He lay down on the bed and closed his eyes.

An hour later, he was in the sanctuary of Izumi Baptist Church, shaking hands with the Japanese pastor and feeling well enough to push on. Maybe it was the few moments sleep he got, but whatever it was, he could at least function.

And he did, for the three weeks he was assigned there. He was even fairly pleased with the sermons he preached. Still, fear and anxiety never really left him. They sat perched in the back of his brain like night hawks, tensed to swoop in and attack their quarry at the first sign of vulnerability.

As if to hold them off, to keep them at bay, Gordon began stockpiling ammunition. Nearly every other day, he would seek out a pharmacy and add to his drug collection, which by now was quite diverse. Along with Dexamyl and Doriden, it included various brands of barbiturates and even a bottle of sake. Yet he took nothing.

*I'm too far from home to do it, too far from home.*

Even as he said the words to himself, he could not understand why he was saying them, could not understand what distance had to do with abstention. Lord knows, he needed something to calm himself.

He needed it more than ever as he was preparing to leave Japan for a visit with missionary friends in Hong Kong. The anxiety and fear returned with a vengeance, making him almost physically ill. He was distraught, near panic, as he packed his bags to go. He wondered if he could even make it to the airport, and he knew he couldn't stay. This was not home. This was as far away from home as he could get. He could die here.

So he went to the airport and to Hong Kong. He visited his friends for a few days. He visited various pharmacies. All the while, he told himself that he was one step closer to home. Just two more stops: first Calcutta, then New Delhi.

New Delhi had been added to the itinerary in Japan, at the Crusade, by Dr. Akbah Haqq. Dr. Haqq headed Billy Graham's missionary team in India, and he had insisted that Gordon visit him for a week, promising, among other adventures, a peacock hunt in Kashmir.

Gordon left Hong Kong as he had arrived, apologizing to his missionary friends for his subdued mood, explaining only that he didn't feel well.

He climbed aboard the waiting TWA plane, closed his eyes, and prayed for a smooth flight to Calcutta. He prayed that the night sky and the steady drone of the engines would envelop him and lull him into much-needed sleep.

He got a thunderstorm instead, a big one that bounced the plane around like a toy, giving another dose of misery to an already miserable man. During the whole flight, his despair abated only once, briefly, when he was looking out the window at the same moment lightning lit the sky. He saw a wondrous sight.

The Ganges River has many mouths that feed the Bay of Bengal east of Calcutta, and Gordon saw them from above in the lightning's flash. To most people, they would be merely the many rivulets of a wide river delta. Gordon knew them as the people below knew them: the Hairs of Siva, one of the great Hindu gods. In that brief moment of intellectual lucidity, he contemplated the fact that the definition of an object depended upon whose eyes were looking at it. He wondered if these might truly be the hairs of a god. Who was he to say they weren't?

But it wasn't his God. His God was the father of Christ, and as far as Gordon was concerned, Christ was the only way. He couldn't revel in that thought just now. He was too wrapped up in himself, in his own depression, to turn to the only one who could save him.

Calcutta was worse for him than Hong Kong. By now his depression and anxiety had worsened. Zachariah Patnaik did everything in his power to show Gordon a good time, taking him on tour after tour throughout the city and its environs. Nothing could shake the demons that tormented him, not even his friend's description of the upcoming tiger hunt.

It was to be a big hunt. Sixty beaters had been hired to drive the tiger from the brush. Porters were employed to carry the camping gear. An excellent guide had been found.

A Bengal tiger was a great trophy then, a hunter's dream. Gordon, two American missionaries, and Zachariah were facing the distinct possibility of bringing one to ground.

But Gordon begged off. He told Zachariah he was ill, and he asked him to call Dr. Haqq in New Delhi and explain why he couldn't go there either. With that, he packed his bags, caught a cab to the airport, and boarded an Air India plane for home.

In his coat pocket was a drug he had never tried, Placidyl. It had been given to him by a missionary doctor in Calcutta, one of Zachariah's friends. "They'll help you sleep," she had said, "and if you sleep, maybe you'll feel better." He had resisted taking them, just as he had resisted taking any of the bag full of drugs he had collected on this excursion, because he was too far from home. He didn't know what being too far from home had to do with it, he just knew he was too far.

On the plane now, headed home, he considered the Placidyl. *What an interesting name. 'Placid.' I could use some placid right now.* He didn't take it. Too far from home. Still too far from home. Home was getting closer. He would make it, if he didn't go stark raving mad beforehand.

The first stop for the jam-packed 727 was Bombay. A few people got off, some because it was their destination, a few to stretch their legs. Gordon Weekley stayed where he was. He didn't get off in Bangkok either. Or in Sophia, Czechoslovakia, or Cairo or Rome or Frankfort or Paris.

He got off in London, but for only a few moments, and he didn't stray far from the plane. He was going to New York on it. Then Charlotte. Then home. And sleep.

There were three passengers on the last leg of the journey. Nine thousand miles down, three thousand miles to go. Somewhere over the Atlantic, Gordon finally fell asleep. And he dreamed.

He dreamed of his childhood, of its warmth and comfort. Of mother and dad and grandmother and grandfather. And Katie, the housekeeper, the nurturing black member of the family.

Katie knew every important story in the Bible, and little Gordon heard them all, sitting at the kitchen table while Katie cooked.

"Oh, you should have seen the boat Noah built," said Katie. "Forty cubits long. Now I don't know how big that is exactly, but it was big. Had to be to get all those animals on it."

"Why did he take two of every animal, Katie?"

"Well, now, there's a question your daddy will answer for you one day, little boy." She sang, too—spirituals, her strong voice filling the kitchen and drifting down the halls and throughout the house, reaching the ears of all those who inhabited it.

The Weekley house was a house empty of sin. There was no dancing, no drinking, no cigarette smoking, and not a playing card to be found. Gordon smoked off and on, mostly off, from the time he was fourteen, but he would never have dared smoke in front of his parents or grandparents.

Grandfather spoke little, letting his actions do the talking. He was a good man who lived a good life, much of it on the steel rails of the Southern

Railroad. He was an engineer. Five days a week for thirty-seven years he rose at four in the morning to make the run from Atlanta to Macon and back.

It was a thrill for young Gordon to ride with his parents and grandmother out to Henderson's Crossing on a Sunday afternoon. He dreamed of it now. He was waiting for the Crescent Limited, waiting for the first sign of smoke on the horizon, for the rumble in the tracks. He was waiting for the familiar face of his grandfather, leaning out the window of the engine, cap cocked back on his head, eyes behind protective goggles, a red bandana fluttering from around his neck.

Suddenly the train was there. The old man was waving from the cab. The whistle was singing hello. The ground was shaking beneath the feet of the Weekley family, and beneath the wheels of the Model-T Ford beside them.

Gordon dreamed, too, of summer days when his grandmother would awaken him at dawn. Together they would walk through two hundred yards of morning dew in a meadow behind the house and listen in the distance for grandfather's train to whistle good morning and goodbye as it made its way on down to Macon.

Now, sleeping on the plane on the way to New York, he saw his father's face as it was then. He was friendly, outgoing, a happy man dedicated to his job, his family, and his church. He had been a deacon and treasurer at Capitol Avenue Baptist. Later, when the family moved across town to First Baptist, his Greek and Latin training helped him build a tremendous following as a Sunday School teacher, a teacher who knew that one day he would have a preacher for a son.

The son woke but stayed in a dreamlike state of mind and thought of Furman and his years there. He thought of friends in the dorm and in classes. He thought of Harold Miller that first day in freshman Greek, the young professor who looked much like a freshman himself but who proved to be the most dynamic teacher Gordon ever had. Young Gordon Weekley turned out to be Dr. Miller's best student ever, and after that, his student assistant.

Those were the days filled with long hours of study that never seemed arduous. And the nights of theological discussions and arguments—and card games—and laughter.

Then came graduation with honors, and after that, a year as principal of a high school in Simpsonville, South Carolina. With so many men gone to war, there was a need. The twenty-three-year-old man from Atlanta filled it quite competently. He returned after he got his diploma for yet another year.

He preached, too, during that off year and during his upper-class years at Furman. He preached in small churches in small communities near Simpsonville and Greenville. He loved it. He loved it all. And he had it all, all the talents it took to be a great preacher, a great teacher, a great bringer of the Word. Why then was he so miserable now, so scared, as he woke up to the sound of wheels touching concrete over American soil?

Norma Lou met him at the Charlotte airport.

"Norma Lou," he said, embracing her, "I'm sick, real sick. Get me home."

Halfway there, she turned her eyes from the road and looked at him slumped against the passenger side door.

"Was it the trip," she asked, "or was it the drugs that did this to you?"

With what little strength he had left, he unzipped the small bag that lay on the seat between them. He pulled open the flaps and revealed the cornucopia of pills—green pills, red pills, multi-colored pills, a pharmacy in a bag.

"I didn't take any of them," he whined. "I was afraid to. I was too far from home. Too far. I could have died there. Norma Lou, just get me home. Just get me home."

"We're almost there," she said softly.

Home. Home at last. Safety. Sanctuary. He would be all right now. The world was out there, but he was here on Addison Drive, with Norma Lou. All he needed now was a good night's sleep.

He dragged himself and his little bag into the bathroom, and after placing it on the toilet seat, he frantically rifled through it. His hand fell on the bottle of Placidyl, the powerful drug the missionary in Calcutta had given him. *A barbiturate. Sleep.* He filled a paper bathroom cup with water, popped his first Placidyl into his mouth and went to bed.

He slept soundly for the first time since he had left America, but he slept only for a few hours. Waking at about three in the morning, he wandered into the bathroom to urinate. Standing there relieving himself, he saw the bottle of Placidyl on the sink where he had left it.

*I was going to take one of those before I went to bed. I guess I'll take it now.*

He filled a paper bathroom cup with water, popped his second Placidyl, and went back to bed. It is possible, probable, that two hours later, he arose again and went through the same exercise.

It was early, just after sunup, when Norma Lou shook him.

"Gordon, Gordon," she said, "wake up. Eddie Vosburgh's father died in the night. Eddie needs you."

Both Eddie and his father were members of the church, close friends of Gordon, but Gordon would not go to the younger Vosburgh this day. Gordon could not wake up. Norma Lou might just as well have been talking to a dead man.

---

"Where am I?" he asked, opening his eyes to an unfamiliar ceiling.

"Peachtree Hospital," answered the nurse.

"How long have I been here?"

"Three days."

He closed his eyes and searched his brain. He saw himself taking a Placidyl in the bathroom of his home. He saw his father walking down an Atlanta street, carrying a bag of groceries. *Why would I see my father walking toward his house?*

He saw his old friend and former classmate, Dr. Roy McClain, pastor of First Baptist in Atlanta, talking to Norma Lou. He saw himself being strapped down on a table while a doctor he had never seen before stood over him.

*Why can I remember nothing else? How did I get here? I was in Charlotte. Who is that doctor?* Roy entered the room.

"Roy, Roy, what am I doing here? What's gone wrong?"

"You've been through a tough time, old buddy. They're going to fix you up."

"Fix me up! Am I broken? Roy, isn't this a psychiatric hospital? Why can't I remember anything?"

"Gordon, listen to me," he said gently. "Norma Lou drove you to Atlanta. You apparently took some Placidyl, probably an overdose. She had to get you out of Charlotte, probably to protect you."

"From what?" Gordon demanded.

"From people finding out what happened to you."

"Nothing happened to me. I took too much of a sleeping medication. It was an accident."

"Of course it was an accident, but this whole thing goes deeper than that. It has to do with your depression, your anxiety, your dependence on medication."

"What do you mean, dependence? What are you talking about?"

"Gordon, this isn't the time. All you need to know right now is that you're in good and loving hands. I got you in here. Your doctor is one of the best. He'll help you."

"Why can't I remember any of this? Please, tell me that."

Roy reached out and put his hand on his friend's shoulder.

"You've been suffering from something called dissociation reaction. You've had some treatment for it."

"What kind of treatment?"

"Electroshock."

---

The Providence congregation was shaken. Most people had noticed changes in Gordon in recent years, that he sometimes seemed speeded up, jumpy, even in the pulpit, that he sometimes slurred his words in conversation and couldn't sit still for more than a few minutes in committee meetings. It was attributed to hard work. He was told more than once that he was taking on too much of a load, even by the very people who were putting that load on him—people who wanted Providence to go further, faster. Nervous exhaustion was the diagnosis that came back from Atlanta, and just about everybody bought it.

Dissociation reaction was the operative phrase in Atlanta. Repeated electroshock treatments over the next several days relieved his anxiety but not his appetite for drugs.

Having been given a prescription of rest, Gordon went after his release to Lake Lure in the North Carolina mountains, to a cabin offered to him by a fellow minister. Norma Lou and the three oldest of his four boys joined him there.

She stayed for a couple of days and then went home to their youngest child, John. Gordon and the boys stayed almost two weeks, fishing a little, hiking a little, but mostly doing a lot of nothing—except, in Gordon's case, thinking.

He could not bring himself to believe that drugs were the major cause of his depression. The psychiatrist had said it was not only the use of them but the withdrawal from them. That night in Seattle, as he was about to board the plane, he knew he would make this trip without his little companions in his system.

"That knowledge," said his doctor, "triggered the anxiety and the depression, and as days went by, your physical withdrawal symptoms made things all the worse."

But, Gordon thought, had the psychiatrist not also said that years of overwork and the enormity of the around-the-world trip were contributing factors ? *I am not an addict. I will never believe that. I need more medication than most people simply because my tolerance level is higher.*

The depression issue haunted him. He did not recall experiencing it in the years before he started taking drugs. Maybe drugs *were* a factor. But maybe not. His mother's side of the family, he knew, had a history of depression.

Louise Weekley's brother, Barney, despondent over the death of his mother or tormented by some unknown demon, took his life. He was thirty-seven.

Uncle Burt's wife had left him to raise two sons on his own. It was difficult at first, but after a while he found another woman, whom he deeply loved and whom he lived with outside of marriage. When his first wife returned from California years later, she put pressure on Burt for reconciliation, too much pressure for him to endure. In 1937, torn between a wife and a lover, Gordon's uncle Burt leapt from a railroad bridge in southeast Atlanta.

Electroshock sometimes causes amnesia, but all Gordon forgot was the several hours between going to bed in his house and waking up in Peachtree Hospital. Even at that, he remembered seeing his father carrying those groceries. Norma Lou later told him that she had taken him first to his parents' home and then on to the hospital. Gordon's father was not there when they arrived nor when they left for Peachtree. He had walked to the grocery store.

The days at Lake Lure passed with Gordon in alternating states of depression and calm. He was anxious to get home to the new house on Country Lane. It had been finished in his absence, and Norma Lou had moved the family in. He had dreamed of the day the house would be ready, and he regretted not being there to see it.

The disappointment of that missed moment was offset by the open-armed reception he got from his congregation, a congregation who knew nothing of his addiction. Nevertheless, Gordon decided to remain clean. The anxiety and the depression were worse than anything he had ever experienced, and if abstinence could relegate those devils to their own private hell, he was willing to give it a try. Although he was certainly not addicted. Certainly not addicted.

# TEN

He did well for eight months, things pretty much got back to normal, except for an occasional day of depression. By the middle of 1964, Sunday School attendance climbed to 650 and church membership reached nearly 800. Plans were drawn up for a $300,000 educational wing. The church's six choirs continued to enhance Providence's reputation for excellence in music. The baseball and basketball teams won league championships.

In the midst of all this, Gordon Weekley decided that it would be all right if he occasionally took a Dexamyl and a Doriden. But only occasionally. He had heard of another young doctor just starting his first practice not far from Charlotte. He went to see him and did not come away empty-handed. The young doctor saw a hard-working preacher who needed something to help him sleep and something else to help him get going in the morning. For occasional use only, of course.

That night, Gordon walked into his bathroom, fished the prescription bottles from his pocket, filled a paper cup with water, and downed a Doriden. Then he hid the bottles from Norma Lou and from himself. He found them three days later and took a Dexamyl. By the time the week was out, he was back on his regular schedule: Dexamyl by day, Doriden by night.

He knew he had the young doctor hooked and knew he would be going back to him again and again—but not on a regular basis. He had to find other doctors, in other towns. He had to spread himself around.

Thus began the odysseys of Gordon Weekley. He went to places like Gastonia and Clover, small towns about twenty miles from Charlotte. Some days he drove farther, as far south as Columbia, South Carolina, a hundred miles away, and as far north as Richmond, a distance of almost three hundred miles.

He drove to a South Carolina town called Chesterfield, too. There he found what he guessed was the town's only doctor, a kindly old gentleman who enjoyed passing the time of day. Gordon hit him with his standard story.

"I'm a minister," he said, "on my way to [in this instance] Myrtle Beach, and I've left my medicine kit at home. I wonder if you could accommodate me?"

The doctor did, and in the course of that first day's conversation, the doctor revealed that he had a sister who was a missionary in Japan.

"Really?" Gordon said. "I just got back from Japan. What's her name?"

When the doctor told him, Gordon was astounded.

"You're not going to believe this, but I had dinner with her and her husband in their home in Tokyo."

It's a small world where friendships are often easily made. This friendship between the minister and the physician was sealed instantly. Gordon was to return to Chesterfield many times.

Once he even went there with his three oldest boys, on their way to the Masters' tournament in Augusta, Georgia. Augusta is 160 miles south-southwest of Charlotte; Chesterfield is 50 miles east-southeast. It took them a long time to get to the tournament.

In late June, Norma Lou and the kids went back home to Indiana for a family reunion. Gordon couldn't go. The Japan trip, the hospitalization, the recuperation at Lake Lure had kept him too much out of the pulpit. And Norma Lou's presence around the house had kept him from his favorite form of recreation more than he liked.

"Have a safe trip," he said, kissing her and hugging the boys. "And call me the minute you get there."

"We will," she said, slowly backing the car out of the drive.

He stood watching and waving until a curve on Country Lane took them out of his sight. Then he turned, walked back in the house, went straight to the bathroom, stuck his hand deep into the recesses of the linen closet, and withdrew a bottle of Dexamyl. Party time on Country Lane.

Quite a party it turned out to be. He started every morning with the Dexamyl and continued throughout the day. Every night, he took the Doriden. From where he stood, as the days passed, he was handling it quite well. He loved the daily burst of energy the morning upper gave him.

He gave what he considered to be a fine sermon on Sunday, July 5, and afterward accepted a luncheon invitation from Mr. and Mrs. Claude Thomas. It was a pleasant affair. Gordon was alert, charming, and talkative. The only hint of a sour note was his picky appetite.

"Gordon," Mrs. Thomas said, "don't you like fried chicken?"

"Oh, yes, I love it. Particularly yours. It's just that I had a huge breakfast this morning."

Gordon lingered after lunch for a polite length of time, thanked the Thomases for a fine meal, and drove home.

It was not unusual that he decided to forego supper that night. He had missed many suppers in recent years, and every single one since Norma Lou left. It was not unusual, either, that he skipped breakfast the next morning. But he also skipped lunch, then supper again, then breakfast. He just stopped eating.

Days passed, then weeks. He continued to perform all the functions preachers were expected to perform—visitations, sermon preparations, committee meetings—but his emotional and physical demeanor was changing rapidly. His words were heavily slurred in the early mornings, waking from Doriden-induced sleep. Then, when the Dexamyl and coffee kicked in, he was a whirlwind, moving rapidly through the day from one project to another but never lingering on any of them very long. If he had a scheduled hour-long counseling session, he would be out of it in ten minutes and on to something else. If he had a luncheon meeting planned, he changed it to midafternoon so he wouldn't have to explain his abstinence from food.

His sermons were short, rapidly delivered, and aimless, leaving his congregation to wonder what he had been talking about.

Norma Lou had returned in mid-July, but her presence did not mitigate his behavior. He was on a roll. Popping pills like candy. Taking no sustenance other than black coffee.

"Look at yourself in the mirror," she pleaded.

He did. He saw the same thing he had always seen: the successful pastor of one of North Carolina's fastest growing churches. He was experiencing the delusion addicts almost always experience. And delusion is the mother of denial.

By mid-August others were seeing something quite different. His weight had dropped considerably. Clothes hung on him like drapes. His eyes were hollow and his cheeks sunken. He was still not eating.

Finally, by September, he was not doing the things pastors were supposed to do. His visitations dropped off. He canceled several of his meetings. Once on a Sunday afternoon, he called his choir director and requested an all-music evening service even though he had been scheduled to preach.

On Mondays, his day off, he hit the road, searching for and finding more doctors with more pills. Often as not, he was on the road other days, too. He was taking up to a half-dozen Dexamyl a day now and three Doriden. He continuously had to replenish his supply. Even when his supply far exceeded his demand, he continued to stock up.

Pill gathering became a game for him. He would try to get some virtually every time he arrived in any town, even if he was there on church business, and even if he was traveling with someone else.

He was traveling with Arthur Smith, the renowned country singer, in late September to Fayetteville, North Carolina. Arthur was to give a talk there at Snyder Memorial Baptist Church. Jim Cammack was pastor and a good friend of Gordon, and so Gordon had decided to go along.

When they reached the church, Arthur occupied himself with a few fans who had arrived early while Gordon and Jim retreated to the pastor's office to chat. Not long after the conversation began, Gordon looked at him and said, "Jim, I'm taking some medication, and I left home without it. Do you have a doctor I could call so that maybe I could get what I need before we start back to Charlotte?"

"Why, yeah, sure, I guess so." He jotted down a number, and then left the room to attend to some business. Gordon made the call, and the doctor agreed to contact a pharmacy just down the street from the church. Just to make sure everything was on the up and up, the doctor called Jim Cammack back to verify the story.

In the few minutes before Arthur's talk was to begin, Gordon slipped out the side door of the church and picked up his merchandise.

On the return trip to Charlotte, there was no danger of Arthur Smith falling asleep at the wheel. Beside him sat a very animated, very talkative, very euphoric Gordon Weekley. He praised Arthur up one side and down the other for his wonderful talk that evening. He told him how delighted he was that Arthur belonged to Providence Baptist. He talked of the future of the church and the great plans for it. He talked. And he talked. And he talked. He was still talking when Arthur let him out of the car in front of his house, talking so much he failed to notice the bottle of pills he left on the seat.

By the end of the month, he weighed 126 pounds. He looked like a survivor of Dachau. Congregation members were concerned that he had some dreaded illness. Others thought he was simply overworked. A few were coming closer to the truth.

Through it all, Gordon remained blissfully ignorant of becoming an issue in the church. True, he was getting daily admonitions from Norma Lou and more and more questions about his health from concerned friends, but he thought he was fending them off quite well, and handling his drug intake quite well, too. He believed that his tolerance level was higher than most people. He believed that he was taking what for him was a normal amount. Norma Lou's concerns, he felt, were nothing more than the wailings and gnashings of a woman caught up in a marriage that over the years had grown into something less than perfect.

Her lack of deep involvement in the goings on of the church had hastened the weakening of their bond to each other, and her recently announced desire to start college again had weakened it even further. She had begun college in Indiana before the young preacher from Atlanta stepped into the pulpit of her church that Sunday morning in 1946. Now she had resumed it at nearby Wingate College. Gordon was against it, believing then that a woman's place, particularly a woman married to a preacher, was in the home and in the church.

He attributed none of the problems in the marriage to his use of drugs or to his immersion in the activities of his pastorate. So even though his ears heard the voices of concern, his mind was deaf to them and his eyes blind to the face in his mirror.

On the first Sunday morning in October, he delivered a sermon that was unusual not in its content but in its length. Usually he took no more than twenty minutes to get his message across. This time he took fifty. When he glanced at his watch and realized it was nearly twelve-thirty, he was stunned. He quickly wrapped up his talk and issued the call to invitation. While the organ was playing and the congregation was singing, Gordon was silently, desperately trying to gather his wits. He quickly shuffled through the pages of his text. *It's not any longer than my other sermons. What happened? Why is it almost twelve thirty?*

He looked up and scanned the faces of his congregation. None of the faces he saw showed concern or discomfort. He didn't see the face of Jarvis Warren.

A few days later, Jarvis called.

"Gordon, a couple of the deacons and I are having a little meeting at my house tonight. We'd appreciate it if you'd join us."

"Be glad to," Gordon said and thought nothing more of it. He was often a participant in deacons' meetings.

Earlier that day, Jarvis and fellow deacons Al Edwards and L.B. Mauney had arrived at Wingate College, some twenty miles east of Charlotte. At the administrative office, they asked to speak to one of the students who was in class there at the time. The three men were ushered into a small conference room to await the student's arrival. A few minutes later, Norma Lou Weekley opened the door. When she saw who was waiting there, her eyes filled with tears, and she said, "I knew you'd come someday. I wondered when it would be."

At eight o'clock that evening, Gordon pulled into the driveway of Warren's home and was surprised to see Norma Lou's car there. He mounted the steps, rang the bell, and was greeted by a grim-faced chairman of the board of deacons.

"Is Norma Lou here?" asked Gordon.

She was. She was seated on the couch in the living room between Edwards and Mauney.

The shocked pastor started to speak, but Warren interrupted him.

"Pastor, we're a committee of three, chosen by the board. I'll get right to the point. You're in trouble, Gordon. Something's very wrong with you. We don't know exactly what it is, but we do know that things can't go on this way."

"There's nothing wrong with me," Gordon said.

"Pastor, please, this is hard enough for us. Listen to me. We want you to take a leave of absence, six months if you need it, to get yourself straightened out. We love you. We'll continue to pay your salary. We just want you to get better."

"I'm telling you, there's nothing wrong with me," Gordon almost shouted.

"Gordon, all the deacons know there's something wrong with you. All the congregation knows there's something wrong with you. And Norma Lou most certainly knows that something's wrong with you. Most likely it has something to do with your medications."

Shock, fear, and anger assaulted Gordon. He turned and looked at Norma Lou with cold, hard eyes, as one would look into the face of a betrayer.

His mind was racing, looking for a means of escape. "Look," he said, "of course I'm taking medications. I've had to because I've had trouble getting to sleep at night. But these are *prescription* drugs. I'm under a doctor's care. Now, I'll admit they may have altered my behavior somewhat. I'm sure there must be some side effects, but..."

"Why don't you tell it all, Gordon?" she said.

In a heartbeat, he covered the few feet that separated them and stood glaring over her.

"You be quiet," he said. "Do you want to ruin me? Is that what you want, do you want to destroy my career?"

"Nobody wants that Gordon," Jarvis said, "especially Norma Lou. What we want is to get you well. We want you to go back to Atlanta, to Peachtree Hospital. We bought you an airline ticket. Your bags are packed and in the trunk of Norma Lou's car."

The strength of Warren's delivery and the firmness in the faces of the other deacons convinced Gordon there was no escape from this indictment. He was trapped. Trapped in the indictment, but not yet trapped into Peachtree. He couldn't bear the thought of Peachtree.

"All right," he said desperately, "maybe I do need some time off. Maybe I am overworked. I'll take the leave of absence, but I won't under any circumstances go to Peachtree Hospital. I don't need a hospital. I need rest."

His mind was racing, searching for alternatives to hospitalization. He knew they would never simply let him go away alone, to the beach or to the mountains.

"Harold Miller," he said suddenly. "I'll go stay with Harold Miller. He's my former professor and best friend. He's head of the Classics Department at Bucknell. He'll let me stay with him. He'll make sure I get the rest I need."

The deacons argued. "Gordon, you need more than rest. You need medical attention."

"I'll get it. I'll get it there. But I'm telling you, I need mostly rest. I am not going to Peachtree. Do what you want with me. Say what you want. I'm not going."

The argument raged back and forth for the better part of an hour, and finally the committee gave in. He would go to Bucknell, go to Harold Miller. And he would go first thing in the morning.

Norma Lou drove back to the house. Gordon followed. She, of course, was alone. He had misery for company. Two cars, one trailing the other through the empty streets of south Charlotte. Two lives, once joined, now separated, with car lengths between them. Norma Lou accelerated slightly. The gulf widened.

Back home, each avoided the other, wandering from room to room until they finally met in the kitchen. His anger was deep, too deep for words.

"We're just trying to help you," she said. "Can't you see that?" He didn't answer.

"Those pills, the ones Arthur found in his car; he gave them to Tom Burnett." Tom Burnett was a doctor, and a deacon and a good family friend. "He had them analyzed. They know."

"They know what?" Gordon said. "That I take some medication?"

Norma Lou turned away. They did not speak for the remainder of the evening, nor did they speak the next morning. Gordon got up, got dressed, and walked to his car. Norma Lou followed him down the driveway.

"Call when you stop for the night," she said flatly.

"I will," he said finally and with deep weariness.

There were no kisses, no hugs, no I-love-you's, from either of them. He simply got in his car and left, wondering whether she wanted him to call because she would miss him or because she wanted to make sure he was headed in the right direction.

He called that night. Steve, his oldest son, answered.

"Hello, son," Gordon said. "I just thought I'd let you know that I'm in a motel in Virginia. I'm going to take my time getting to Lewisburg and see a little scenery. I'll call tomorrow."

He hung up, raised himself from the bed he had been lying on, and went to the window overlooking the street. He watched the steady stream of Charlotte commuters heading home in their cars.

He returned to the bed, opened his shaving kit, and poured his pills on the spread. He separated the uppers from the downers and calculated how many days' supply he had left. *Enough for three more days on the road,* he said to himself, *and then two more days at Lewisburg, just to get myself acclimated there.*

His math done, he took two Doriden, laid back on the bed and waited for the euphoria to sweep over him. He was asleep in thirty minutes.

The following morning, he awoke groggy and wondered for a moment where he was. Then the reality found its way into his brain, followed closely by depression. He dressed and went downstairs to the motel restaurant. He ordered coffee. When it came, he used it to wash down a Dexamyl.

He stayed three days in Charlotte, and except for morning coffee, he never left his room. He couldn't risk it. God knows what his deacons would do if they found him still in Charlotte. He sat tight and savored the sweetness of his uppers and downers.

His anger had pretty much left him now. He decided he indeed did need a rest. And it would be good to see Harold Miller again, to spend long hours in the company of the man who was his best friend. But he worried about what lay ahead with the psychiatrist or medical doctor at Bucknell. He worried, too, that he was losing the ground he had gained in his nine years of Providence ministry. He worried that people would think less of him, but he did not worry about it too much because the drugs wouldn't let him and because no one other than the deacons suspected he had a dependency problem.

*Besides,* he thought, *I don't have a dependency problem, no matter what Arthur or Tom Burnett might think. I'm overworked. I'm tired. My congregation knows that. They'll understand. They've understood before.*

---

At sunrise the fourth day, he rechecked his drug supply and confirmed that it was time to leave for Lewisburg. He packed his bags, paid his bill, got into his car, and drove north. At dusk, he arrived in Maryland and called home just as he had every night since he left. Just as he had every night since he left, he talked to Steve. He told him where he was and that he expected to arrive in Bucknell within the next day or so. The following morning, headed toward Lewisburg, he debated whether or not to spend one more night on the road. By midday, when he reached Harrisburg, paranoia had seized him.

*Maybe I've taken too long to get there. Maybe the deacons are meeting right now, deciding this trip wasn't such a good idea. Maybe they're going to call ahead and arrange to have me shipped to Peachtree. Maybe they haven't done anything. Yet. I've got to get to Lewisburg, fast, before they do something.*

He worked his way impatiently through the Harrisburg city traffic. Clearing the city limits, he slammed his foot down hard on the accelerator and started up the valley along the Susquehanna River. Fifty, sixty, seventy, eighty, ninety,

ninety-five miles an hour. He was flying. Although anxiety still rode with him, exhilaration did too. His Dexamyl-saturated brain felt no fear of the highway patrol or the sharp curves that wound alongside the river.

*Life is good,* he thought, taking in the magnificent mountains on either side of him. *God created a beautiful world.*

The beauty did not end at Lewisburg, but the exhilaration did. He had come and there was no turning back. At the south end of town, he crossed a bridge that clattered under his tires, and after only a few yards more, he pulled up in front of Harold Miller's apartment. It was on the main street of this college town of some six thousand inhabitants, a brick, three-story building built, Gordon guessed, sometime in the twenties and housing probably no more than six tenant families. The street was tranquil and tree-lined, and behind the apartment, the land sloped a few hundred yards to the Bucknell campus.

Harold was there when he arrived. And after the usual hugs and handshakes, they settled down in the living room to talk.

"A lot of people, myself included, are very concerned about you, son," Harold said.

Gordon didn't respond.

"Jarvis Warren has called several times, and Dr. Tom Burnett. As a result of those conversations, I've arranged for you to have an extensive examination by a Dr. Waitman, here at the university. He's first-rate, Gordon, and I feel sure he'll help you get to the bottom of whatever the problem is."

Gordon, still feeling the effects of his Dexamyl, countered and parried gracefully. Smiling at his good friend, he said, "Harold, I've simply worked too many hours, too many days, too many years without rest. Taking this church to where it is hasn't been easy. It's extracted a heavy price. I'm exhausted. And I think there will be nothing better for me than to simply rest here for a few weeks. Then I'll be fine."

"But—" Harold interjected.

"Don't worry," Gordon said, "I'll see your Dr. Waitman. I wouldn't want to disappoint Norma Lou or any of the other folks back home."

With that, the conversation took another course. The two men drifted back to better times, times at Furman, when the young professor of Greek and the boy with the hunger for knowledge became best of friends.

They talked into the night, never again mentioning Gordon's problems.

Harold was a gentle, almost shy man, who demonstrated a deep love for his protege, his "son," as he called him. Gordon knew that his surrogate father would not voluntarily go any further into the matter of the affliction. He would simply be a friend. A friend was what Gordon desperately needed right then, because the next day would be his last day on drugs.

He took the first of his two remaining Dexamyl about seven that morning and the second about one o'clock. He spent the day lounging around the apartment, enjoying the final pleasure-filled hours.

When Harold returned from his lectures late that afternoon, he found Gordon in an easy chair, reading.

"Let's walk," he said.

"Walk where?" asked Gordon.

"Anywhere, let's just walk. I do it every day. It's good for you. Come on."

They walked across the campus, through the quaint little town, back past the apartment, over the rickety bridge and into the countryside. Gordon thought he had never walked so far, but he kept up, bouyed by the Dexamyl in his system.

That evening, he even ate a little. After dinner, the two men alternated between talking and reading. But as the evening slid away, so, too, did the euphoria. Gordon began to feel restless, anxious. He knew that there was no Doriden waiting for him in his room.

He went to bed about eleven, but he might just as well have stayed up. He did not sleep, not for one minute. He stared at the ceiling. He got up. He paced back and forth. He got back in bed. He felt the same fear he had felt in the Seattle airport and on the flight to Japan. He was terrified. He closed his eyes.

*Please, God, if there's something wrong with me, get me through it. I can't do it without you.*

Suddenly his ears were filled with a tremendous rattle and a roar. He felt as if the walls were caving in.

"What's happening?" he said, wide-eyed. And then he knew. It was a truck. An eighteen-wheeler rolling across the rickety bridge and up the road beside the apartment, rerouted because of the detour on Highway 15.

Gordon had heard the trucks before and the cars and the rattle, rattle, rattle of the loose boards on the bridge, but now tonight without the medication to soothe him, the sound was unbearable. He covered his ears with his hands.

*Please God, no more trucks, please,* he pleaded.

But more came, two or three every hour until four in the morning. Then they slacked off. Still he could not sleep. Sleep just wouldn't come. He rummaged through his shaving kit, hoping that one Doriden lay hidden in a crevice somewhere. There was none. He lay there, facing the window, listening to the night and waiting for the cold gray of dawn.

It came, and at midmorning he found himself being escorted into the office of Dr. Waitman at the university medical facility. Waitman explained that he would put him through two days of testing and then they would talk.

And so it began—the blood testing, the X-rays, the punching, the probing. For a normal man, it would have been an uncomfortable situation; for a man in the first stages of withdrawal, it was agonizing, particularly because this man had not slept in two days.

He did not sleep the third day, either. When he arrived in Waitman's office for consultation, he felt awful. He must have looked that way, too, because when Dr. Waitman looked up from the chart and into Gordon's eyes, he said, "You're in pretty bad shape, but I guess you're no worse off than our town drunk."

The words cut Gordon. They were spoken not bitterly but clinically. Still, there they were. The Baptist minister, the rising star, the honor student, the man who had everything, was now no worse off than the town drunk.

"My God, what do they think is wrong with me? Can't they see that I'm just worn out?"

"I'm not going to give you any medication, and I want you to assure me that you won't take any on your own. What you need is abstinence and rest."

*Rest? How can I get any rest with those damn trucks driving through my bedroom,* he thought. But he said nothing.

"This is not going to be easy," the doctor said, "but you have to try. It's the only way."

He left the medical building and walked across campus to the apartment. He was mad with desire for a Dexamyl. This was the third day. He had been without sleep since the first night without Doriden. *This isn't fair. No medication and no sleep either. I can't make it.*

He reached the apartment and began pacing, back and forth across Harold's living room. *God, I'd give anything for a Dexamyl.* He checked his shaving kit again. Nothing.

At four, Harold returned from class and they walked. At six, they had supper, and Gordon ate reasonably well. He longed for sleep, and shortly after he had eaten, he excused himself and went to bed.

Sleep did not come; only the trucks came. Like demons from hell, they filled up his room and his senses with their unbearable noise. *I cannot stand it!* Gordon screamed silently. *I can't do this.*

He lay awake the rest of that night, his mind alternating between the terror of the trucks and anger at the people who sent him away. *Why are they doing this to me? What have I done to deserve it? Somebody there wants to get rid of me, make me quit? Maybe Norma Lou's behind it all. Whoever it is, they won't get me. Never.*

The following day, his withdrawal was more acute. So too was his anger. He unloaded it on Harold that evening and for many more evenings to come. He talked during their walks, he talked while Harold made supper, he talked as they sat in front of the radio before bedtime. Harold mostly listened, offering only friendship, love, and support in his soft-spoken way. He neither agreed with Gordon's paranoid ramblings nor disagreed with them. He was simply there for him.

The bed Gordon did not sleep on was the only one in the small apartment. Harold spent his nights on the couch. He didn't sleep much either, because Gordon was constantly up and down. If he happened to catch Harold with his eyes open, he would snare him in a conversation.

Seven days passed, and still Gordon hadn't slept. He was seeing Dr. Waitman every other day for urine and blood tests and weighing.

"Doctor," he said, "it's obvious I'm not taking drugs. You know that by the tests. But look at me—I'm so depressed I can't stand it. Please, in the name of God, give me something. I swear to you I won't abuse it."

Waitman remained firm, and Gordon left his office as mad as he had ever been at anyone in his life. He returned home to a waiting Harold Miller.

"That son of a buck doesn't want me to get better. He doesn't care. I'm going to die, and he doesn't care."

"Easy, son," said Harold, putting his arm around his friend's shoulder. "We'll get through this together."

"Are they calling you, Harold?" he asked. "Jarvis, Tom Burnett, Norma Lou, are they calling you at your office to check up on me?"

"Well, yes, I've had a couple of calls. But they're concerned, Gordon. They love you."

"Love me? If they loved me they wouldn't have done this to me. They don't love me. They're trying to get rid of me."

"Son," Harold said quietly, "we all love you. Someday you'll understand that."

"It'll be a cold day in hell when I understand that," Gordon said.

Another seven days passed. Urine samples. Blood tests. Trucks in the night. Pacing. Paranoia. And sleeplessness. Gordon by now was at the end of his rope, venting anguish to himself, to God, and most especially to Harold Miller. In lucid moments, Gordon could see that he was taking a toll on his friend, but he could not stop himself. And the kindly professor never complained. Daily, he followed the same routine. He would return home, take Gordon for a long walk, prepare dinner, and then settle in on the couch and listen to the rantings of a withdrawing drug addict.

One night, in the middle of the third week, the routine changed. Harold returned from classes two hours later than usual, and with barely a word of greeting to Gordon, changed into his pajamas and robe and proceeded to cook dinner. Gordon, sensing Harold might be angry, retreated to the bedroom.

After a half hour or so, Harold appeared in the doorway.

"It's ready," he said.

They ate in silence. Harold seemed to be somewhere else and at the same time seemed to be concentrating very hard on the ritual of eating. He cut and chewed his food methodically, as if it were a recently learned skill.

Nothing was said through the entire meal. When it was over, Harold picked up the bowls and both sets of dishes and sat them on the counter beside the sink.

"Aren't we going to wash them?" asked Gordon.

"Not now," was the murmured answer. Harold turned and took a somewhat circuitous route to the sofa, unceremoniously flopped himself down on his back, and fell asleep.

*My God,* thought Gordon, suddenly realizing what was happening, *he's drunk. Harold Miller is drunk. I've driven the poor man to drink.*

Gordon did not sleep again that night, but he noticed that his friend did.

The following morning after his urinalysis, blood test, and weigh-in, he made yet another appeal to Dr. Waitman.

"Doctor, in the name of God, give me something. I can't go on feeling this badly. There's just no purpose in it. Please, I'm begging you."

Waitman took a deep breath and then relented.

"All right, I'll give you some Ritalin. It's a little like an amphetamine. It'll help you feel better. But I'm going to dole these out to you very sparingly. Very sparingly."

For the first time in weeks, Gordon felt elation. He almost ran back to the apartment and, safely there, washed down the pill and waited for the euphoria. It came. But it was so lacking in intensity that he barely felt it. Still, it gave him hope that somehow he might be able to get through this most horrible period of his life.

He was somewhat calmer when Harold arrived that evening, but only somewhat. Neither discussed the events of the night before, and they settled into their normal routine. Gordon was still anxious, still depressed, but his conversation was more rational, less animated.

Late that night when the Ritalin wore off, the depression and anxiety returned full bore. And the sleeplessness was still there. It was always there.

The morning after the twentieth consecutive night, Gordon slipped into his jeans and flannel jacket and walked out into the brisk October air. He was so tired he could barely move, but he was hoping a walk would wear him down finally to the point where he could sleep.

He crossed the rickety bridge down from the apartment and set out slowly for the countryside. There, unencumbered by buildings, the north wind whipped freely down the Susquehanna Valley, pushing him along, encouraging him to go forward.

*I'm shuffling like an old man whose time has almost passed. My Lord, I'm only forty-three. And there's nothing medically wrong with me. Why am I here? Why can't I sleep? What do the deacons have against me? What does Norma Lou have against me? Am I going to lose everything? What have I done to deserve that? I was a loving son, a good student, a faithful husband, a servant of the Lord. I've never willingly hurt anyone. I've tried to love everyone.*

Tears filled his eyes.

*I'm worn out, that's all. If I could sleep, I could get my strength back and I'd be fine. But will they believe that back home? Will everything I've worked for be gone when I get there? Have I ever not visited a sick bed? Have I ever failed to drive through the night to be on hand when a newborn arrived? Have I ever stood over an open grave without feeling the same pain of loss as the friends and family members there with me? What have I done that's so wrong, except work too hard? Is banishment and chastisement my reward? God, help me.*

On the morning after the twenty-first sleepless night, he lay on his back looking at the ceiling and listening to Harold tiptoeing around the kitchen. Finally the front door opened and closed, and he was alone. He closed his eyes. He did not hear a truck. He did not hear the wind beating against the window. Instead, he saw an old friend, a member of his congregation in Masonboro, and the old friend was walking toward the church cemetery, past the clam-shell cross, down into the little valley, then up the far hill among the tombstones.

Startled, Gordon opened his eyes. "A dream," he said excitedly. "A dream. I was sleeping. I was actually sleeping."

He had slept only a few minutes, but there was hope now. Later that day, he slept again, briefly.

When Harold returned that afternoon, he was greeted by an excited and optimistic Gordon Weekley.

"I slept Harold, I slept."

And he ate, too. A good supper.

"Let's walk," said Gordon after they had finished the dishes. "And after that, I'm going to bed and I'm going to sleep."

When they returned from their evening sojourn, Gordon slipped into his pajamas, turned out the light and dropped to his knees, just as he had every evening before. This time, his conversation with God contained no wailings, no gnashing of teeth. *Lord, I do love you. And I bring this whole experience to make it an offering. Please accept it. Take and manipulate all the factors of my life that have in any way reduced my service to Thee and short-cut my loyalty.*

He crawled into bed and pulled the covers tight against him. If trucks passed in the night, he did not hear them. If the wind howled, he took no notice. He slept all the way through the night. He awoke with the sun, still fearful, still a little depressed, but refreshed. He was thinking more clearly than he had in months.

In the weeks that followed, he fared better. He no longer took the Ritalin. He no longer lashed out as strongly against the forces that put him here in the first place. He gained weight, up to 136 pounds. He got good reports from Dr. Waitman; he was "improving."

On the Thursday before Thanksgiving, he took a morning walk. He walked all the way through Lewisburg, then back past the apartment and down to the rickety bridge whose loose boards rattling under the wheels of the big trucks had caused him so much consternation.

He leaned over the railing and gazed into the quiet, easy-moving waters of the Susquehanna. There in the brisk Pennsylvania air, on the rickety bridge, a deep calm filled him. "I surrender Lord," he said. "If all this is part of Your plan, I surrender to it." He turned and, stuffing his hands into his jacket pockets, trekked back up the hill to the apartment.

"What do you think, son?" asked Harold, a few nights later. "My mother wants me to come to Washington for the holidays. Shall we go, or would you rather we stay here?"

"That would be nice; let's go. And Harold, I think I'll just go on home from there."

"You know it's not going to be easy, son," Harold said, putting his hand on Gordon's arm.

"I know."

"Just remember, God's with you. He's always been with you. You're a good man, Gordon. The best. Whatever's waiting for you, you can handle it. You have to believe that about yourself."

"I will. I don't mind telling you I'm scared—scared I'm going to lose my family. Scared I might lose my church. But I'm trusting in Him and His plan."

"Are you still angry?"

"No. No, not angry. I guess I did need a rest. I just don't think it was handled well. And I'm afraid they think I was worse off than I really was."

"You were in pretty bad shape, son. I've got to tell you that. I also want to tell you that I love you. And so do the people back home. They'll be waiting for you."

"I hope so."

Early Friday evening, the day after Thanksgiving, Gordon's blue 1961 Chevrolet turned off Country Lane, rolled across the bridge he had built with his own hands, and started up the long driveway toward home.

*It seems that I've had a lot of bridges to cross lately, he thought, and the biggest one's yet to come.* He wondered if he would ever set foot in the Providence pulpit again.

Just then, his eyes caught a crudely lettered sign nailed to a tree alongside the drive. And a few yards farther, another. And another. They were welcome home messages from his children, strung out like Burma Shave signs along a highway.

He stopped the car in the drive, jumped out, made his way quickly up the walk, and opened the front door to the greatest sight he had ever seen: four grinning children, love all over their faces. Instantly, they broke ranks and rushed him, covering him with hugs and kisses. Tears filled his eyes as he enveloped them all in his arms.

"Daddy's home," he said, "daddy's home."

With the four boys hanging on to him, he straightened up from his bent-over hugging position and stood face to face with Norma Lou. Both hesitated. Both stepped forward. Both reached out to embrace. Both cried. And then they walked arm in arm into the den, followed by the four little dancing Weekleys.

Daddy was home.

ELEVEN

His next reunion, on Monday night in a large room above the sanctuary, would not be such a happy one. Gordon had not preached that Sunday, had not, in fact, left the house since his return Friday evening. But he had taken calls, dozens of them, from well-wishing congregation members who had somehow found out he was back.

Now it was Monday, and now the meeting Gordon had dreaded but approached with an aura of calm was beginning. There were twenty-one people there: Jarvis, the entire board of deacons, and Gordon.

Everyone shook his hand and welcomed him back warmly, some more warmly than others. Then they got down to the business of deciding whether or not Gordon Weekley would again stand in the pulpit at Providence Baptist Church.

*Who will be the executioners?* he wondered.

Almost as if he had read Gordon's mind, Jarvis suggested the meeting begin with each person in the room taking a few moments to express his feelings about Gordon's situation.

The tension in the room was thick. A man's job was on the line, maybe even his entire career, but each man had been asked to speak his heart. Each man did. Some, in soft, even compassionate tones, said Gordon had outlived his usefulness. Others said the same thing less kindly but without anger.

And there were those who honestly admitted that they didn't know what should be done with their pastor. On one hand, they appreciated all that he had done for them, and on the other, they felt disappointed, hurt, by his recent behavior.

One man said perhaps the church had grown too big for Gordon. "You're a one-on-one pastor, Gordon," he said, "and now there are nine hundred of us. Maybe you're taking on too much. Maybe it would be best if you found a smaller church."

"Now hold on," said another. "Has anyone here considered the possibility that what happened to Gordon was our fault? We were the ones who wanted a great church. We were the ones who put the demands on him. He's done the work of three men—and he never complained."

"I agree," said another. "And it wasn't just the big demands of a growing church. It was all those little personal ones, too. If one of our family members got sick, we expected Gordon to be there. If a baby was born, we expected him to be in the waiting room. If we knew of some family that might want to consider Providence, we sent Gordon to visit them. If we had a personal problem, we called Gordon. I think we're as much at fault as he is."

"Whether it's our fault or his," said another, "there's no excuse for turning to drugs. If Gordon stays, I have no choice but to leave. As you know, some of us have wanted to form a new church anyway. The Mecklenburg Baptist Association has its eye on that land over on Sharonview. And I'm telling all of you that there's an excellent chance of something happening. In fact, it's going to happen whether he stays or goes."

The possibility of a church split was not news to Gordon. Jarvis had approached him on the matter some months before, and he had been against it. His argument had been that Providence was too small to be birthing a new church. "Maybe later," he had said.

*Maybe later is now*, Gordon thought, as the tribunal continued and each man spoke his piece. *Or maybe I'm gone. Maybe tonight is my last night as pastor of this or any church.*

The hours dragged on. Ten o'clock. Eleven. Midnight. One. The moment for a vote was almost at hand, maybe only half an hour more. Gordon felt like he was on death row and hoping the governor would call.

At a few minutes after one, Arthur Smith spoke.

"Fellows," he said, "it's very late. I don't know if we're going to resolve this any time soon. And we're all tired, maybe too tired to make a proper judgment. So I'd like to put a motion on the floor. I'd like to move that we allow Gordon back in the pulpit one more time, next Sunday."

That's all Arthur said. He didn't say why Gordon should occupy the pulpit. He didn't suggest a course of action following the sermon. He simply moved that the man be allowed one more hour in the pulpit, and the motion passed.

Relief washed over Gordon. A stay of execution. A chance.

When he got home, he went straight to his study. He was so excited he didn't even begin to think about sleep. He began, instead, thinking about his sermon. It had to be great. It had to be perfect. Everything was riding on it.

He switched on the little desk lamp, slipped into his chair and shoved a piece of paper into the typewriter.

*Where do I start? What do I say? Help me, Lord. The drugs. The medications. I'm going to have to address that. I'll have to admit to the congregation that I've had a problem even if I don't really believe it. The deacons believe it, and the word will be out to everyone else. I have problems, no doubt about that. I've pushed too hard, taken the church too far too fast. It's beaten me down. But I'm ready now to lead again. I care so much for this church, these people. I've had a setback. I'm over it.*

He buried his head in his hands and after a long moment spoke aloud to his Maker.

"Dear Father, give me the words to say to these people. I've been broken and now I'm restored. But how will they know that? What can I say to them that will renew their faith in me? I surrender to you, Lord. I need you now like I've never needed you before. If it's Thy will that I continue in this pastorate, please, give me the words."

It was a prayer not so very different from the prayers of others in desperate situations. Prayers that say in effect, *Get me through this, Lord, and I'll be a good person from now on*—or at least until the next time.

The words for Gordon's sermon began to come late the next afternoon. He had gone to bed at four in the morning with a blank page still in his typewriter, but he had slept well. Now the words were coming. He hated having to admit to drugs, but there was no alternative. That was a given.

He wrote, and as he was writing, he wished for a Dexamyl. He knew, though, that his Dexamyl days were over.

By Wednesday, his rough draft was done. By the end of the day Thursday, he had refined and distilled it to twenty minutes. He had paused often during this four-day process to take walks and turn paragraphs over in his mind, but he'd never left the confines of Country Lane. He wasn't going anywhere until Sunday morning, and he especially wasn't going to the church until then.

The church came to him often that week in the form of well-wishers. Some six or seven families came calling. He cherished their visits. It was good to see friendly faces, loving faces, supporting faces.

By Saturday, it seemed that Sunday would never arrive. By Sunday morning, it had arrived too soon. He awoke at five and was showered, shaved, and dressed by six. He was waiting for the Sunday paper when it came, and for the next hour, he pored over it, remembering nothing he read.

By eight, the family was stirring. Gordon joined them at the breakfast table at eight-thirty. Little was said—small talk mostly, between husband and wife. The kids were unusually quiet.

Finally it was almost nine and time to go. As he stood up and started to leave the table, his son David looked up from his plate and said, "It's going to be a good day, Dad."

Gordon looked down at him, smiled, and nodded. And then he was gone.

He arrived at the church parking lot at nine-fifteen and went straight to his office. He put his hand on the knob and tentatively pushed open the door, almost as if he expected to see someone else seated at his desk. The room was empty and just as he had left it. It was the first time he had seen it in over six weeks. He wondered if he would see it again.

He pulled the sermon out of his pocket, went to his desk, and sat down. For the next hour, he read and reread the words he had so diligently and prayerfully crafted. He considered searching the desk drawers for a Dexamyl. He needed one now more than ever. Just one. The last one. Just to get through this sermon. Somehow he resisted the urge to look. At ten forty-five, he left the office and walked up the hill to the building that housed the sanctuary. *"He maketh me to lie down in green pastures: he leadeth me beside the still waters. He restoreth my soul…"*

He stopped just outside the door leading to the altar and stood quietly and alone for a few moments. *"For thou art with me; thy rod and thy staff they comfort me."*

Just beyond the door, he heard the shuffling and whisperings of the gathering flock. After a few moments, the human sounds were superseded by the organ prelude. He had heard it many times before— Bach's "In Thee is Gladness." It was Gordon Weekley's cue. He opened the door, walked the few steps to the pulpit, and took his place in the chair that he had not occupied since early October. He looked out over the congregation. There wasn't an empty seat. The pews were more tightly packed than he had ever seen them, and plenty of people were standing.

He felt his heart pounding in his chest. His hands were shaking. *Am I all right?* he thought. *I must be. I'm fine. A little jittery. I'm okay.*

He stood up, stepped forward, and lifted his arms. The congregation rose as one.

*Praise God from whom all blessings flow,*
*Praise Him, all creatures here below,*
*Praise Him above, ye heavenly hosts,*
*Praise Father, Son, and Holy Ghost.*

He bowed his head and delivered the invocation. He did not hear the nervousness in his voice, although he felt it in his throat.

When he opened his eyes he called for hymn number 68, "As With Gladness Men of Old." They sang all four verses and sang passionately. Gordon had selected this hymn specifically for its final verse. The words came ringing back to him from the voices in the pews:

*Holy Jesus, every day*
*Keep us in the narrow way;*
*And when earthly things are past,*
*Bring our ransomed souls at last*
*Where they need no star to guide,*
*Where no clouds Thy glory hide.*

He got through the reading of the scriptures and he got through the morning prayer. The service was moving smoothly now, belying the anxiety of the pastor. The tithes and offerings were next, and then an anthem, "The Glory of the Lord."

When the last strains of Handel died, the minister rose again from his chair and stepped to the podium, facing those who had prayed for his return, facing those who wished he were somewhere else.

"While your lives have probably run more along the course of normalcy during the recent days since I last stood here in this sacred place, I have wandered through an experience of deep and profound significance.

"So often have I longed for some sudden deepening of my spiritual life to match the ever-increasing challenge of this beloved pastorate. I used to think that such an experience would take the form of tragedy which, when redeemed by God, would be shot through and through with a new power. Or it could take another form: the reclamation of God in the life of one who was possessed by great evil. And when that blackened heart was purged, the soul would blossom forth into a flaming witness for him.

"One of my dear friends in the ministry was lifted out of the path he was traveling a few Thanksgivings ago when his entire family was wiped off the roster of the living by a terrible auto crash which smeared mother, father, and sister into unidentifiable corpses along a South Carolina highway. Today, a symbol of God's redeeming grace, he is a great powerhouse for the Lord.

"Another preacher, who was once wanted in three states for major crimes, was gloriously transformed by God so that he is now one of the most effective evangelists that I know of in the ministry. Out of his heart, once scarred and stained with evil, there flows now the compassion of Christ. Out of a mouth which fired volleys of oaths and profanities, there now flows the message of redemption.

"Little did I know a few weeks ago that a time of enforced solitude and retrospection, soul searching and reappraisal, was about to break on me. 'God works in wondrous ways, His mysteries to perform.'

"For many of you, this will be told for the first time: It will tell you of one who needed a new and shaking confrontation with God. Of a challenge and its acceptance. Of a warning and a whole network of holy resolutions with which to heed it.

"Having made the foolish error of attempting for the last few years to apply myself to my duties in the same manner I used nine years ago when our church was one-tenth its present size and failing to realize that such was a physical impossibility, I resorted to the misuse of two medications which had been prescribed for me. One: a capsule primarily for the control of weight but prescribed for me for the secondary effect it produced, that of a source of energy. The other: a capsule used to provide inducement of sleep.

"Because of my tolerance of these drugs after that much use, I seized control of the administering of them and gradually edged down into overuse. This caused an inordinate loss of weight and other very undesirable side effects, imperceptible to me in the extent to which you saw them.

"The deacons and Personnel Committee were represented in a meeting with Mrs. Weekley and me and expressed their extreme concern for my physical well-being, asking that I take a mandatory leave of absence to correct this.

"For five weeks, I have withdrawn from the local scene here for that purpose, submitting myself to physicians at Bucknell University for a thorough physical examination and guidance to me for the safeguarding of the future of my health.

"What they did was remarkably rapid, as I trust you can see. But this is only the surface evidence of what has happened. I committed myself to four weeks of most intensive normalizing of my physical status; a thorough report of this entire sequence of events, their findings, their recommendations, their prognosis was forwarded to our deacons and Personnel Committee and has been interpreted for them by one of our deacon doctors.

"Unfortunately, in the framework of human nature, many very wild and distorted ideas have been rampant among our people since this thing was sucked up into the vacuum of lack of knowledge, for as conscientiously as I tried to keep our leaders appraised of the situation, for one reason or another, it was not possible to transmit all the facts to all of you with the great distance between us and with my absence.

"Now that I am back, I am happy to state that the preceding week has given me time for allaying much of the speculation regarding this event, which was clouded by the haze of the unknown.

"I have been astounded by the milieu of totally unfounded, illogical, and twisted information under which many of you have been laboring. I have stated what the case was, and I would like to declare for complete clarity a positive and categorical denial that anything else comprised part of this incident.

"I shall be most happy to share any portion of my experience with any person in our congregation who wishes to know more or to ask questions. And included in that will be the offer of the medical report.

"As thrilling as the physiological restoration has been, it is not the significant portion of my story, by far.

"Having pushed myself into a corner and having gone into a place of virtual solitude, I was happy to see that three days and nights put me out of the woods and into the clearing, and from then on, the physiological part of my time away was routine: eating, sleeping, walking; eating, sleeping, walking.

"I was staying in the apartment of my dearest friend, who is head of the Department of Classics of Bucknell. Since he was up on the university campus most of the day, my time started to drag heavy on my hands. There was no television, no daily paper, no familiar faces.

"At first, the silence was deafening. Then I found it to be gradually unfolding as the marvelous envelope in which I should hide to read the Word of the Lord—and in which He spoke back in accents clear and strong. Prayer followed this and I found myself speaking to Him more articulately than in a long time: best of all, in this framework of Scripture and prayer, He was speaking more loudly than ever.

"One of the strong impressions of those early days: I was led to see that this was meant to be a true spiritual exile.

"I received a letter from a cherished friend of the years, Dr. James Blackmore, whose account of an incident in the life of Stanley Jones was timed to come to me just at the right moment. Under the thrilling impetus of this, I began to search the Scripture for others who had been temporarily put on the shelf by God for restorative purposes. I read of Elijah and his retreat. I read the stories of some of the prophets and their withdrawing from the affray of life. I read with new revelation of the many, many times Christ had turned aside for the restoration of prayer. I turned especially to the Arabian desert experience of Paul and saw him emerge from it renewed.

"This was God's clear message.

"And each day it became clearer. It could never have happened here; I had to withdraw and turn aside. Whoever could think I would leave the busy pastorate and make time for this?

"But the truth is that we won't make time for God until (like Stanley Jones) we have to be thrown down. And when one is thrown down on his back, the only way he can look is up.

"As I have looked up in the days since then, I have seen many, many things. I have seen with new eyes my life in the context of His will. In this, I received a glorious refresher course, the plan of salvation—only this time, instead of preaching it for the edification of others, I was being made a single actor on the stage, and Christ, the only other actor, replaying His role as Savior.

"This embraced sin: no longer was I acting in the role of a pastor. No longer was I working on pastoral prayers; I was praying afresh the prayer of the sinner—and, my friends, this prayer should not escape us daily. 'Lord, be merciful to me, a sinner.' It can't be made any longer or more simple than that. It loses its power when it is adulterated. It is basic to the core of Divine Truth. It embraced confession of sin, and grappled to my soul now, more than ever, ever before were those words of I John 1:9—'If we confess our sins, he is faithful and just to forgive us our sins, and to cleanse us from all unrighteousness.' And again, Proverbs 28:13—'He that covereth his sins shall not prosper: but whoso confesseth and forsaketh them shall have mercy.'

"So I spent many days, and when the lights had been snuffed for the night, I spent even more valuable hours then in a great spiritual housecleaning.

"This- experience was beginning to go far, far beyond weight gain, lab tests, doctor's appointments. I was down to the wire in a rendezvous with God. I was being led through the whole gamut of renewal. Having worked on the matter of sin and confession, I came to the inevitable result of confessions: forgiveness.

"Oh, what a sweet word that is; what unutterable glory one has when he has gone through the fires of purging to come out on the other side knowing God has dealt not only with the immediate error of his life but also with all past error, clearing the whole adding machine of everything that was in it. Never was that tremendous incident of Peter more clearly understood and more deeply loved in this heart of mine than as it fit into my experience of these days.

"How often have I preached from this, and it was not unreal to my heart then—but don't you have times when the pages of the Bible suddenly jump at you, become transcendent?

"Three times the Lord asked 'Do you love me?' Twice Peter responded with his mouth. The third time he responded with his soul. I'm so glad God gave Peter that third chance. What would the course of Christian history be otherwise? Isn't this a parable of our lives, because of our frailty, yes, even ministers? We answer without total heart.

"Then there comes a time when we are given that additional sweet call of God: Peter, really, do you? Gordon, really, do you love Me? Denial, partial denial, then at last a breakthrough, a time of 'full-filling.' I'll never forget the Friday night I knelt beside my bed and answered the Lord more deeply than ever: 'Yes, Lord I do love you, and I bring this whole experience to make it an offering. Please accept it. Take and manipulate all the factors of my life that in any way have reduced my service to Thee and cut short my loyalty.'

"Many of you know that the earliest beginning of my problem was restlessness at night, the inability to 'turn off problems; this was the start of it.

"That night was my first night of deep and peaceful sleep. It had been my fleece.

"I awoke the next morning and went into my friend's room smiling (and I did not have a strong habit of smiling minutes after arising). I was happy because I knew something deep and wonderful had happened.

"Then that afternoon, I was out walking along the banks of the beautiful Susquehanna river, and as I rested my arms on the railing of an old wooden bridge looking down into the lazy waters of that river, there came over me a sudden and complete relaxing of the tensions of concern. That new-found surrender. There came something wholly new and wonderful—at least, for a very long time, I had needed this, much of the time thoroughly unbeknownst to me—a surrender, an inner yielding to the grip that life so often has upon us. And from that hour, all the processes of restoration were amazingly speeded. From that hour, a new spiritual look. From that hour, a new calm with which to face *this* hour.

"The greatest proof of my experience is that during the days and nights of this week—the most critical week, I suppose, of my life—a week which would have formerly been borne with the greatest agitation and emotional pain—this week has been one of inner calm, of sound and peaceful sleep, of expectancy and grace.

"Again and again and again, there has gone through my heart the phrase, 'The Gospel is the good news of new beginnings.' I apologize for the chagrin and embarrassment and for the concern and inconveniences which this abrupt pause in my life has brought to many of you.

"Through all my adult life, I have been aware that somehow in human nature there is the thought: 'Ministers should be impeccably strong and different.'

"Well, dear friends, in a way this is true, to be sure. But often we have to find consolation in that great and reassuring verse of Scripture: 'God knoweth our frame, that we are dust.' There is no ministerial exemption from this. We too can grow weary in well-doing; we too can stumble—but we too, like the laity, can get up and stand tall again, taller than before. I come this morning to sit at the table of which I have been the waiter, the servant; I must now eat the bread of humility and contrition.

"I have gone away into a time with God in a deeply personal need. That need has been gloriously met. God, I found, has had a concern about me just greater than even yours or my family's. He has forgiven and restored. And now there surges in my heart and soul a desire greater than I have ever felt to move out in His ministry with the joy of this ringing in my heart, with a desire more intense than ever to preach His unsearchable goodness.

"I come to you for the same forgiveness He so generously administers, the forgiveness you too seek in life. What an experience this could be for people and pastor.

"I drove home last Saturday. Along with my congregation, I had missed my family terribly during this experience of renewal. As I drove down the gravel road that led to the house, I came presently upon a crude little sign, tacked to a tree. I thought it at first the advertisement of some land to sell.

"Then, I saw these words: 'Say, where have you been...We've missed you, Dad.'

"The car went around a slight bend in the road and there appeared another sign, 'See you in a few feet...hurry up,' and 'just around the next turn.' Banner over driveway, 'Welcome Home.' A final sign was the climax to this great parable on the Gospel of New Beginnings which my sons and their mother were so innocently working out.

"For he's a jolly good fellow.. .just a little more Dad.' The comma had been left out—what they meant was 'just a little more, and you'll be home, Dad.'

"But those words have been blazing in front of me all week—just a little more Dad. Just a little more Dad, just a little more consecration— just a little more dependence on God and not things, medications, personal strength. I want to show God, and you, for His glory, what can be done even when a minister falters."

It was finished. He stood silent for a scant moment, trying to read the faces. They told him nothing. He wanted to scream, "Do you love me, do you accept me?" Instead, he cleared his throat, picked up the hymnal, and referred them to number 451, "O Zion, Haste."

"As we sing, please pay particular attention to the words of the last stanza. They tell us that sometimes we pay a heavy price for being Christians, but that God will repay us in turn. And if any of you would like to come forward today to accept Christ as your personal Savior, to give your life to Him, we welcome you at this altar. Also if any of you would like to transfer by letter to the Providence family, or if some of you would like to simply come forward as a reaffirmation of faith, the arms of God are open to you."

The notes from the organ poured out in familiar four-four time, and the voices of the congregation raised, singing:

*O Zion haste, thy mission high fulfilling,*
*To tell to all the world that God is Light;*
*That He who made all nations is not willing*
*One soul should perish, lost in shades of night.*

Gordon wondered if anyone would come forward this day, but he supposed not. Who would join a church or come forward as a candidate on a day when its pastor's future was in the balance? Who would come forward in a reaffirmation of faith when faith in the church's leader had been diminished?

Arthur Smith would. And did. And so did the Howard Byrums. And the Harry Bacons. And so did virtually everyone in the crowded sanctuary, singing as they came. "...Tell how He stooped to save his lost creation, and died on earth that man might live above...."

Down the aisles from out of the pews on either side they flowed, a stream of young and old, of charter members who had been with him so long, of newer members who had quickly come to love him. The flow stopped, a logjam of people in front of the altar as the first arrivals reached Gordon, hugged him, embraced him, shook his hand. On and on the organist played, back through the hymn again and again.

"Good to have you back, pastor."

"We love you, pastor."

"Welcome home, Gordon."

Never before had he seen such a sight, not even in the great Billy Graham Crusades in Africa and South America. It was noon when he issued the call to invitation. It was one-fifteen by the time everyone had made it back to the pews, everyone except eight people who had chosen this day to transfer their letters of membership to Providence—and a ninth person, a young man, who had come forward as a candidate for Baptism. His name was David Weekley.

At one-thirty, the church finally cleared. As the joyous worshipers made their way across the parking lot to their cars, someone stopped Jarvis Warren and said, "He looks good Jarvis. I think he's going to be all right."

"I wish I could agree with you," Jarvis answered sadly.

In the grip of delusion, Gordon had believed every word he preached that day. In truth, his soul was a long way from being restored.

Things did get better for him in the weeks that followed, at least in terms of his addiction. His powerful sermon had brought him back into the fold, and no subsequent deacons' meetings were held to discuss his future. Nevertheless, he understood that even though he was widely loved and almost universally forgiven, he was walking on thin ice. He couldn't afford another episode like the Pennsylvania exile. He knew Jarvis would be watching him closely. He knew Norma Lou would be doing the same. He knew, too, that the road ahead would be bumpy.

The first bump was not long in coming. Dick Ungerbuehler, who had been a part-time director of music and came on full-time in early 1964, was gone before that year's end. Oscar Whitescarver, the respected and highly competent minister of education, left his post shortly after Ungerbuehler's departure.

The movement to form a new church was growing, too, but Gordon did not resist it nearly as passionately as he had in the past. From a logical point of view, he felt that Providence with its 967 members was too small to be birthing another church, particularly in light of the fact that a new, larger, and expensive sanctuary was not too far down the pike.

Of equal, perhaps more, importance, was the fact that a split would signify a lack of faith in his abilities to lead. He had been told as much in the deacon's meeting when he returned from Bucknell. Not everyone who wanted to form a new church lacked confidence in Gordon. But many did.

On the other hand, if those who lacked confidence left, the remaining congregation would be behind him. He had to admit that though he loved every one of his members, even those thinking of leaving, the thought of a united congregation was not unappealing.

## TWELVE

By the spring of 1965, the church had returned to near normal. Rev. Dean Kaufman of Nashville had accepted the post of minister of education, and Helen Ann Connell was named minister of youth. The spring wasn't dull, though—at least not for Providence member Tackie Vosburgh.

She had just picked up her two children and two others at Cotswold Elementary School and was driving by a First Citizens branch bank on Randolph Road near the church when one of the FBI's ten most wanted men decided to make a withdrawal. The robber, William Coble, was running from the bank parking lot with a police officer in hot pursuit toward Woodlark Lane, a residential street that intersected Randolph and on which lived two of Tackie's closest friends. She saw Coble, stepped on the gas, sped past him, turned right on Woodlark, and spotted her friends in a front yard. She rolled down the passenger-side window and yelled, "Get in your houses. There's a bank robber headed this way."

"God help us," said Carolyn Leonard, one of the friends. "There he is."

And sure enough, there he was, waving a pistol, running straight toward Tackie's car.

"Lock your doors and roll up your windows," she screamed to the four kids in the back seat. They did, but it didn't matter, because Coble fired. The bullet went through the front window, through Tackie's right thigh and into her left.

"Get out of the car," Coble yelled.

He didn't have to say it twice. Tackie stumbled out, jerked open the back door, and reached for the kids. By the time she got two of them out, Coble was behind the wheel.

"Wait," she demanded, "the children, let me get these children."

"Hurry up," he snarled.

She grabbed the remaining two, and Coble took off. He didn't get far. Not knowing the neighborhood, he turned into a dead end street, and before he could get turned around, he was face to face with Charlotte's finest and a Providence member named Duane Bruch. Bruch, too, had been driving through the neighborhood and had seen the pursuing officer on foot. He stopped his car, the officer jumped in, and away they went after Coble.

Tackie's wounds were serious but not critical. The story might have ended there, but it didn't.

A few weeks later while awaiting trial in the city jail, Coble received a visitor, Gordon Weekley. Gordon wanted to know if there was anything he or his congregation could do to help the imprisoned man. That visit and the letter he received must have surprised Coble.

Dear Mr. Coble:

There have been many thoughts and prayers running through my mind and heart these past few days. I have thought of all the many people involved and how much worse this episode could have been. You certainly showed compassion for us by letting the children and me out of the car.

My foremost prayer from the very first hour has been 'Thank you, God, thank you'— over and over as that long night slowly passed. I realized more and more that our Lord was watching over us. He took care of so many of his children—including you. I do not think you meant to shoot me. I believe you were desperate for a mode of transportation and I happened to be there. The police told me that you said you were sorry you shot me. I want you to know that I have no malice towards you. There are many reasons to be thankful. We have three little girls, and one of them prayed the night of the accident that 'God would be put into Mr. Coble's heart.' This is the prayer of many, and shall continue to be.

Mrs. E. B. Vosburgh, Jr.

Tackie later visited the man herself and gave him a Bible. Such was the nature of the Providence people and their pastor.

It is also the nature of Baptists to spawn, and that summer the much talked-about spawning of Carmel Baptist became a reality. At the regular church conference in June, Jarvis Warren reported to the congregation that the Mecklenburg Baptist Association had committed to buying the land. Providence was being asked to come up with $28,000, half the purchase price.

"The deacons and the finance committee unanimously recommend that we go ahead," said Jarvis.

The pastor asked the congregation members to think about it, pray about it, and be prepared to vote on it at the next meeting. Gordon knew in his head something that he had always known in his heart: an affirmative vote was inevitable. This congregation of doers would have supported a new church even if things had not been rough with him. Maybe he had hastened the process a little, but it would have happened.

On July 11, Jarvis brought the matter to the floor of the church for a vote along with the suggestion that Providence use the money in its own building fund to pay part of the $28,000. When the meeting began Providence had $6,000 in the fund. They gave it all.

Gordon tried to look on the bright side. A new Baptist church would be a welcome addition to any community, particularly a growing area like Charlotte. And the fact that Carmel was born from Providence Baptist certainly says something about the success of the mother church. With that in mind, he managed not to think too much about the Carmel situation.

By late July, his weight had climbed to 150 pounds. People were no longer looking at him with disbelieving stares. He was working as hard as he ever had, and he was not seeing much of his family. Even on the rare evenings he was home, Norma Lou was cloistered in some room studying.

He was not worrying a lot about job security, but he didn't feel completely comfortable about it either. He often found himself recalling the words of his good friend and church leader, Tom Pfaff. Over lunch one afternoon not long after Gordon's return from Pennsylvania, Tom said, "Once there's a crack in the foundation, the eyes of people will always, occasionally, be focused back on that crack."

Gordon knew people were watching him and wondering if the crack would expand, but he felt good. The church was continuing to grow, and the deacons were already talking about forming building committees as early as next year, which meant that the permanent 900-seat sanctuary would likely be completed by the end of the decade.

*I've proven myself,* he thought, as he sat at the desk in his church office one steamy Carolina August afternoon. *I've come through the Carmel thing. I survived Pennsylvania. I've done well in the months I've been back. I think now I can handle whatever comes along.* He strode out of the office and got into his car.

In less than thirty minutes, he was standing in a phone booth in the middle of a small town north of Charlotte going through the Yellow Pages. His finger found the name of a pharmacy a few blocks away, and he decided to give it a try. It was a typical modern-day drugstore with the drugs in the back and everything else under the sun on the shelves and in the aisles. None of the displays tempted Gordon Weekley. What he wanted was behind the counter. When he got to that counter, he was relieved to see that the pharmacist was a man in his late fifties.

Pharmacists over fifty had proven to be the easiest marks, and this one was no exception. In the several months since his last indulgence, Gordon had not forgotten his litany: "...Charlotte minister... on my way out of town... forgot my shaving kit with medications in it... don't know any local doctors... can you help?"

The pharmacist helped, with Doriden and Dexamyl. Gordon Weekley was back in business.

*Now remember,* he said to himself on the return drive to Charlotte, *these are rewards. I'm only going to take them once in a great while, when I feel like I've earned a break.*

He stopped at a gas station, got change from the attendant, and pulled a soft drink out of the vending machine. The attendant was in the mood for conversation, but Gordon politely explained that he was in a hurry and quickly got back in his car and back on the road.

He placed the drink between his legs and flipped the top off the Dexamyl bottle with his right hand, steering with his left. He shook a capsule out on the seat beside him, and with the dexterity of someone who had done this many times before, he retrieved the cap from the seat, snapped it on the bottle with his thumb and forefinger, and stuck the bottle back in his pocket. He groped, found the capsule, and brought it to his mouth. Reaching down again, he wrapped his hand around the soft drink, lifted it to his lips, and drank, sweeping the capsule into the body and the mind of Gordon Weekley.

By the time he found himself in the late afternoon Charlotte traffic, the old euphoria was back. He made his way out Providence Road to Country Lane, parked the car in the driveway and bounced to the front door of the house.

When he walked in, he encountered no wife or children, so he went straight to his study and hid the pills behind some books on the shelves. Then he sought out Norma Lou. He found her in the kitchen making supper and kissed her hello. Usually he would return at this hour to the study to read and write, but this time, he flopped in a chair at the table and struck up a conversation—one that turned out to be one-sided. He rattled and rambled and didn't keep quiet long enough for her to respond if she had wanted to. The Dexamyl was running his mouth.

After several minutes of his nonstop verbosity, she turned from peeling the potatoes and gave him a long, curious look. He caught it and realized that he had probably talked too much.

"I've got a little reading to do," he said, "and I'd better get to it."

He ate dinner that night, although he was not at all hungry. He ate enough, he thought, to discount any suspicions Norma Lou might have. Later, he took a Doriden.

He did not take anything the next day, or for the next several days afterward. He lasted, in fact, about a week.

*This is no problem,* he said to himself one morning in his church office, *I can control this.* He took another Dexamyl.

He took another the next day. And the next. And the next. He followed them all up with nightly Doridens. He observed Norma Lou as carefully as he assumed she was observing him. He noted nothing in her behavior that would indicate she knew about the drugs.

Perhaps her guard was down now since he had agreed to see a psychiatrist. The sessions seemed meaningless to him, though. He did almost all the talking, while the man we shall call Dr. Schmidt did almost all the listening. When Gordon asked him for a diagnosis after several sessions, Dr. Schmidt told him that along with depression, he had free-floating anxiety—a fear of being afraid. Gordon was not convinced. *If I have anything,* he thought, *this man's not going to fix it.*

After two weeks, he checked his weight. He had lost five pounds. He vowed to eat even though he was repelled by the sight of food. In the sanctity of his study one evening, he was shocked to discover his supply was running low. He needed to replenish, and soon. The next morning, he got in his car and headed west. Somewhere out there in the direction of the mountains was a doctor or a pharmacist with a sympathetic ear.

Highway 74 from Charlotte to the Asheville area high in the Great Smoky Mountains was dotted with small towns. The first was Gastonia, but he didn't stop there. He wanted to get farther out, farther away. Kings Mountain was next, and Kings Mountain was definitely out. Everybody knew everybody there, including him. He remembered with a smile the telephone operator who had received a call for him, had seen him walking toward the drugstore, and had put the call through to there. Shelby was out, too. He had preached there frequently when he was a pastor in Kings Mountain. So on he went, past Forest City, and finally to Rutherfordton.

He stopped at a phone booth on the outskirts of the town and flipped through the Yellow Pages. Then he remembered that one of his best friends from college and seminary lived there and preached there. He decided Rutherfordton wasn't a good risk.

He turned north on Highway 221 and traveled up into the mountains toward Marion. He had a college friend there, too, but this friend was a doctor. They hadn't seen each other since Masonboro days, when Gordon was in his first pastorate and the doctor was taking his internship in nearby Wilmington.

The office was easy to find, and Gordon was ushered right in. There were handshakes and hugs and how-are-you's and how-are-the family's, and after a few minutes of those pleasantries, Gordon slid smoothly into his forgot-my-shaving-kit-with-the-medication-in-it litany.

"I'll be more than happy to call those in for you," said the doctor, "and all you have to do is walk right around the corner and pick them

That's exactly what Gordon did. He didn't even have to pay for them. Two large bottles, one with uppers, one with downers, compliments of a good and trusting friend.

He was into them now. Not a day passed without uppers or a night without downers. In a matter of only a few weeks, his weight dropped like a stone. His eyes hollowed. His daily activities became frantic. At his desk, he would hop from one topic to another—a few minutes on his sermon, a few minutes on a committee report. And then he would be up and out and on his way to the hospital or someone's home. But sometimes, in the car, he would forget where he was going and have to stop and check his appointment book.

The one thing he could not forget was Carmel Baptist. It returned to his mind over and over. It was a frontal assault on his ego. He was losing part of his family and it hurt, although he tried not to show it.

After Providence had voted the start-up money, Gordon sent out a news release. In it he described the generosity of the mother church in giving up $6,000 of its own building fund. The release resulted in a story on the front page of the local section of The Charlotte News. It also brought an admonishment from Bill Edwards, one of the church leaders.

"Gordon, what you wrote is not quite true," he said. "Yes, that was building fund money, but you know as well as I do that it's not necessarily money allocated for the new sanctuary. We always have a building fund kitty whether we're planning on building or not. Why did you say that in the paper?"

Gordon knew why he had done it, but he was not about to tell Bill Edwards that he had been trying to put a good face on a bad situation, to cover up the main reason for Carmel's existence: his failings as a pastor.

*How did I fail them?* he agonized silently. *I've given my life to them. They're family.*

"Look at yourself in the mirror," Norma Lou said to him one night in August. "You're on them again. You can't hide it from me. You're going to ruin your life, my life, the kids' lives. You're going to ruin everything."

"Stop it, stop it," Gordon shouted. "I'm not ruining anything. Look at this house. Look at this sixteen acres of land. Look at those two cars in the driveway. Look at the size of the church. When I look at myself in the mirror, I see a very successful pastor and a good family provider. What do you see when you look at me, Norma Lou? I'm seeing Dr. Schmidt regularly. What more do you want from me?"

Norma Lou had voiced her confidence in the doctor's abilities, but Gordon had trusted him even less since the day Schmidt had said he would not be on the way to a full cure until "you can look me in the eye and tell me to go straight to hell."

"I'll never do that," Gordon had said. "That's not the way I deal with people."

"Well, you're going to have to start doing it."

Gordon had heard that indictment all his life: too much sugar, not enough salt. But that's the way he was, and that's the way he was going to stay.

"Deny you're taking drugs. Deny it," said Norma Lou.

"I don't have to deny it," he said, and stormed off to his study. He flopped in his chair, put his elbows on the desk, and rested his chin on his hands. After a few minutes, he got up, walked over to the bookshelf, and fishing behind a row of books, latched onto the bottle of Doriden.

---

At the September church conference, Ed Echerd announced that anyone interested in Carmel Baptist was invited to a meeting the following Sunday. The announcement was delivered without fanfare, matter-of-factly, but the words knifed into Gordon's soul.

*It's happening,* he said to himself. *It's happening. What could I have done to stop it? What did I do to cause it?*

He could not get over the irony, either, that Ed Echerd, the man who was largely responsible for wooing him from Kings Mountain, was now the man delivering a message that would take some of this church away from him.

All the following week, his Carmel obsession continued. The only respite from it was no respite at all. It was Norma Lou's cold anger. She was getting under his skin, accusing him daily of using drugs. He pleaded with her to leave him alone, but she wouldn't let up. When she indicted him for putting stress on the children, he countered that she had done her share by her constant harping and by the selfishness she exhibited in pursuing a college degree instead of spending time with the kids. Finally, they would expend their words for the evening and sit silently across the room from each other. He wondered on more than one of these occasions how two people seated so closely together could be so far apart.

*The world is 25,000 miles around,* he thought, *and she's not ten feet away. She's 24,999 miles and 5,270 feet away. A world apart. And what of the others, the ones that are going to Carmel? How far apart from me are they? And how many of them are there?*

It didn't take him long to find out. The following Sunday, when the members-to-be gathered under the giant oaks on the five and a half acres that would be the foundation for Carmel Baptist Church, a lonely figure stood quietly apart from them at the far corner of the property. He watched and he counted, almost to a hundred. Then he left, wondering how Providence would be able to fulfill its own ambitions for an addition to the fellowship hall and the new sanctuary. He wondered too if this event signified the beginning of the end of his popularity as a minister.

If it did, one couldn't tell by the enrollment figures. By the time Providence got around to selecting its building committee members in the spring of 1966, Sunday school enrollment was over eleven hundred and church membership over a thousand. The Carmel attrition had been a blip on the growth chart and nothing more.

One of the people selected for the building committee was Al Edwards, who co-chaired the building committee for the first sanctuary. Al had brought the golden plow to the ground-breaking for that sanctuary, and had also been one of the four people at Jarvis Warren's home who confronted Gordon with his drug problem on an evening in October in 1964. Some thought Al Edwards wanted Gordon Weekley out of the Providence pastorate, but Gordon didn't think that. Though his relationship with Al was strained, he readily agreed that the man belonged in the important post of chairman of the building planning subcommittee.

Edd George didn't think he belonged there. George had been a loyal supporter of Gordon before, during, and after his exile to Pennsylvania. Gordon had heard that George made a vow during the exile that the Weekley children would get college educations should their father be unable to resolve his addiction problem. Gordon couldn't have had a better friend.

"I can't believe you're letting Al Edwards chair that subcommittee," Edd George almost shouted at Gordon. "The man's out to get you, you know that."

"Edd," Gordon said, "I know Al and I aren't getting on all that well right now, but he's a good man, and he's certainly a qualified man for the building committee. For me to disapprove his appointment just because he disapproves of me would be an act of vengeance and un-Christian. Let's just drop the matter."

Edd didn't let the matter drop. At the regular church conference on the evening of August 28, 1966, he made a motion to remove Al Edwards from his committee position. Tom Pfaff, overall chairman of the building committee, made an intervening motion that the matter not even be considered. Pfaff's motion passed 52-30. Gordon was relieved. The crisis had passed. Apparently George's anger hadn't.

Gordon now felt a gap widening between himself and the man who had so loyally supported him. George no longer called or visited him, no longer spoke to him unless he had to. Gordon hated what was happening. His was a ministry of love. He truly believed in the concept of church family. He ached inside when he felt that someone in his congregation was put out with him, and it was an ache that even his nightly Doriden didn't squelch.

His intake was escalating now. By winter, he was popping as many as eight Dexamyl a day and three or four Doriden. He was constantly on the road resupplying himself. During his workday, he overlooked routine details, forgot to sign letters and return phone calls. He missed appointments with fair frequency. Even some of his sermons didn't have the compelling messages people were so used to hearing. But every time he got too close to the edge, he somehow recovered. If he gave a bad sermon one Sunday, he came back with a very good one the following week. If he missed an appointment and knew about it, he made sure he kept every appointment for the next several days.

He never, however, failed to see those who truly needed him: the ill, the depressed, the families contemplating separation or divorce. That part of him was ingrained. So he hung on, pastoring adequately as far as most observers were concerned, but very poorly to those few who felt he must certainly be on drugs again.

And any hopes he had of reconciliation with Edd were to vanish in January of 1967.

## Thirteen

It started in Sunday School, in the men's fellowship class. Edd George, class teacher Mercer Blankenship, and two other class members, Jim Royster and Hollis Baxter, decided among themselves to integrate the class with their wives. Mixed classes weren't commonplace in Southern Baptist churches, but the group nevertheless went ahead without conferring with the Sunday school superintendent or any other church staff member.

Gordon was bewildered. He was opposed to mixed adult classes, largely because of his traditionalist upbringing. Still, he couldn't understand why the families hadn't come to him or to Sunday school superintendent Bryan Coates or minister of education Dean Kaufman before they integrated the class.

The answer came a few days later, on February 3, 1967, when Dean Kaufman looked up from his lunch at Bailey's Cafeteria and saw Mrs. Jim Royster standing over him.

"Jim and I would like to meet with you," she said.

"I'd be happy to," he said, thinking that maybe now some definitive discussions about the Sunday school class could begin. When he arrived at the Royster home that evening, he was greeted not only by the Roysters but by the Georges and the Baxters as well.

It was not a good meeting, and it was not, as Kaufman had thought, a meeting about Sunday school. It was about Gordon Weekley. As Kaufman was later to report to a special meeting of the deacons, this small group was out to get Gordon removed from the pulpit. Gordon wasn't necessarily the only target, because part of Kaufman's report included a threat that unless he kept his skirts clean, he would be the next to go.

At this same deacons' meeting, Jim Hayes dropped another bombshell. He said he had heard some members of the dissident group discussing a plan to get forty families to withhold pledge money and throw the church into a financial crisis unless their demands were met.

The deacons were shocked and saddened. Their church, built on love and sacrifice and compromise and cooperation, that had brimmed with confidence and optimism, that had done everything it had set out to do, was in danger of being torn apart. Certainly there had been disagreements before on how much should be spent on buildings or missions or the size of Sunday school classes. Certainly tempers had flared—but always, always in the spirit of family, always with the greater good of the church foremost in mind.

This was different. This situation was a vessel filled with bitterness and hostility. It had to be resolved, exorcised, at once. After hearing the reports of Kaufman and Hayes, the deacons called Gordon to the meeting. They gave him a unanimous vote of confidence. The next thing they did was arrange for a subcommittee headed by Arthur Smith to meet with the dissident group.

The meeting was held on February 18 in deacon chairman Smith's office. According to the minutes, the four readily admitted that they wanted Gordon out. They also admitted discussing among themselves the possibility of asking forty families to withhold pledges, but they claimed that the discussion never evolved into a plan. Then they promised to back off their personal crusade for Gordon's removal if the deacons would handle it instead. Mercer Blankenship was reported to have said he was re-evaluating his position on Gordon.

Four days later, Smith's subcommittee reported on the meeting to the board of deacons. Once again, Gordon came away with their full support. The Sunday school issue was still unresolved, though, and Dean Kaufman came away from the meeting deciding it was showdown time with Mercer Blankenship.

A short time later, Kaufman confronted Blankenship and asked him to get his class back to normal or resign as its teacher. Blankenship declined to do either. On March 22, the deacons met again. Several of them stated that the dissident group was still actively lobbying for Gordon's removal. Kaufman reported that he had gotten nowhere with Blankenship.

It is the nature of gentle Southern people to leave exits open for their adversaries, to give them ample opportunity to recant harsh statements and retire from the battle with their dignity intact. Now, after eight long weeks, the exits finally closed. The deacons decided to take the matter before the entire congregation at the regular church conference scheduled for April 2. A letter went out from deacons' secretary Paul Godfrey to the church membership explaining the two issues to be discussed and requesting that each member attend and support the pastor and the church policy regarding Sunday school.

The meeting was scheduled for 6:30, but it was not even six o'clock when Gordon looked out from a church office window and saw in the twilight a line of Buicks and Fords and Chevrolets on Randolph Road, turn signals blinking like beacons, waiting to pull, one after the other, into the church parking lot.

By 6:15, the sanctuary was full and people were still coming. Those who couldn't find seats found places to stand along the walls. Since this was to be a conference and not a service, there was no organ prelude to fill the sanctuary air in the remaining minutes before the scheduled start time. Instead, there was the hum of hundreds of voices exchanging whispered greetings or speculating about the purpose and probable outcome of the meeting.

Silence suddenly covered the congregation like a blanket. The pastor was in the pulpit. For a moment, he studied the crowd before him, looking into the faces he had known so long and so well. He considered the irony that here he was, the minister of Providence Baptist Church, presiding over a meeting to discuss a proposal to remove from the pulpit the minister of Providence Baptist Church. This time, he did not feel the cold stab of fear he had felt that night at Jarvis Warren's home. This time, the deacons were here to ensure that he did not leave. Still, it was embarrassing and awkward to be on trial, to be tried by the very people he loved. As his eyes fell on Edd George, he wondered how a man could be so unfailingly loyal one day and so opposed to him the next. And all because of Al Edward's appointment to the building committee.

"Let us pray," the pastor said. After they prayed, the minutes of the previous conference were read and approved. A church nominating committee was selected. Then a motion was made to employ Mrs. Mercer Wilson as a community missionary, and that too was approved. It was all so ordinary it could have been any church conference on any Sunday night—until Arthur Smith stepped forward to preside over the remainder of the meeting.

In his melodic Southern drawl, he explained the two issues the deacons were bringing before the congregation. Then he turned to Charlie Patterson and asked him to read the minutes from the February and March deacons' meetings so that the congregation could be fully apprised of what was going on in their church.

Patterson stood up, cleared his throat, and read the chronicle of events that led up to this, the most critical night in the history of the church. People leaned forward in their seats, coughs were suppressed, even the few children who were there stopped squirming and listened, somehow knowing this gathering was too important for them to test their parents' patience. When he finished reading, seven typewritten pages later, everyone there knew for the first time the depth and the scope of the dissenters' efforts to remove Gordon Weekley from the pulpit. Patterson paused for a moment after the reading and then read again, this time a statement from the deacons:

After careful and prayerful consideration of all the information which has been presented to or has come to the attention of the Deacons, the Deacons stand firmly behind the Pastor, Reverend Gordon Weekley, and can find no reason for requesting his resignation. The Deacons thereby recommend to the church that the dissident members involved to secure the resignation of the Pastor refrain from any further efforts to secure his resignation and any other efforts which would prove detrimental to the effectiveness of his ministry and the spiritual welfare of the members of Providence Baptist Church. The continuation of such efforts could lead to prompt disciplinary action by the Church, as provided in the Church's constitution. It is hoped sincerely by the Board of Deacons that harmony will be regained, that we may all move forward in Christ's program at Providence. Furthermore, we wish to extend the Christian hand of fellowship to these dissident members, asking that they join us in doing the best job possible for the Lord at Providence and around the world.

The meeting was opened for motions and discussions, with a man named Charlie Myers acting as parliamentarian. Patterson still held the floor and introduced a resolution that "the Men's Fellowship Class be and remain a male class and that this class be visited by females on certain occasions only." That brought Hollis Baxter to his feet, and the battle was joined. He objected to the resolution and stated that the deacons had done certain "things" in recent months that indicated to him they were really less supportive of Gordon Weekley than they appeared to be.

Max Howie, a deacon, followed, speaking out in favor of Gordon and the Men's Class and asking the dissidents to give specific reasons for their discontent. Before he could get an answer, Wendell Wilmoth was up, offering a substitute motion that the church give the deacons and pastor a vote of confidence. Bruce Shannon seconded.

Charlie Myers called for discussion and got a speech from Mrs. Marge Schnakenberg in favor of the pastor and a similar one from Doug Broadway. Then it was Edd George's turn, and he built his case against Gordon by stating that pledges were $3,000 in arrears and that recent church growth was not good compared to other churches in the area.

Another member stood up and said he wanted to know what "things" Hollis Baxter had been referring to concerning the deacons' support of Gordon Weekley.

Baxter said Dean Kaufman had come to Providence for less money than he had been making at his previous church because the deacons had made certain promises to him, telling him that "things were not as they should be" in the pastorate.

Kaufman was on his feet in a flash. Struggling to control his anger, he looked straight at Hollis Baxter and said the reason he was at Providence was because "the Lord wanted me at Providence."

The meeting was heating up. Tension was rising. Bart Hodges rose from his seat and challenged Edd George on his figures, stating that Providence was $500 ahead of last year's pace and claiming that Providence was doing just fine in comparison to other area churches' growth.

George rejoined the fray and disputed Hodges on both counts. Back and forth they argued until, finally, Bill Williams got the floor, bringing a message of love, his love for the pastor, and saying that even the people who had left to form Carmel still loved Gordon Weekley.

Myers, the parliamentarian, called for a vote on Wendell Wilmoth's motion in support of the pastor and the deacons. "Will those who are in favor of a vote of confidence for Reverend Weekley and the deacons indicate by standing," he said.

Now the suppressed coughs came out. Now the audience that had been rigid and rapt with attention, stirred and shuffled. Now Gordon Weekley would find out exactly where he stood with his church. It did not take him long. Like a wave off the coast of Masonboro, they rose, men, women, and children standing up to be counted—virtually the entire gathering.

They had not forgotten who was always there when they needed him. The lady in the back row remembered that Gordon had stayed with her through the long night at the hospital, the last night of her husband's life. The young couple remembered who was there in the waiting room for the birth of their child. The once estranged husband and wife remembered who counseled them back to each other and to God.

They all remembered something. Gordon didn't know whether or not any of them had tears in their eyes, but there were tears in his.

"Thank you," said Charlie Myers to the congregation.

*Thank you,* thought Gordon Weekley to the Lord and to these friends who had risen to support him.

"Those opposed," said Myers.

Those opposed were the dissident four families. They stood. And they stood alone. Twice in three years, Gordon Weekley had faced his congregation with his future in the balance, and twice he had not only survived but triumphed. He considered himself a very fortunate man.

The audience was buzzing now, basking in the temporary relief of the tension. People were shaking hands, patting each other on the back, smiling, much like they did on Sunday mornings when the benediction had ended and the preacher had made his way up the aisle to his greeting place at the front door.

Arthur Smith quickly brought them back to attention, and the second issue, the matter of the Sunday school class, was brought back up for discussion. Here the dissidents fared far better. Bart Hodges called for Mercer Blankenship's resignation, but Blankenship, Baxter, and Mrs. Jim Royster fought back, with Mrs. Royster making the point that mixed classes did in fact exist in some churches within the Southern Baptist Convention.

Back and forth the argument flowed, and as the clock inched its way toward ten, it became apparent that the issue would not be resolved this night. Mrs. Jane Stoker moved that the class remain male, with females being allowed to visit on occasion. Blankenship objected, and he was joined by Mr. W.B. Sharpe who stated that Providence needed a Fellowship Class of men and women, and that the class needed Providence.

When Mrs. Stoker's motion was brought to a vote, it was defeated. Sharpe again rose to his feet, this time asking that the motion to remove Mercer Blankenship be tabled and sent back to the deacons for discussion for thirty days. The motion passed, 133 to 100, and a weary Providence congregation went home.

At the next church conference, on April 22, Arthur Smith read a deacons' recommendation that Mercer Blankenship be retained as class teacher and that the class remain male. The recommendation was largely due to Blankenship's statement to the Deacon Program Committee that he was not, nor had he been, associated with any group seeking the pastor's removal. The deacons further recommended that the Church Council study the matter of couples classes and bring a report of its recommendations to the church at large.

Smith then read a letter dated April 21. It was from Mercer Blankenship and contained his resignation as teacher of the class. In May, the Roysters left to join Pritchard Memorial Baptist Church. In June, the Baxters joined Myers Park Baptist.

## FOURTEEN

With the crisis behind it, Providence Baptist Church turned its attention to raising money for its building expansion. Because of the large sums required, the church sought professional fund-raising help. That brought Marshall Thompson of the Ketchum Corporation to Charlotte.

Ketchum was renowned for its ability to solicit funds, and Thompson was one of its best people. One method he used was a series of small banquets hosted in Fellowship Hall by the preacher with some ten to fifteen families in attendance. The purpose was to convince every church member that he or she was an important factor in the future of Providence Baptist Church. It made people feel good and it worked well—as it should have, because each member *was* indeed important to the church.

The dinners were friendly and fun. As they all sat around the table in the original church building that now served as the Fellowship Hall, Thompson and Gordon excited them with blueprints and word pictures of the new sanctuary.

There was also another portent of the future that no one except maybe Norma Lou took note of: the chicken and peas sitting untouched on Gordon Weekley's plate.

Summer brought no change in Gordon's habits. He continued to take pills, believing himself invulnerable to addiction although he certainly was an addict. As fall approached, he spent more and more time on the road looking for and finding his treasured pills.

Meanwhile, the building campaign was moving along nicely, and new members were steadily showing up on the rolls. Everything seemed normal to those on the outside looking in, and things felt normal to Gordon, too. In fact, if it hadn't been for Norma Lou's constant harping, life for the Providence pastor would have been ideal. She begged him to get help. He refused to acknowledge that he needed it.

She shouted at him. He retreated to his den. She gave him the silent treatment. He ignored it.

On the morning of November 12, at the completion of the 8:30 church service, a deeply concerned Arthur Smith found Bryan Coates in the Sunday school area and steered him quickly to a quiet corner.

"Bryan," he said, "something's very wrong with Gordon. I don't know what we're going to do, but I know what we can't do. We can't let him get into that pulpit and preach the eleven o'clock service."

What Arthur had seen was a pastor repeatedly losing his place in the text and slurring his words, a pastor who was clearly not in command of his material or himself.

Bryan immediately sought out Dean Kaufman, and the two of them then found Gordon's son Steve.

"You two are going to have to get him away from here," said Dean. "I'll handle the service."

Bryan and Steve went to Gordon's office and knocked on the door. There was no answer. They tried the knob. The door was locked. They decided to wait.

At 10:45, Gordon stepped into the hall.

"Dad," said Steve, taking his father's arm, "we're going home."

"What are you talking about?" Gordon snapped. "I've got a sermon to preach."

"Not today, Dad. Come on."

"Son, I'm not going anywhere except that pulpit."

"You're going home, Dad," Steve said, tightening his grip.

Gordon tried to pull away, but by now Bryan had his other arm.

"Let go of me. Let go of me!" he shouted. But they didn't let go. They didn't let go when he told them they had no right to do what they were doing. They didn't let go when he told them they were trying to ruin him. Only when they got him into Steve's car did they let go.

With tears welling in his eyes, Bryan Coates walked back into the church. Already, the sight of his pastor being shepherded away was etching itself permanently in his mind.

The next four days were hell for Gordon. He knew he had to be in trouble with the deacons. Surely there would be a meeting in which he would be called to task. But as it turned out, a meeting was something he would never have to deal with.

On November 17, he awoke to the sound of squirrels chattering as they rustled through the leaves beneath the window in the cool, fresh morning. It was 8:30. By now, there should have been sounds in the house and smells of coffee and bacon. But he heard only the squirrels.

He propped himself on his elbow, waiting for something familiar to reach his ears and his nose. Nothing. Then he was moving, throwing on his robe and racing down the stairs. Something was wrong. Halfway down the steps, he stopped and stared in disbelief and fear at what he saw. Norma Lou was struggling to get a large suitcase out the front door.

"Where are you going?" he shouted as he crossed the foyer and followed her out into the yard. "For God's sake, where are you going?"

She did not answer, did not even turn to acknowledge him. She went on to the car, parked heading out, ready for a fast escape. Using her knee for a prop, she lifted the heavy suitcase into the trunk, slammed the lid, and took her place behind the wheel.

He stood ten feet away, frozen. As his eyes followed her from the rear to the front, he saw David and John, the youngest of the four Weekley children, sitting silent in the back seat. Steve and Dan had already left for their classes at East High School. Norma Lou slammed the driver-side door and started the car.

Gordon quickly covered the ground between them, grabbed the door handle, and pulled to open it. It was locked.

"Norma, Norma, don't do this," he screamed. "We need to talk, we need to talk now."

The time for talk had passed. Staring straight ahead, ignoring him, she put the car in gear, and it started to move forward. Gordon stepped close to the fender, put one hand on the windshield and the other on the side mirror, and tried with every muscle in his body to keep the car and the people in it from leaving.

"Stop, stop, stop," he screamed.

She did not stop. She gradually accelerated until the car's momentum pushed Gordon aside and left him coughing in the dust as it traveled down the long gravel driveway and over the bridge he had worked so diligently, so lovingly, to build. Then the car and his family were gone up Country Lane. Through the clearing dust and the nearly leafless trees, he watched with glistening eyes and clasped hands until his wife and his children disappeared from his sight and from his life.

He turned and dashed back to the house. Gripped by fear and hyperactivity, he moved quickly from room to room. He was swinging into action, but his actions were aimless. His brain was too besieged to guide him.

*Where is she going? Is she leaving for good? What'll the church say? They won't accept a divorced preacher. Why did she go? We didn't even talk. How can I go on without a family? She's trying to destroy me. She's paying me back for something. How can I preach this Sunday? God, God, God, what's happening to my life?*

"I've got to think," he said. "I've got to have a plan. I've got to stop this."

He pushed open the bathroom door, turned on the cold water, filled his cupped hands and brought them to his face. With closed eyes, he groped for a towel. He patted himself dry, then dropping his hands to his sides, he looked in the mirror.

"My God," he said aloud as he stared at the image in front of him. "My God."

What he saw there was a stranger. A hollow-eyed, sunken-cheeked, old man.

"What have I done to myself?" he cried. "What have I become?"

He knew then what Norma Lou had known, what the deacons had known, what those closest to him had known for years. He had to act. He had to do something. He did not know what. He wandered the house. He wandered the sixteen acres. Finally he walked to his bridge and looked down Country Lane, hoping to see the car making its way back home.

"I'm so glad you're back," he said, rehearsing his lines. "And I hope you will find it in your heart to forgive me for what I've done to you and the children."

After a while, he realized that the car was not coming. Not today. Maybe not ever. He returned to the house and fell to his knees and prayed. He prayed for God's help, prayed for Norma Lou's return, prayed for all to be well again. When he arose, he was not calmed. He resumed his wandering, pacing, fear clutching his heart.

"Schmidt," he said at last. "Schmidt can help me."

He dialed the psychiatrist's number, got the receptionist, and pleaded with her to put him through to the doctor. After a few long minutes, Schmidt's voice came on the line. Gordon quickly explained what had happened and begged to see him that afternoon. Schmidt agreed and Gordon hung up.

At least now there was a glimmer, a small one, of hope. Maybe Schmidt could tell him how to get her back. He knew where she was; she was at her mother's house in Belmont. He would go there just as soon as he found out what Schmidt wanted him to do. For now, all he could do was wait. He was too distraught to drive. He would have to wait for Steve and Dan to get home. One of them would have to take him to the doctor. For now and for the next several hours, he was alone with his guilt and his fear.

*This absolutely cannot be happening to me. I worked so hard, I tried so hard never to hurt anybody, never to let anybody down. I worship God, love him with all my heart. Why has it come to this?*

Still in his pajamas and robe, he wandered out of the house and into the wooded back yard. He chose a tree, and pressing his back against it, he slid slowly to the ground. He bent forward and put his head between his knees.

He closed his eyes and let his brain take him back to the places he had been and to the things he had done. He saw himself receiving his Royal Ambassador Plenipotentiary award, only the second ever given in the state of Georgia. He saw himself walking on stage at the Boys High graduation and accepting the H.O. Smith scholarship for academic excellence. He saw Harold Miller, teaching him Greek at Furman. He saw his mother and his father, and the pride in their faces as he told them of his induction into Hand and Torch. He saw the seminary in Louisville and the little church in Columbus, Indiana, and the pretty choir girl, smiling and signaling for him to, for goodness sakes, sit down. He saw Sonny Smith, scrapbook in hand, saying to him in front of an adoring congregation, "This, Gordon Weekley, is your life." And now his life had come to a broken man in pajamas under a pine tree behind an empty house in Charlotte, North Carolina.

"Dad?" He looked up. It was Steve. He struggled slowly to his feet, trying to put dignity in his movements.

"Steve," he said, brushing the pine needles from his robe, "you need to take me somewhere. I have an appointment."

An hour later, showered and dressed, Gordon Weekley found himself seated across the desk from his psychiatrist. He had his game face on now, his preacher face, the face he had waked up with and gone to bed with every day for over forty years. It was a face Dr. Schmidt had in earlier sessions said he wanted to change. He wanted to see anger in Gordon Weekley's eyes. Fire.

Gordon thought again of the indictment that he was too much sugar, too little salt. He had a too-much desire to please, a too-little desire to say no. But he could not change and would not change, and Schmidt would not change him, not even now, with Norma Lou on the run and his life in disarray.

"I'm not surprised she left you, Gordon," he said. "I told her to leave a long time ago."

"You told her what?" a stunned Gordon Weekley shouted.

"In my opinion, it's the only chance you have to get well."

Gordon exploded in fury. "My wife leaving me, taking my family, tearing our lives apart? Do you think that's going to make me well? Damn you. Damn you to hell."

It was an anger Gordon had never before known, and had certainly never verbalized. Now there was nothing left to say. For a long moment, the two men sat silently facing each other, one glaring. He had finally done what the psychiatrist had told him to do some time before: Look him straight in the eye and tell him to go to hell.

But it was too late.

"Give me some Valium," Gordon demanded.

"I told you you'd never get drugs from me, Gordon."

"Man, can't you see I'm dying. I've lost everything, everything. For God's sake, give me some Valium."

Another moment passed in silence. And then, for whatever his reasons, Schmidt reached in his desk drawer and pulled out a prescription pad.

*That's the last I'll see of him*, Gordon thought, making his way down the steps and out to the waiting car, *but at least I've got something to help me get through this.*

Steve drove him to a drugstore, and then the two of them headed out Randolph Road.

Steve, the bewildered and fearful son, kept both hands on the wheel and looked straight ahead. The anguished father clutched his bag of Valium in one fist and pounded the other continuously against his forehead, saying over and over, "Why... why... why..."

When they got home, Gordon was screwing the top off his Valium bottle as he walked through the front door. He had the pills in his mouth by the time he reached the kitchen sink, and without pausing to get a glass, he downed them with water straight from the faucet. He went to the phone and placed a call to Marvin, Norma Lou's brother.

"Marvin, you've got to come talk to me. You've got to tell me what's going on."

There was a long pause on the other end of the line, and Gordon heard Marvin say, "I'll come."

It took him forty-five minutes to get there, and by the time he arrived, Gordon had made up his mind what he had to do.

"Marvin," he said, before the man had gotten out of his car, "take me to her."

Marvin shrugged, let him in, and backed the car out of the driveway, turning it in the direction from which he had just come. It was evening when they arrived at the modest frame house on the tree-lined side street in Belmont. Leading the way and without bothering to knock, Gordon entered and went straight to the living room, Marvin right on his heels.

Norma Lou was there, playing the organ. Her mother sat in an easy chair a few feet away. Neither acknowledged his presence. He felt like a ghost, an apparition. He turned his head from one to the other, but neither would return his stares.

"Norma," he finally said, "I've got to talk to you."

"Mother," Marvin interjected, "would you come with me to the kitchen."

Norma stopped playing, went to the sofa and sat down. She looked straight ahead past Gordon to a spot somewhere on the wall.

Gordon slowly approached her, looking straight into her eyes, hoping for some glimmer of recognition. Then he did something he had only done before for his God. He got down on his knees in front of her.

"It won't do any good," she said to the wall.

And it didn't. Marvin took him home. Back in his empty bedroom, he pulled off his clothes and slowly worked his way into his pajamas and robe. This had been the worst day of his life, and now he was facing the worst night. He sat on the edge of the bed for several moments, trying to gather his thoughts, trying to formulate some plan to get his family back together again. No plan would come. He was engulfed by a hopelessness and depression that neither he nor the Valium could overcome. Finally he got up and walked down the hall to Steve's room. He found him there, studying.

"Son," he asked, "will you do me a favor?"

"Sure, Dad, what is it?"

"Will you sleep with me tonight?"

"Well, gosh, Dad, I..."

"Please. Please do this for me."

"All right, Dad."

Steve followed him into the room, got into bed, and in a short time was sound asleep. His father tossed and turned all night, sleeping for only brief periods, then waking suddenly, fearfully, checking to see if his son was still there.

When the sun finally rose, Gordon's eyes were wide open. He slipped quietly out of bed so as not to waken Steve and padded down the stairs to his study. He seated himself in front of his typewriter, pulled out a piece of paper, and began typing a letter he had already written in his head in the darkness before the dawn.

November 18, 1967
To the congregation of Providence Baptist Church
My dear friends,

It has been a glorious experience to serve you as your pastor during the past twelve, nearly thirteen years. As we have labored together since this church was formed, God has rewarded our efforts and a potentially great and powerful church has come into being.

At this time, under the advice of my doctors, and following a thorough physical examination, I am forced to conclude that I must tender my resignation as your pastor and let God lead you to another minister who will lead you on to higher and greater things in that part of His vineyard...

I shall pray for you as you seek your new minister and shall follow the progress of Providence Baptist Church in my prayers always. Thank you for the many kindnesses shown me during these years; you have blessed all the Weekleys in more ways than we could ever count.

God's richest blessing on each family of the church.
Sincerely and affectionately yours, for Christ's sake,
Gordon Weekley

He pulled the letter from the typewriter, placed it in his lap, and stared at it for several long moments. The silence in the house was absolute. He had never felt more alone. Finally, he folded the letter, put it in an envelope, and took it with him into the kitchen. He made coffee. He carried his cup and the envelope to the table near the window, sat down by them, and waited for Steve to wake up.

When the young man appeared about an hour later, Gordon handed him the letter and asked him to deliver it to the church. Then he went upstairs and started packing.

Christ made a journey into the desert, Buddha to a forest, Mohammed to a mountain top, and each returned a changed man. Gordon Weekley's journey was on Interstate 85, south to Atlanta. What lay beyond his immediate destination, he did not know. He only knew now that he was going home to his mother and his father, and that his son was driving him there.

He looked over at Steve, and in the midst of his own grief, felt deep pity for the teenage boy caught up in the melodrama—the obedient son, obviously dazed and frightened, yet carrying out his supporting role without question. Gordon's hand went out and landed softly on Steve's shoulder.

The nearly five-hour drive brought them to the front of the elder Weekleys' apartment. When Louise opened the door, she couldn't have been more surprised.

"My goodness," she said with a broad smile, "what brings you all here?"

The smile faded when she saw the look on her son's face. He made his way past her. Gordon's father appeared from the kitchen and greeted his son and grandson warmly while at the same time looking to Louise as if he were trying to find in her face a reason for this unannounced visit. He likely saw what Gordon saw: a nervousness, a slight trembling in her hands, signs that her maternal instincts were telling her something was very wrong.

"It's Norma, Mother," he said. "She's left me and I don't think she's coming back."

"Oh, no," she said, moving backward, feeling for a chair, crumpling into it. "Please Gordon, please, don't use that word in front of me. Don't say 'divorce.'"

He didn't say it, but he made it quite clear that reconciliation was, at this point, an impossibility. Next, he told his parents about his pastorate. Then, choosing his words carefully, he told them about his drug problem.

"Some of what's happened may have to do with those medications I've been taking," he said. "They've gotten my system all out of whack, but that's something I can correct."

He knew that with each terrible revelation, he was driving the nails deeper into his parents' own crosses. He hated himself for what he was doing to them, and he felt their pain more deeply than he felt his own. The model son, the golden boy, the boy who could do no wrong, had done everything wrong. He had lost his wife, his kids, his church, and even control of his own mind.

The silence in the tiny apartment was broken only by the tick of a clock on a shelf in the corner. Nobody moved. Mr. and Mrs. Weekley, their faces bleak, held fast to their chairs. Gordon, the prodigal son, stood bowed and broken in front of them, and Steve stood almost behind him. Gordon looked at the fading flowers in the carpet beneath his feet that had once covered the floor of the living room on Virginia Avenue. He remembered a time when the roses were so red he could almost smell them.

*I've let everybody down, everybody.*

The next day, Sunday, Gordon put Steve on the train back to Charlotte. On Monday, at Louise's advice, he saw her doctor. It was all anybody could think of to do.

"You're anorexic," the doctor said, "but aside from that, and considering what you told me about your drug use, you're in pretty good shape. Still, I think maybe it would be wise if we checked you in to the hospital for a few days and gave you a more thorough exam."

*Why not? I can rest there and I won't have to sleep on the roll-away in the apartment.*

An hour later, he was at the admissions desk at Georgia Baptist Hospital, answering the standard litany of personal history questions and watching the clerk check blocks on the form.

"Have you ever been a patient here before?" she asked. A routine question. He did not answer.

"Have you ever been a patient here before?" she asked again, looking up for the first time from her admissions form.

"Yes." He was almost whispering. "I was here once before. August first, 1921. I was born here."

The three days of tests turned up nothing other than a reaffirmation of the anorexia diagnosis. Nor did those three days of rest and relative seclusion give him any clue about what he would do next with his life. He was lost, totally lost. Never before had he faced the future without a map.

On Friday morning, his cousin Sara picked him up and took him to her house to stay. He loved Sara, was closer to her in many ways than he was to his own sister. She had spent most of her childhood in the Weekley family home, having lost her mother, Louise Weekley's sister, in a tragic bedroom fire when Sara was only eighteen months old.

Sara brought consolation to Gordon, not judgment. They spent several days enjoying each other's company, walking the neighborhood in the afternoons and watching television at night. In the days they spent together, she offered him only one piece of advice.

"Next time you're with Aunt E," which is what Sara called Louise, "I want you to take out a cigarette and light it."

"Are you crazy?" he asked, suddenly leaning forward in his chair. "Why don't I just go ahead and break all ten of the commandments in front of her. That wouldn't upset her as much as my smoking."

He had smoked intermittently over the years. It was not uncommon then for ministers to smoke. Most of the men in his congregation did, and so too did many of the women. Smoking on the front lawn of the church after services was a ritual shared by nearly every church in the land. It was the socially acceptable thing to do, and Gordon had most definitely wanted to be socially acceptable. But he had never smoked in front of his mother. Smoking was to her a vice, a bigger vice perhaps even than card playing.

He had seen her reaction to card playing in Masonboro. Louise was there for a visit, and one evening while the family was sitting around the kitchen table, Gordon mentioned to Norma Lou that some friends were coming over the following evening for a game of canasta. As soon as the words left his lips, he realized he had made a terrible mistake. Louise bolted from the table, went to her room and started packing. She would not stay under the same roof with people who played cards. It took all the begging Gordon could muster to keep her from boarding the train back to Atlanta, including a promise to cancel the card game. And now Sara wanted him to smoke in front of her?

"What are you driving at?" he asked her.

"You know perfectly well why I want you to do it," she said gently and with a smile. "You can't go on trying to please everybody all the time, and it's time you showed some independence."

He trusted Sara and her instincts. The following evening after finishing dinner with his parents at a cafeteria on Lenox Road, Gordon went to the coffee urn and refilled his cup.

*Sara,* he thought, *I hope I don't live to regret this.*

He returned to the table, sat down, and as casually as he could, pulled out a Salem. As he struck the match and held it to the cigarette, he glanced apprehensively in his mother's direction. She returned the glance, but her face showed nothing, not surprise, not disapproval, nothing. He was astonished. It was the first time in his adult life he had willingly defied her, and he had gotten away unpunished.

A few days later, Gordon got an early morning call from Dr. Posey Downs, a Providence member and close friend.

"Gordon, I don't know what your plans are for today, but whatever they are, change them. I've canceled all my appointments, and I'm flying down to see you."

*I wonder what he wants.*

As it turned out, he wanted nothing other than to spend a few hours with the exiled pastor. Gordon met him at a gate at the airport, and they retired to a coffee shop just off the main lobby. They talked about everything they could think of except Providence Baptist, drugs, and Gordon's family. When the autumn afternoon sun started to set, Posey stood up, put his arm around Gordon's shoulder, and said goodbye, looking affectionately into his former pastor's eyes.

Gordon lingered a few moments in the coffee shop, then walked to the large window in the lobby and watched through his tears as the plane taxied down the runway and lifted into the blue and orange sky. Posey Downs had made a one-day, five-hundred-mile round trip at great expense simply to tell Gordon Weekley that although he was gone, he was surely not forgotten. He waited until the plane was a small dot, and then made his way to the parking lot and headed home to Sara's.

On the way, he spotted a small shopping center and a few minutes later found himself standing in front of a drugstore counter.

"Hello," he said to the man in the white coat, "I'm from Charlotte, North Carolina, here in Atlanta for a ministerial gathering, and it seems I've come away without my prescription drugs."

The weeks and the addiction dragged on. He didn't know what to do with himself. Sara, thankfully, was in no hurry to get rid of him. His parents weren't pressuring him. Yet he knew he had to do something. He had to get on with living. He was at least functional now, having cut his consumption in half, and he felt that he could soon win the battle on his own. He missed his family terribly, and he stayed in touch with the boys through frequent phone calls. He did not speak with Norma Lou.

Winter came, and although the weather was gray and forbidding, his spirits were lifted one day by a call from Bill Crawley, another Providence member.

"I've heard about a job opportunity, Gordon, and it could be a good one."

"Good news," he told Steve on the telephone one evening in March. "I've got a job, a good one. I'll be coming back to Charlotte."

"Mom," he heard his son say, "Dad's coming home. He's got a job."

There was silence on Steve's end of the line, and then Gordon heard a voice he had not heard in a long time. "Hello," she said.

"Hello, Norma. I found a job, a very good one. They tell me I can make seventy-two thousand dollars a year."

"That's wonderful, Gordon."

"It's with the United States Research Corporation, a new company. I'm a regional director. I'll be headquartered in Charlotte. Oh, Norma, I think I'm turning the corner. This is the opportunity I've needed. Maybe we can put things back together again. There's nothing I want more."

There was a long pause, an eternity of silence.

"Maybe we can," she answered finally.

Three weeks later, he was home again at the house on Country Lane with Norma Lou and the kids. He launched himself into his work, renting a small office on Myers Street in uptown Charlotte and advertising for sales people to come to work for his company.

His job was to train them and send them out into the field to sell, and to recruit even more sales people. United States Research Corporation was a pyramid-structured company. The broader the base of sales people under Gordon's jurisdiction, the more money he stood to make. He was $2,500 in the hole to start with because of a company stock investment required of all managers. Posey Downs had loaned him the money, offering without being asked.

Gordon was genuinely excited about this opportunity in his life. He backed off even further from his drugs, taking only a few Dexamyl and Doriden now and again. This, he felt, was his last chance to salvage his marriage and to establish a career. He knew in his heart that Norma was taking him back for the security, the income he could now offer. *And who can blame her. We have four kids and a mortgage.*

He yearned for the warmth they shared so many years ago, but that warmth had begun to wane long before, even before his introduction to drugs. It wasn't there now. *Maybe it will come back if I can make this job work out.*

It was not his fault that the job failed. The company itself was failing. It never really got off the ground. By July, Gordon could see the handwriting on the wall. He was crushed. Without that job, without that potential for significant income, he knew his welcome home would wear out fast. He would no longer be an asset, but again a liability. Evenings he dragged himself home from the futility of the office and sat silently in the study, sometimes staring for hours at the rows of

theological books on the shelves that had helped him to climb to such great heights and were now closed to him.

The only respite from his pain was the Dexamyl and the Doriden, and he began taking more and more of them. He no longer even hid their presence from Norma Lou. Soon he stopped going to the office every day. On the days he didn't go, he took only Doriden, the downer, in an attempt to sleep away his depression.

"Maybe," he said from his bed one morning as she sat sewing in a chair across from him, "maybe I should get some help."

He had just taken his third Doriden in the last hour and a half, and even he knew that was too much. She put down her needle and thread and looked straight in his eyes. He had her complete attention.

"Where?" she asked.

"Remember Toni Griffin? She was director of education at Providence Methodist."

"I know her."

"Well, two or three of her brothers and her father own a psychiatric institute in Asheville. It's called Appalachian Hall. Maybe Toni could get me in there."

"Maybe she can," she said, rising. "I'll call her." She hurried to the downstairs phone.

For the next two hours, Gordon, still in his bed, heard snatches of what seemed to be several telephone conversations. Finally, he heard Norma's quick steps on the stairs, and she burst into the room.

"You're in," she said, hurrying to the closet and pulling a suitcase down from the shelf.

"When?" he asked, bewildered.

"Now. Today," she answered. "They're waiting for you."

# FIFTEEN

Three hours later, Gordon found himself sitting alone in a small office 143 miles from Charlotte waiting for someone to orient him to his new surroundings. Norma Lou had left for a motel with a promise to join him the following morning for an interview with his assigned psychiatrist, Dr. Bill Griffin.

His ears took in the muffled hubbub of people passing by in the hall beyond the closed door. They were, he assumed, doctors and nurses on their way to cope with one troubled soul or another in a building that was filled with them. Soon footsteps would come for him. He prayed they would come sufficiently armed to save him.

The following day, Norma Lou came back. He listened limply as she poured out their story to Dr. Griffin. She told of a marriage gone bad, a pastorate gone bad, a life gone bad. Then she was up and leaving. Their goodbye was awkward. No kiss. No embrace. They simply looked at each other for a second, and she was gone.

Through the window of Dr. Griffin's office, he saw the car pull away from the building. He followed it just as he had followed it that day on Country Lane, until it disappeared in the trees lining the long driveway.

"Gordon," Dr. Griffin said, putting his hand gently on his shoulder, "I have some other patients to see, so why don't you wander around a bit, get yourself acquainted with the building and the grounds. You got in so late yesterday you really didn't have much of a chance to see everything. I'll catch up with you around three."

Appalachian Hall was so beautiful it could have been a mountain resort hotel, which is exactly what it had been. Built in Norman architectural style before 1920, it was five stories tall, finished in beige stucco, and fronted with a hundred-foot-long stone porch where hotel guests and now patients could sit on wooden rockers and soak up the beauty of the immense tree-studded lawn and the majestic mountains

beyond.

It was located slightly above the little town of Biltmore, just south of Asheville, a city of some 60,000 people, the most famous of whom had been the author Thomas Wolfe. The Griffin family had purchased the building and grounds in 1931, two years after the stock market crash had brought the roaring twenties to a screeching halt. In 1943, the Navy leased it from the Griffins and had used it as a convalescent hospital until 1946.

It didn't take long for Gordon to discover that his vision of a mental institution did not match the reality of Appalachian Hall. It operated very much like a fine hotel. His room was not large but comfortable and well appointed. The meals in the dining room were superb.

The Griffin family treated their patients like guests and offered them a variety of amenities and activities, including billiard and ping-pong tables, a card room, bowling lanes, a softball field, and volleyball and tennis courts. There were group day trips available to nearby mountain attractions, and woodworking and other crafts.

Still, Gordon knew that neither he nor any of the other patients were here for a vacation. The Griffins were highly respected, highly skilled professionals, and they had created the environment for one purpose: to make the sick well. Even casual activities such as the pick-up softball games were part of the therapeutic process.

For the first couple of weeks, he met with Dr. Griffin every day as the two of them struggled to get to the root of his addiction and his depression. The sessions dropped back to once weekly, with the remainder of Gordon's time given over to rest and relaxation. He found himself living in a pressure-free environment. Nothing was asked of him except that he get up out of bed every morning at seven. He spent hours reading, walking the grounds, talking with new friends.

He had very little contact with Norma Lou. In his entire stay, she would visit him only twice. When he called home, he talked mostly to Steve or Dan and the two younger children, David and John. The few telephone conversations he had with her were brief how-are-you ones and nothing more.

He did get packages from her. Boxes of his clothes and books arrived frequently, and by the end of the second month, his room was cluttered. His closet was filled to overflowing, and he had to walk a maze of boxes to get from the bathroom to his bed.

He knew what she was doing, knew that she was severing the cord. He thought it was only a temporary severance, and that when he got well, they would be a family again.

He was getting at least a little better, he thought, getting by without Doriden and Dexamyl, though he missed them both terribly and was terribly depressed. If he measured himself against his peers, he was certainly doing better than the alcoholic textile magnate who arrived by chauffeured limousine at the end of Gordon's first month.

The man was from a small town near Charlotte, and he was no stranger to Appalachian Hall. His family sent him there often to dry out, he told Gordon. Although he was enormously wealthy, he had not lost his rural folksiness. He was affable, talkative, comfortable with himself—the kind of man who would be equally at ease in the presence of dirt farmers, governors, or preachers.

"Come walk the grounds with me," he said to his new-found friend one morning. "I'll show you something."

The two men strolled across the dew-wet grass and into a stand of trees some thirty yards beyond the north side of the main building. They stopped beside an old oak with a rot hole the size of a wall safe six feet up its trunk.

"My chauffeur is very loyal," he said, reaching into the hole and pulling out a sealed fifth of Jack Daniels. "May I offer you a drink?"

Gordon shook his head. "No, thanks. I've never had a drink in my life."

"Good," the man said laughing, "then you won't be sneaking out here and stealing mine."

Gordon didn't have to steal what he wanted. It was waiting for him in Asheville. All he had to do was get there. And get there he did, at the end of his third month, when it was felt that he had progressed sufficiently to merit off-campus passes.

*I can handle it now,* he thought, as the bus pulled to a halt at the Asheville station. *I'm really not an addict anymore.*

Thirty minutes later, he was in an ophthalmologist's chair complaining of burning eyes and explaining that he was there in town on church business.

"I can't find a thing wrong with your eyes," the doctor said.

"Well," Gordon answered, "I'm probably just reading too much. I'll tone it down a bit. Oh, by the way, doctor, I seem to have left Charlotte without my shaving kit."

He returned to Appalachian Hall, checked in, and immediately set out for the stand of trees. *I wonder what else is out here,* he thought as he slid the prescription bottles under a rock not far from the Jack Daniels oak.

The cycle began again. Dexamyl in the mornings and afternoons. Doriden at night. The void in his heart carved by depression was once again filled with a sense of well-being. When after a week or so, the supply ran out, he made another foray into Asheville. He had a sore throat this time, a real one, so it was with a great deal of confidence that he strode into a doctor's office he found on a side street just off Patton Avenue.

The waiting room was small, about the size of a walk-in closet. The chairs were hard plastic supported by aluminum tubing. The nature scenes on the wall might have come straight from Woolworth's. The magazines on the table bore last year's dates. It was obvious to Gordon that this was not one of Asheville's most successful practices.

"You're right," the doctor said, peering over the depressor he held on Gordon's tongue, "your throat looks angry."

He wrote a prescription for penicillin. And he wrote prescriptions for Dexamyl and Doriden simply because Gordon asked him for them. It would not be the last time this all-too-willing doctor would be seeing Gordon Weekley. He would return again and again over the next several weeks.

What drugs he didn't hide in knotholes or under rocks he kept in his room, lined up, one capsule after another, on top of a door frame on the inside of his closet.

Thoroughly medicated now, he began to enjoy his days and nights at Appalachian Hall, particularly those euphoric moments late in the evenings when the Doriden collided with the remaining traces of the Dexamyl.

It's possible he could have gone on for months. As it happened, he opened his eyes late one night and looked directly into the face of Dr. Griffin.

"What are you doing here?" he slurred.

"Gordon, you're on the floor. You fell out of bed. They called me at the house."

"I'm all right. I'm fine."

"I wish you were, my friend. You're on drugs again. You probably have them right here in the room—not that anyone could find them with all the clutter in here."

"I'm not on drugs," he lied.

"I'm putting you on lock-up," he said, not unkindly. "You don't leave me any choice."

Not even the drugs could overcome the despair and embarrassment he suddenly felt. Until that moment, he had imagined himself on a plane with Dr. Griffin. Two intellectuals. Two professionals. Two highly educated men working out a problem together. Now he knew differently. Now he remembered that the reason he volunteered to go to Appalachian Hall in the first place was because he was a failure.

Lock-up, as it turned out, was not much different in appearance than the rest of the institution. Occupying most of the third floor, it featured a large common area with comfortable furnishings. The patients slept two to a room and spent most of their time reading or watching television and movies. It was the ultimate low-stress environment, but in the two weeks he was there, it did nothing to alleviate the depression Gordon always felt immediately after coming off drugs. Nor did it alleviate his craving, which by now had taken such control of his life that he decided it would never really leave.

Dr. Griffin was not yet ready to believe that. He approached Gordon with a proposition.

"I'd like to try insulin sub-shock," he said.

That was not what Gordon wanted to hear, recalling the electroshock treatments he had in Atlanta.

"The insulin shock," he asked, "what does it do?"

"Interestingly enough," Dr. Griffin answered, "it causes your blood sugar to drop and your heart rate to increase, but the end result should be a relaxing feeling. We use it primarily for anxiety, but sometimes for depression. I can't promise it will be effective."

"Well," Gordon sighed, "I don't suppose I have anything to lose. Let's do it."

They did it the next morning, in the infirmary. Under the watchful eye of Bill Griffin, a nurse placed an IV of insulin into his arm as he lay on a bed. By the time a substantial amount of the insulin entered his vein, he was supposed to fall into fitful half-sleep that would last for an hour or so.

He watched the bag slowly drain itself of its contents and waited for the promised sleep to come. It never did. It came for the lady next to him receiving the same treatment, but Gordon was nearly as wide awake as he had been when he entered the room. And hungry as a horse. He had never wanted food so badly as he did now.

He got it, but not before a nurse handed him and the lady beside him big containers of Karo Syrup and instructed them to drink it all. Its purpose was to counteract the insulin, negate the shock.

Every morning for the next several days, the procedure was the same: insulin, Karo Syrup, breakfast. Every morning Gordon awoke

hoping this would be the day the weight of depression would be lifted. It was not to be.

To make matters worse, he had a phone call one afternoon from a Providence member. It was a courtesy call really, and the caller mentioned son David's tonsillectomy.

"What do you mean 'tonsillectomy'?" Gordon asked, alarmed.

"Well," answered the caller, "I understand he's having his tonsils out, today or tomorrow, I think."

"This is too much," he thought. His own son was having an operation and she didn't even tell him.

He quickly got off the line, threw a few clothes into a bag, and caught the next bus to Charlotte. By nine o'clock that evening, he was walking into David's room at the Eye, Ear, Nose and Throat hospital. David was asleep. Norma Lou and her mother, Mrs. Atkinson, were there, sitting in chairs beside the bed. The collective response he got from the two women was a glare.

"What are you doing here?" Norma Lou asked flatly.

"Norma, he's our son. He's having his tonsils out."

"He's had his tonsils out. This morning. He's fine."

"But don't you think I should have been here?"

He got no answer.

The tension was broken momentarily when David stirred and opened his eyes. "Hi, Dad," he said, managing a weak grin.

"Hi, son, I'm sorry I couldn't get here sooner. You're a brave little man, getting your tonsils out."

"I suppose you'll be spending the night," Norma said, not kindly. "Mother and I are staying here. I'll call Steve to come get you and take you back to the house."

"Never mind," he said, "I'll get a cab." Saying goodbye to David, he turned and walked out of the room.

The cab took him to a drug store on East Independence Boulevard where a young pharmacist behind the counter listened patiently to Gordon's patented story but didn't relent. Gordon pressed the issue and finally, an older pharmacist, overhearing the debate, instructed the younger man to give Gordon three Dexamyls and two Doridens.

He thanked his benefactors and hurried off into the night, heading uptown. He had no idea where he was going or why he was going in that particular direction.

He stopped at a restaurant, found a booth, and ordered a cup of coffee. He used it to down two of the Dexamyls, then stared out the window at the passing cars, waiting for the medication to take effect.

It didn't take long. Although it didn't erase the humiliation he had felt in David's room, it did at least make him more decisive and more confident in himself as a man. He decided that despite Norma Lou's hostility, he would go home. She had, after all, suggested it. And besides, it was as much his house as it was hers.

He called Steve and told him where he was. Within a half-hour, he was back on Country Lane.

Home again. It felt good to be there. Even Norma's coldness couldn't override his joy at being on his own turf, a joy enhanced by the Dexamyl.

He prowled the house like a prospective buyer, peeking into rooms, opening closet doors, rekindling memories of better times. When he had finished his tour, he took a Doriden and retreated blissfully to the sanctuary of his study. Sitting at his desk, looking at his books lining his shelves, he let himself believe for a moment that he was pastor of Providence again. That everything here at the house was all right. That things between him and Norma Lou were normal. That nothing had ever happened.

The moment passed, and in the throes of his Dexamyl/Doriden high, he began to consider the present. He would be going back to Appalachian Hall tomorrow, leaving the house and family once again in Norma's hands. She was in complete charge of both now, and he knew that. It seemed to him in these contemplative moments that the more dependent he had become on drugs, the more self-sufficient she had become. That was understandable, but it seemed to him now that she was comfortable in her self-sufficiency. She had discovered power and she was not about to relinquish it. Not ever.

*What's she going to do with this house?* he suddenly asked himself. *What's she going to do with the boys? She's planning something. And it doesn't include me. I'm going to be left with nothing, no one.*

It was a terrifying thought that became even more terrifying as the hours passed. *I have to do something,* he thought. *And I've got to do it now.*

It was one-thirty in the morning when he picked up the phone and called Allen Bailey. Bailey was one of Charlotte's most respected attorneys and an active layman at First Baptist. Gordon knew him—not well, but well enough to be on a first-name basis.

"Allen, I've got to talk to you immediately," he said to a very sleepy listener.

Somehow Bailey managed to convince him that "immediately" could wait until nine o'clock the next morning at the attorney's office.

*That's not going to be soon enough,* he thought after he'd hung up. *I've got to do something now. Tomorrow might be too late.*

For some reason he thought then of Arthur Ross, the friend who years before had given him money for the African Crusade.

*Arthur will help me. He helped me before.*

He went to the phone, called a cab, then hurried to the front porch to wait for it. When finally it came, he told the driver to take him to the Dilworth section, an older residential neighborhood near uptown.

Usually he took his Doriden as the Dexamyl began to wane in his system. This night he had taken them virtually on top of each other, and the uppers and downers were waging war in his system. He was stoned.

At 3:30 a.m., they pulled up in front of Arthur's house.

"Do you want me to wait?" the cabbie asked.

"No, no, Arthur will take care of me," he slurred.

An eternity later, Arthur Ross opened the door and the fallen pastor stumbled in.

"Arthur, you'll take care of me," he said, slumping into a chair.

Arthur's wife, Ida, was up now and she joined him on the couch across from Gordon. Together they listened as he ranted and raved about the outrageous fortune that had befallen him.

"She thinks she's got the house," he said. "Didn't tell me anything about David. Wants me out. Allen Bailey will help us. You and Allen and I, we'll stop her."

On and on he went, interrupted occasionally by a frustrated Arthur Ross who was trying to make sense of the one-sided conversation.

Finally Ida managed to get Gordon into the kitchen for coffee, and she kept him there for some time under the ruse that the brew was not quite ready.

When she could detain him no more, he got up from the kitchen table and wandered into the living room. There he found Arthur and Henry Crouch, the pastor who had replaced him at Providence.

The next thing Gordon knew, it was evening. He was in the day room at Appalachian Hall, and Dr. Griffin was talking to him.

"How's your son doing?" he asked.

"Fine. Very well, thank you."

"That's great," said Griffin. "You must have had some time of it down in Charlotte. You want to tell me what happened?"

"What do you mean?" asked Gordon. "You know, with Arthur Ross."

"Well, yes," came the confused answer, "I went to see Arthur, something to do with Norma, I think."

"And?"

"And," stammered Gordon, "after that I don't remember."

"You don't remember anything?"

"Nothing."

"Well, I got a call from Henry Crouch early this morning. He told me he was putting you on a bus to Asheville. He said you were in pretty bad shape, and wanted to make sure I would be aware of your coming. A couple of my people met you at the bus station. We didn't want you to end up in Knoxville or somewhere."

"Dr. Griffin, I'm sorry."

"For what," Dr. Griffin asked.

"For everything."

"We'll keep trying," the doctor said gently.

---

It was spring, and the mountains around Asheville and Biltmore awoke from their winter's sleep and covered themselves with coats of green. Flowers popped out of their beds at Appalachian Hall. Grass grew. Rebirth was everywhere—except in the shattered soul of Gordon Weekley. The insomnia had come back, the insomnia that had led to his introduction to Doriden ten years before. Night after night, he lay awake in his bed, giving the demons of depression who tortured him during the day the opportunity to work overtime. They did their job well, assaulting his mind with a litany of failures. The loss of his wife. His children. His church. His profession. His self-respect.

For Dr. Griffin, it had been a winter of discontent with his patient's lack of progress. The counseling hadn't helped, nor the insulin shock, nor the long restful days Appalachian Hall offered its patients.

"Gordon, my friend," he said one afternoon in April as they sat together in his office, "knowing who you are and all the good you've done for so many people, I would have been very proud to have helped you. The truth is I haven't helped. As much as it pains me to say this, I don't believe Appalachian Hall is the place for you. So in the next two or three weeks I'm going to dismiss you. Please contact whoever you need to and make arrangements for them to come and get you. I'm sorry, truly sorry."

"I'm sorry too," Gordon said with his head bowed, his hands clasped, his eyes staring at the floor.

### Sixteen

It was a sad departure for a sad man. Certainly he did not want to spend the rest of his life at Appalachian Hall. He wanted to get well. And yet this place had become home to him. He had friends here, a nice room, wonderful food. He had the mountains which he had come to love.

His mother, his sister, Mary, and her husband, Aubon, arrived on a Sunday. As Gordon helped them load his bags into the car, he was overwhelmed with a deep sense of shame. His mother's son, the golden boy, the honor graduate, the minister of the Gospel, had flunked out of a mental institution.

They drove to Atlanta, to Mary and Aubon's house on Marlin Drive. Gordon would stay there until whatever was going to happen to him happened. Until he either got well or got worse. Since both Mary and Aubon worked, his mother would stay there, too, because somebody had to be with him at all times.

"Can I help you unpack?" she asked him in his room that evening.

"No, mother, I can do it."

She left the room and closed the door behind her. When her footsteps faded in the hall, he unzipped his shaving kit and took out a bottle of Dexamyl he had gotten from an Asheville doctor the previous Friday. He had, he figured, a three-week supply if he went lightly. He also had a limited supply of Carbitral, a sleeping medication Dr. Griffin had reluctantly given him during the most severe stages of his insomnia.

*Go easy,* he thought. *If they find out I'm still taking this stuff God knows where I'll end up.*

For the next several weeks, he took only enough of the two medications to keep the demons of depression at bay. He was high, but not high enough, he figured, to be discovered.

He spent his days reading and sitting. He had no earthly idea what he was going to do with his life, and didn't much care. His mother spent her time sewing, watching television, and watching Gordon. It troubled him that he had forced her away from her apartment and her daily routine of visiting friends and working on church projects, but there was nothing he could do about it. There was nothing he could do about anything, it seemed.

His supply of drugs ran out, and desperation began to set in. He fought off the urge, went into withdrawal, and a few days later came out on the other side. Nobody said anything about his irritability during the withdrawal period, but then nobody knew that he had been sneaking drugs.

Nobody said anything about the depression that followed either. The family did their best to cheer him up, but they never admonished him or openly discussed depression with him.

He lasted a few weeks before he could stand it no more. He had to have something. He had to have Dexamyl. And he had to have Doriden.

There was no doctor within walking distance of the Marlin Drive residence. He couldn't take a bus anywhere because he would be gone too long and be discovered. He rummaged through his mind trying to come up with some way to find a fix before he went crazy.

Then he remembered Stewart Long, a classmate he hadn't seen since high school. He knew through mutual friends that Stewart was a surgeon, and a good one.

"Stewart," he began his telephone conversation, "long time no see." From there he engaged his friend in a few reminiscences about their school days together and the mutual friends they had seen or heard about over the years. Then he launched into his trusty story about inadvertently having left his prescription drugs at home.

"Aubon," he said to his brother-in-law the following morning, "I wonder if you might run me over to Northdale Pharmacy this morning? I need to replenish some of my toiletries."

He had selected Northdale because of its size. It was large, and its many aisles were stocked with everything from beach balls to car wax. In a place this size, one man could easily get out of sight of another for a few moments.

"Aubon," Gordon said, clutching his shaving cream and deodorant, "it's been so long since I've been out of the house, do you mind if we take a few moments and browse?"

"Not at all," he said. They began slowly making their way down the aisles, working their way from the back of the store to the front, looking at this and that. Finally Aubon spotted an item that interested him. As he held it in his hands and examined it, Gordon casually walked away from him. He rounded the corner of the aisle and headed toward the back, toward the pharmacy counter.

Since the prescription had been called in day before, he knew it would be ready, and with no other customers at the counter the transaction would take only a few seconds.

"Weekley," he said.

"Weekley, Weekley," the pharmacist answered, turning toward a box bulging with filled prescriptions.

"Weekley, Weekley," he said again, thumbing slowly through the white paper bags.

*God*, thought Gordon, *everyone in Atlanta must be sick*.

"Weekley, Gordon?"

"Yes, yes, Weekley, Gordon."

He quickly paid the pharmacist, stuffed the bag into his windbreaker pocket, and turned to see if Aubon was anywhere in sight.

He was. He was at the front of the store, a hundred feet away. And he was looking directly at Gordon.

Nothing was said about the incident on the way back to the house. Aubon was a gentle, quiet man, and even though he had opened his home to Gordon, he apparently wasn't going to tell him how to run his life.

Gordon, meanwhile, figured he had better go very easy on the drugs. Aubon, after all, hadn't seen the bottles, just the bag. *Maybe he'll think it's some ordinary medication they prescribed at Appalachian Hall.*

For the next several days, he took just enough Dexamyl to give himself a mild glow and just enough Doriden before bedtime to slightly dull the sharp edge of depression that was always with him now.

Nobody in the house seemed to notice a change in his demeanor. If they did, they didn't say anything. He began to feel more confident about the incident at Northdale Pharmacy, so he increased his dosage— significantly.

While the amphetamine in Dexamyl is a strong stimulant, the amobarbital is a barbiturate-like depressant. So too is the glutethimide in Doriden. After only a few days of heavy dosages, the depressants usually win the battle. The user becomes drowsy and groggy even while high on the amphetamines.

Gordon Weekley was high, drowsy, and groggy late one night in his bed when he suddenly decided he needed a cigarette. *Crash*, went the lamp from the night stand as he rolled to his feet. *Boom, boom*, went his body against the walls as he staggered down the hall to the living room. *Thud*, went the honor graduate, the minister of the Gospel, as he collapsed to the floor near the sofa and rolled over on his back.

He wanted that cigarette. He reached up from his prone position and reconnoitered the top of an end table with his fingers, knocking over another lamp in the process. He found the pack and the matches and brought them back to his chest.

He fished out a cigarette, and after repeated attempts, finally found his mouth with it. Next came the matches. Strike one. Strike two. Strike three. He could not for the life of him manage enough hand-eye coordination for the flame and the cigarette to meet.

After several more tries, he let his hand fall to his sides and stared straight ahead at the ceiling above him, the Salem still dangling from his lips. It was then that he saw Mary and Aubon and his mother.

*They're viewing my body*, he thought sadly. *I'm dead and they're viewing my body*.

Finally Aubon bent down, found the matches at Gordon's side, and struck one.

"Here, Gordon. I'll light it for you."

He smoked his cigarette lying on his back with Aubon kneeling beside him holding an ash tray. The two women said nothing, but even in his stupor he could see the look of anguish on his mother's face.

He stayed in his room the next few days, occasionally hearing snatches of the conversations of a family trying desperately to decide what to do with him.

They had found his pills and taken them, leaving him nothing to do except wallow in his depression and wait for someone to tell him what was coming next. No one ever came.

He knew he could no longer stay there. He was an embarrassment, and if his mother's heart wasn't already broken, he was breaking it now.

It was then that he thought of his cousin, Charles Weekley. Charles was an executive with the Singer Corporation in Atlanta, but at the time was in Greensboro, North Carolina, on business. Maybe he could wangle a job for him, something, anything, to get him back on his feet.

He said goodbye to his family and caught a bus to Greensboro. He had called Charles and asked if he could come talk to him. When he got an affirmative answer, he scheduled his trip so he could arrive in town the evening before the meeting. He needed one more day and night with his Dexamyl and Doriden, and the following morning, he would face the world cold turkey.

Under the influence, the bus trip was almost enjoyable. When he arrived at the Travelodge, he popped his Doriden and basked in euphoria for almost an hour, until sleep finally claimed him.

His conversation with Charles the next day went well, and he learned of an opening in Singer's Anderson, South Carolina, operation.

"I've scheduled an appointment for you down there for tomorrow afternoon," Charles said. "Is that all right?"

"You bet it is," answered an almost exuberant Gordon Weekley. "I'm heading for the bus station right now."

The interview the next afternoon went well, Gordon thought, and the personnel manager promised to call him the following day.

He gave the man the number of the Anderson motel he was staying in, and retired to his room to await the verdict.

*This might be my last chance,* he thought, lying on his bed that night, *but I feel good about it. I really do think I'm going to get this job.*

He slept late the next morning and would have slept longer if the phone hadn't wakened him.

"Hello," he said, trying to sound bright and chipper.

"Mr. Weekley?" the voice on the line asked.

"Yes, yes, this is Gordon Weekley."

"Mr. Weekley...Gordon...this is Bill Johnson. Listen, I'm sorry to have to tell you this, but I just don't think this position is going to work out."

"Oh, I see," said Gordon.

"But I certainly enjoyed meeting you yesterday, and we'll keep your resume on file."

"Well," said Gordon, taking a deep breath and forcing a smile on his face, "I certainly understand and maybe we'll connect somewhere down the road. Thanks for calling me, Mr. Johnson."

Defeated, he cradled the phone on the receiver and stared at himself in the mirror on the far wall.

*What do I do now? What do I do now?*

Doug Broadway decided for him. Broadway was a longtime friend and a longtime member of Providence. Like so many members, he had stayed loyal to his former pastor and deeply concerned. He was concerned enough to drive to Atlanta in the late spring of 1969 and make him an offer.

"Gordon," he said, "I'm leaving Bridge's Furniture and opening my own store. I'd like you to be one of my salesmen."

*A salesman? I couldn't sell ice water in the Sahara.* At least it was an opportunity, a way out from under the watchful eyes of his family. And, who knows, maybe it would be a way out from under his depression, though he doubted it.

Most importantly, it would get him back to Charlotte and, he hoped, eventually, back with Norma Lou. He knew he wouldn't be able to push her into a reconciliation. He had years of broken bridges to mend. It would take time, but at least he thought he had a chance.

"Oh, one other thing," said Broadway, "we'll be selling some of this merchandise on credit. So I'll need you to work any past due accounts we may have."

Gordon took a deep breath and accepted the job in the full and firm belief that he would be a failure at it.

The store was housed in an old building in a predominantly black section of west Charlotte. Gordon was housed in the YMCA on East Morehead Street near the heart of the city.

It was a dreary existence. Mornings, he would drag himself to the drab store and do his best to sell furniture to the mostly low-income people who wandered in. Evenings, he would return to his small room on the seventh floor of the building he called home.

Several Providence church members called him either at work or at the Y, and although he always took the calls or returned them, he rarely accepted invitations to visit their homes. He saw his older sons, Steve, Dan, and David, occasionally, but he didn't want to interfere in their lives. He was ashamed of what he had become and of how his addiction had deprived them of normal father-son relationships.

When he was with them, he always asked about their mother, hoping they would relay his inquiries back to her, that he would get some signal of possible reconciliation in return. He didn't.

For the first few weeks on the job, he abstained totally. He wanted to make a go of this career, no matter how distasteful he found it.

He still had some pills left, though, a couple-of-weeks' supply. After a particularly bad afternoon of knocking on door after door of ramshackle houses trying to collect overdue debts, he would turn to his little friends—not to the degree he had in Atlanta, but enough to keep him on the roller coaster of highs on pill days and deep, dark lows on the others.

It didn't take him long to realize that nothing good was going to happen in Charlotte. He was not well, and he was not getting well. He knew it. Doug Broadway knew it. His boys knew it. Norma Lou was not coming back to him.

With the doors to Appalachian Hall closed to him, with no money for another private institution, there was nothing left for him but Broughton.

Broughton was the state mental hospital in Morganton, about seventy miles west-northwest of Charlotte, on the eastern slopes of the Blue Ridge Mountains. He was admitted on October 1, 1969, and it didn't take him long to discover that this was not Appalachian Hall revisited.

Broughton was a government-built, government-run institution, and it appeared to him that the government had spared every expense to make it comfortable. It was brick and wallboard and institutional beige paint. The uniform for patients was khaki shirts and khaki pants. The food was all but inedible.

Who was he to complain? He had brought this on himself. Besides, he had to be some place, and where else was there for him to go?

He went through an evaluation—a medical examination and a few hours of psychological interviews. Other than that, he did nothing beyond sitting around the day room leafing through old magazines or talking to new acquaintances, two of whom were facing electroshock treatments and were frightened. Gordon tried to ease their fears, but having undergone it once himself, there was little in the way of encouragement he could offer them.

Shortly into his stay, he was introduced to Thorazine, and it was definitely not his drug of choice. It's an antipsychotic medication that, in high doses, "reduces affect," acting as a kind of chemical traffic cop that keeps patients going at the same speed: slow. They have less energy. They are less likely to initiate conversations. They shuffle.

Though nobody wanted it—some were already too far gone to care—they all had to take it. The attendants who passed it out made sure the patients swallowed it by checking under their tongues and feeling along the sides of their cheeks. "Cheeking the med," they called it. Once the medication took hold, the ward became the home of the living dead.

Gordon was a living dead man even without the Thorazine. He no longer held out any hope of redeeming himself from his situation. All he wanted to do was lie on his bed, but that was prohibited except on Sunday mornings.

Sundays, he and a very few others went to chapel. The sermons didn't interest him. He couldn't decide whether it was the preacher or the parishioner who was at fault. God was never far from his mind, but He was not foremost there, either. Except for occasional silent prayers, he was reluctant to face his Maker, embarrassed to face Him. He felt like a dog who slinks away from his master after soiling an expensive carpet, hoping the love is still there but fearing the worst.

A few days into his stay at Broughton, he was summoned to the office of the vocational rehabilitation director. When he walked in, the man behind the desk looked up and confronted him with the most riveting and compassionate stare he had ever seen. The director got up, covered the short distance between them, and put both hands on Gordon's shoulders.

"It *is* you," he said. "Gordon Weekley."

"Yes, yes, I'm Gordon Weekley," he said, bewildered.

"You preached at my church, Calvary Baptist, here in Morganton. It was a few years ago, a week-long revival. You remember it, don't you?"

Gordon did.

"When I saw the name on our roster, I wondered if it could possibly be you. That was the finest set of sermons I ever heard."

"Thank you," muttered Gordon, "I appreciate that." He did, but he was mortified, too, to be standing there in a khaki uniform, no longer a member of the society of churches and congregations, no longer an active participant in this world or perhaps even the next. He was an addict and a failure.

He left the office and rejoined the only fellowship he belonged to now, the fellowship of bent and broken minds.

He saw his psychiatrist infrequently and for five minutes at a time. The doctor would check his blood pressure, ask him how he was doing, and send him on his way.

He had few visitors during his stay either. Dr. Henry Crouch, who replaced him at Providence, came to see him. So did Jarvis Warren, the former chairman of deacons who had asked Gordon to his house and confronted him about his drug problem that night in 1964—the man who led the exodus from Providence to Carmel Baptist.

In a way, he was Gordon's adversary, but in a much larger sense, he was Gordon's friend. He proved it by that trip to Broughton.

Another friend and former parishioner, Carolyn Leonard, came one day, too. She drove home crying at the memory of seeing him standing in the doorway of the waiting room in khaki pants a full four inches too short that revealed his white socks and white tennis shoes. She cried, too, about the words a nurse had spoken to her before Gordon arrived from his ward.

"Whatever you do," the nurse had said, "don't give him any money."

Dr. Johnnie McLeod visited with him by accident. She was a Charlotte physician, one of the state's foremost specialists in teenage drug dependency, and a friend of Gordon's. She was leading a group of young people on a tour of Broughton, and as luck would have it, he was sitting in the lobby of the main building reading a magazine when she walked in.

He felt liked a trapped rat and moved the magazine closer to his face. It was too late; she had spotted him. She seemed as surprised as he was at the chance encounter, but she recovered almost instantly and greeted him with warmth and affection.

The meeting lasted only a few moments, but to the embarrassed minister, the seconds dragged on like hours. *Of all the people to find me here,* he thought, *a friend who's also a drug counselor.* He vowed from that day on to avoid the lobby.

He was beginning to realize that if anything was going to change, if he had any chance of getting better, it wouldn't happen here at Broughton. At the end of the third month, he was as depressed as the day he arrived. In all that time, he had done nothing constructive and had received maybe a cumulative thirty minutes of counseling.

On the positive side, he had stayed off drugs longer than any other period since his addiction began. Passes were available for him to leave campus, to go into Morganton, but he never availed himself of them, even though he knew he would have no trouble talking a pharmacist or two out of some Dexamyl and Doriden.

He didn't go, and he didn't know why. Maybe his depression was so acute he no longer cared, or, more likely, the Thorazine had squelched his desire.

On or off drugs, this was no life for him. He thought maybe a change of scenery would break the bonds of his depression, help him get going again.

He told his psychiatrist he wanted to leave and got no argument. His commitment had been voluntary and he was not considered a danger to society, so he was permitted to go. The only question was where.

He decided on New Orleans. Beatrice Collins, an old friend from seminary days, was there. They had sung in the choir together and often hung out with each other after classes. They had even dated, though not romantically, before Gordon met Norma Lou.

Bea was director of the Organ Department now at the New Orleans Southern Baptist Seminary. It would be good to see her and a few other faculty members who had been seminary classmates.

She met him at the train and took him to one of the guest apartments on campus.

"If you're not too tired, I'll show you some of the sights this evening," she said.

He said he thought that would be a fine idea, although it didn't matter to him whether he saw them or not. The mind that once bubbled with curiosity about people and places was in neutral. Nothing interested him. But he went with her, and if New Orleans didn't excite him, he at least enjoyed being in the company of an old and dear friend.

They spent most of their time that evening and in the days that followed reminiscing about classmates and professors and the good times they had at seminary.

Bea was no stranger to his troubles. They had kept up a fairly frequent correspondence over the years, and what he hadn't told her, she had heard from the ministerial grapevine. She was a sympathetic friend and a good listener.

On their last day together, over dinner, he asked her the question he had been asking himself for weeks.

"What am I going to do with the rest of my life, Bea? I'm a drug addict. I'm separated from my wife. I can never ever preach again. I don't have any skills. I don't have anything anymore. And what's worse, if you really pressed me on the matter, I don't much care."

She reached across the table and placed her hand on his.

"Gordon," she said, "maybe you're just not quite ready yet. Maybe you need a little more time. Have you ever considered a halfway house?"

"I don't know what that is."

"It's a transitional place. It's a bridge between the institution and the real world. You live in a somewhat controlled environment, but it's a home environment, too, in a neighborhood, and you're free to come and go pretty much as you like. It might be just what you need."

He called Dr. Schmidt's office from New Orleans, reached one of his associates, and in less than an hour, arrangements had been made for the halfway house.

He took a train to Charlotte and a bus to, of all places, Morganton. He hated the thought of even being in the same town with Broughton, but if that's where the halfway house was, that's where he'd have to be.

It was a one-story frame house close to downtown in a neighborhood that was in transition. The thirty or so homes were virtually surrounded by industry, holding out Alamo-style against a tide of change that would one day sweep them away.

There were eight men there, counting Gordon, and two live-in counselors, a husband-and-wife team. In his first few days, he found that life was not at all unpleasant there. He read and walked during the day and listened to the snores of his roommate at night. The noise was so loud, he swore he could feel the walls shake. He couldn't sleep anyway, so he didn't complain.

After about a week, he began to take stock of himself. He had been several months without drugs—long enough, he thought, to be free from their addictive power. His weight was back to normal and he was in decent shape physically. He saw no reason why he couldn't have just a few Dexamyls and Doridens. As sort of a reward for good behavior. Something to celebrate his emergence from the bland and numbing existence he had known in the institution.

He picked up a phone and called a psychiatrist who had recently left Broughton to establish a private practice. This triumph in drug procurement was probably his greatest. It was like talking a jailer out of the cell-door key. But there he was, an hour or so after the phone call, paying the pharmacist at a nearby drugstore for his beloved pills.

And there he was, an hour after that, glowing with energy as the Dexamyl raced through him. Alive again after all those months.

Alive but not hungry. He picked at his food at lunch and again at dinner.

"You're not eating," said Mr. Jones, the counselor.

"I'm not hungry."

"You have to eat."

"I'm not hungry."

He was only hungry for the Doriden he took later that evening. When the two drugs, the Doriden and the Dexamyl, married in his brain, he was in a state of bliss. The effects were staggering. The staggering he did walking through the parlor did not go unnoticed, either.

"Gordon," said one of his housemates, "if you're on something, you'd better get off it right quick. They ain't going to put up with that around here."

He didn't get off of it. The next morning, he took a Dexamyl, and by late afternoon he had taken two more.

He didn't eat his lunch or his dinner, and late in the evening, he took the Doriden. If he had stayed in his room, he might have escaped notice—but he didn't. This time he was falling-down drunk on drugs, and when he looked up from the parlor floor, he saw the towering figure of a deputy sheriff.

The drive to Broughton was shorter this time than it was before. It was less than a mile.

"Don't worry," the kindly deputy said as they rode through the streets of Morganton. "On an involuntary commitment, the law says they can only hold you for seventy-two hours. If you're okay after that, you'll be back out." He re-entered the institution on March 27, 1970. It would be a while before he would leave it.

He spent the first two weeks on a locked ward, Ward 107, where he was once again placed on Thorazine. At the end of the two weeks, he was moved to

Ward C, but though his location changed, his routine didn't. He'd get out of bed, eat breakfast, and long to lie down again. He read but without much interest. He walked the grounds, and always, guilt and despair walked with him. The days were filled with the same sameness as the time before, except one day in April when an orderly found him on the grounds and told him he had a visitor.

"Thank you," he said, and slowly, dutifully, he made his way to the lobby. He pushed open the door and cast his eyes around the large room. There were maybe a dozen people there, but no one he recognized. The only person who stood out was another of Burke County's finest, a deputy sheriff.

"H. Gordon Weekley, Jr.?" the deputy asked, walking toward him.

"Yes, I'm H. Gordon Weekley," he answered, wondering what this man could possibly want with him.

"I've been instructed to serve you with these," the deputy said, pushing a thin sheaf of papers into his hand.

"Greetings," the top one read. "You are hereby summoned and notified to appear and answer the above entitled civil action."

*What civil action? What could I have possibly done?*

His eyes scanned the page, and in the upper left-hand corner, he saw Norma Lou's name with his name directly under it. Norma's involved, too, he thought, still scanning. Then, in the right-hand corner, beneath some bureaucratic file numbers, he saw the words that described this particular civil action: "Non-Jury Divorce."

*Non-jury divorce, non-jury divorce, non-jury divorce.* Over and over, the words played in his mind.

Trembling now, he looked through the pages. "Wherefore the plaintiff prays judgment on the court as follows:...that the bonds of matrimony now existing between the plaintiff and defendant be dissolved and that the plaintiff be granted an absolute divorce from the defendant...that the plaintiff be awarded the sole care, custody and control of the minor children born of the marriage of the plaintiff and defendant, and defendant allowed reasonable visitation rights with the said children."

She was gone for good. The pretty choir girl in the little church in Indiana. The mother of his children. The comrade in arms who fought by his side that night in Masonboro trying to save the doomed chickens with Vicks Salve.

She no longer wanted him, no longer needed him, could no longer put up with him. If he could have found something to cling to at that moment, he would have. He had nothing to cling to. Not physically. Not emotionally. Not spiritually.

He raised his eyes from the papers, found the deputy's face, and, always the gentleman, thanked him. Then he turned and shuffled back to his ward to contemplate his failings as a man.

He did not contest the divorce. He had neither the energy nor the self-esteem to do it. When the initial pain of loss wore off, he returned to his routine of days filled with emptiness. He would not find out until much later, that on one of those days, December 21, Judge Claudia Watkins signed a decree stating that "...the bonds of matrimony heretofore existing between the Plaintiff and Defendant... are hereby dissolved, and that the Plaintiff and Defendant are granted an absolute divorce one from the other."

In the weeks that followed, he found another addiction: Snickers candy bars. They supplanted the food he no longer ate in the cafeteria. Morning, noon, and night, he couldn't get enough of them. They were the only thing he looked forward to every day.

By the end of his sixth month in Broughton, his candy addiction had pushed his weight to 230 pounds. He was suffering almost constantly from indigestion. Night after night, he slid out of his bed, shuffled down the hall, and asked the night attendant for Maalox.

His psychiatrist, who never in Gordon's entire stay knew his name, ordered an upper G.I. series, and the results showed a hiatal hernia. He was placed on a strict diet, and in a few months both the weight and the hernia went away. Unfortunately for Gordon, the Snickers went along with them.

Gordon had lost virtually everything in his life that mattered to him, and now he couldn't even enjoy the pleasure of a candy bar. He was no longer being counseled either, although he knew that counseling probably wouldn't help. He had never met a counselor more impressive than Bill Griffin, and even he had failed.

On February 12, 1971, he left Broughton for the second time, and once again returned to Atlanta to Mary and Aubon's home. His depression went with him, but he vowed to himself that this time he would stay off drugs.

He knew that he would have to find work. He could not be a dependent forever, but at least he was not totally freeloading on his sister and her husband. For some time, he had been receiving $152 a month in Social Security disability income and $60 a month from the Southern Baptist Relief and Annuity Board. He used a portion of that money to help Mary and Aubon with groceries.

Then, after a couple of weeks of boredom, depression, and halfhearted attempts to find work, he used some of his money to buy Dexamyl and Doriden.

Gordon's family was at wit's end. From time to time, he thought he overheard hushed discussions in which the word "Broughton" was used. Each time he heard it, he would give up his drugs for a few days. If he was going to feel this bad, he'd rather go through it in Aubon's house than in the house the State of North Carolina had for him.

Doug Broadway stepped in. He once again offered Gordon Weekley work, and Gordon once again found himself in Charlotte at the YMCA. He was grateful to Doug for the job and in despair at his prospects for the future.

Later Doug Broadway was to say that after two months he knew he had made a mistake in hiring Gordon. The mistake had nothing to do with Gordon being a poor salesman and everything to do with Gordon being a very sick man.

As always, Gordon tried to put on a good face, but before those first two months had passed, he was back into Dexamyl and Doriden. Desperation and depression had once again given him the courage to seek out doctors and pharmacies.

Some days he would take the pills, some days he wouldn't, convincing himself in that way that he was in control of himself.

The job and his life dragged on, going nowhere. He occasionally accepted dinner invitations from old friends, and he saw his son Dan, who was out on his own, fairly frequently. Steve by now was at Wake Forest but visited with his dad from time to time when he came home on weekends. Other than those few bright spots, life was almost as miserable as it could get.

One evening in late February, he was out riding with Dan, and it got a little worse.

"How's your mother?" he asked.

"She's doing great. She's on her honeymoon."

"I didn't know she had remarried," Gordon said, trying to disguise with his voice the pain he felt in his heart.

Self-esteem was not a problem for Gordon Weekley then. He didn't have any.

One night, Clyde Griffin's ex-wife, Verna, called and invited him to dinner.

"Someone else will be here, too, Gordon," she said. "Her name is Peggy. I want you to meet her."

She was attractive, intelligent, single, a little younger than he, and he liked her from the moment he met her. For a few hours over dinner that evening, his cloud of depression was lifted. He thought he had been almost charming. He smiled a lot, laughed at little jokes, and made sensible observations on the subjects discussed around the table. When he went home to the Y, he went home on a cloud.

He called her the next day and made a date for the following evening. They had dinner at a modest restaurant, and again he found himself making pleasant conversation and maintaining a fair enough level of concentration and energy. She was a devoutly religious woman, so they had plenty of common ground for discussion. But while the night before, Gordon's relatively high energy level had come easily, this time it took a little more effort. Depression was a formidable foe.

They went out almost nightly, and his feelings for Peggy grew stronger. He took her to a basketball game at Wake Forest in Winston-Salem. Young Eddie Payne, who had grown up in Providence Baptist, was one of the stars of the team, and Gordon and Peggy yelled and applauded his every move.

Driving back that night, they talked at first about the game, then lapsed into a tired, easy silence as the car hummed its way along the interstate. Mile marker after mile marker drifted by as Gordon fought a mental battle with himself. Finally, summoning up his courage, he

took his hand off the wheel and placed it on hers. Wordlessly, gently, she slid her hand away from the contact.

The simple movement of her hand was all it took to convince Gordon he'd been rejected.

The next night, with his pill supply depleted and his hopes for romance destroyed, Gordon Weekley went into a liquor store for the first time in his life. He marveled over the number of choices available to the drinking public. He ran his eyes over the hundreds of bottles categorized in their shelves under signs reading gin, bourbon, vodka. He had no idea what differentiated one from the other, but he remembered a name. Four Roses. He had seen it in an ad somewhere.

Back in his room, he slipped the bottled bouquet of roses from the brown paper bag and unscrewed the top. *It sure doesn't smell like roses,* he thought, wrinkling his nose.

He rinsed out a water glass from his nightstand and filled it to within an inch of the top with straight whiskey. It looked like iced tea. *I wonder if it tastes anything like it?* He brought it to his lips and drained fully a third of the glass.

The coughing spell lasted a while. Never had he tasted anything that assaulted his senses so dramatically. *Lord, how can anybody drink this?* he thought, but drink it he did—more slowly, to be sure, but he finished the entire glass, then another and another until the bottle was empty.

He slept like a baby, better than any sleep he could remember.

The next morning, he paid the price. He was groggy. His head ached. His stomach churned. His normal, everyday depression was now overlaid by an unfamiliar nervousness. Still, he made it to work on time and spent another miserable day trying to sell furniture. He decided he was the worst furniture salesman in history. He knew little about the products and cared even less. His brain simply wouldn't absorb what he needed to know about springs, cushioning, and fabrics, even though the information wasn't complicated.

He made it through each day on the secure knowledge that there was a bottle of Four Roses waiting for him at the liquor store on the way home. For the next several weeks, he drank a bottle every night. He drank it the way he thought everybody else did, straight. He would begin about eight, after a light supper at the Y commissary, and drink until there was nothing left in the bottle except glass.

The hangovers diminished and eventually disappeared, but the grogginess and nervousness stayed with him until finally Doug Broadway spoke.

"Gordon, you seem jumpy lately. What's bothering you?

"I don't know," he said. "Maybe I'm not getting enough sleep."

He began to forget things. Customers who had been in the store only the day before were strangers to him. He would pause ringing up a sale and try to remember what it was he had sold. Sometime in the middle of the third week of his binge, he forgot how to write.

"What did you say your name was?" he asked a customer, stalling.

"Branch."

"Right, Branch. I'm sorry, I've been a little forgetful lately."

He stared, pencil poised, at the delivery order in front of him, and he could not make his hand write the word *Branch*, although he could see it clearly in his mind.

"Where do you want this delivered, Mr. Branch?" he said.

"Elm Street. 525 Elm Street."

Elm Street was no better. The fingers simply wouldn't work. Finally, he put down the order and promised Mr. Branch that the furniture would be delivered that afternoon.

That afternoon, March 20, 1972, Doug Broadway fired him, not callously or coldly but with compassion and pity.

He bought three bottles of Four Roses on the way back to the Y. By early evening he was drunk. He stayed that way for the next three days. He kept to his room except for two visits to the commissary for snacks. He spoke to no one, preferring instead to suffer alone in this latest of a legion of setbacks. It must have been obvious to those who saw him that he was as close to dead drunk as a man on his feet can be.

He was a lonely man in a city he had once held in the palm of his hand. Night after night he lay on his small bed listening to the passing cars on Morehead and on nearby South Boulevard and envying the people in them. They had some place to go.

On the fourth day, he awoke sober. He showered and shaved for the first time since the binge began. He selected a suit from the closet and began to dress. He was tying his tie in the mirror when the realization hit him. He was all dressed up with no place to go.

He had no place to stay either, because that morning the director of the YMCA called him to his office and told him in a firm but kind manner that he could no longer remain there.

"I'm sorry, Reverend, but I think you know why," the director said.

Gordon knew why. He only wished the director had called him *Mister* instead of *Reverend* when he said without saying it that he was kicking him out for drunkenness.

He went to see Dan, who by this time had a small one-bedroom apartment on Hawthorne Lane, a low-middle income neighborhood on the east side, not far from uptown.

"Son, I'm going to have to move in with you for a while," Gordon said.

Dan didn't protest. It wouldn't have changed things even if he had. Steve was in college at Wake Forest. There was simply no other place for the exiled minister to go.

Dan's bedroom was large enough for only one double bed. Gordon fixed that by buying a set of twin beds from Doug Broadway.

"What will you do, Dad?" Dan asked. "You just can't sit around."

"I don't know yet, son. I'll find something. At least I have my disability and annuity to live on, so I won't be a burden."

But he was a burden, and he knew it, cramping the style and the apartment of a young single man who dated and, until Gordon moved in, frequently had friends over.

Dan had his life. Gordon had none. He tried his best to stay out of his son's way. He watched the television shows Dan wanted to watch and waited until Dan finished with the newspaper before picking it up. He stayed in bed mornings until Dan finished showering and dressing for work.

By six-thirty, Dan would be out of the house and on the way to his job at Presbyterian Hospital. By nine, Gordon would be in a cab headed for the liquor store at Kings Drive and Morehead Street, a little over a mile from the apartment. When Dan returned in the evening there would be no sign of the booze. What Gordon didn't drink, he hid. What he hid, he drank later, long after Dan had gone out or to bed.

He had gone out early one Friday evening in the second or third week of Gordon's stay at the apartment, leaving him with plenty of time to spend with his Four Roses. He started at seven, and by nine, he was falling-down drunk. He was in the tiny bathroom when he fell backwards into the empty tub.

He lay there for a moment, stunned, and then tried to climb out. None of his parts seemed to work properly. His body seemed to have a mind of its own. He tried throwing his leg over the side, but it wouldn't go. He tried pushing against the tub bottom with his arms, but they wouldn't push. He turned and thrashed and eventually got over onto his stomach, hoping he could get to his knees. He couldn't.

He was scared and sweating. *I'm going to die here. I'm going to die in this bathtub. This is where they'll find me.*

He fought until he could fight no more. Then he laid back, resigned, staring at the ceiling. *How did I get into this?* He had been there a long time and knew that Dan might be back any minute.

*I can't let him find me like this.* Screwing up his remaining strength, he resumed the battle of the bathtub. He relied not on intellect to instruct his body but on mindless frenzy. Then he was out and on the bathroom floor, sucking air as quickly and as deeply as he could get it, relieved and still frightened.

*I've got to get up. But if I get up I might fall again. I might fall in the tub.*

He crawled out of the bathroom, down the hall, and up into his bed. He pulled the covers around him and drew himself into a fetal position. Exhausted, he went straight to sleep.

The next morning he vowed he would never touch alcohol again. He kept that promise until five o'clock that afternoon when Dan left for the evening.

Every day was the same: a trip to the liquor store and a fifth of Four Roses. He never once looked for a job. He was too tired, too depressed. He drank and drank until finally he could collapse on the bed and fall into a deep and forgiving sleep.

"Dad."

He opened his eyes. "Steve, what are you doing here? You're supposed to be at school."

"Dan sent for me."

He looked past his oldest son, at the ceiling. This wasn't Dan's bedroom.

"Where am I?"

"You're in Memorial Hospital."

*The bathtub,* he thought, *they found me there. No, I got out of the bathtub. I made it to the bed. I got up the next morning. I saw Dan. What day is this?*

"What day is this?"

"It's Thursday, Dad," Steve answered.

"What month?"

"May."

*Then this isn't the day after the bathtub. That was two weeks ago.* "What happened?"

"Dan found you last night. He was out on a date, remember, and he had a feeling he should come back and check on you."

"I remember him going out. I don't remember him checking on me.

"He couldn't wake you, Dad. You were lying on top of the bed covers, all dressed. He tried to get you to wake up, to get your pajamas on, but you were out. They brought you here in an ambulance."

Shame overtook him again. He had overdosed on booze. Had scared Dan to death. Had been transported in an ambulance. Had caused his son to be called away from college.

"I'll be all right," he said to Steve. "You need to get on back up to school."

"Dad, one of us, either Dan or I, has to stay with you all the time."

"Steve, no, you can't do that."

"It's okay, Dad, I can drive back and forth. I won't miss many classes at all."

Gordon turned his head away from Steve and closed his eyes.

The following day he was transferred to Presbyterian Hospital. He was embarrassed because Dan worked there.

"Dan, why does one of you have to be constantly with me? I feel better now."

"The doctors are worried about you, Dad. *We're* worried about you."

"Why? I'm okay."

"You're not fooling anybody except maybe yourself. "What do you mean?"

"I know what you were doing. I followed you to the liquor store more than once. How long have you been drinking, about three months? The doctor says you already have liver damage. It's reversible, but you can't drink anymore. Dad, you've got to get yourself out of this mess."

"I will," he promised, "I will."

His general practitioner was the young doctor who had supplied him with Dexamyl and Doriden during the last years of his pastorate. His psychiatrist was Dr. Schmidt, the man who had encouraged Norma Lou to leave him.

Gordon hadn't asked for either doctor. He had not seen them since he left Charlotte in October of 1967. He was not happy to see them now, but the boys had called them, and based on his condition, he had little choice in the matter.

Besides, he really didn't care all that much anyway. He didn't care much about anything.

On the evening of the third day of his stay in Presbyterian, he awoke from a nap to see both Dan and Steve in the room with him.

"Dad," Steve said, "it's time for a family conference."

"What about?" Gordon asked dully.

"About tomorrow," Dan said. "Tomorrow, you're getting discharged and, well," he hesitated, "well, we just can't take care of you."

"Take care of me?"

"Dad, I'm in school," Steve said, "and Dan's working, and somebody has to look after you."

"I can look after myself," he said wearily.

"No, you can't, Dad," said Dan, "and we haven't got the money to send you to Appalachian Hall or Peachtree Hospital."

"Dad," Steve interjected quickly, "we think you should go back to Broughton. We'll take you."

They took him on May 31, 1972. He stayed for almost a year, another year out of a life that had at one time been full and exciting and meaningful, to himself and to the many hundreds who had adored him.

It had been nearly six years since he had resigned his pastorate. He had been hospitalized seven times, his wife was long gone, his kids were grown, and virtually all his worldly possessions were in the one suitcase sitting beside him in the Morganton bus terminal.

He was waiting for the bus to Charlotte, although he knew there would be nothing to do when he got there and nobody there to meet him.

He didn't want anybody to meet him, didn't want anybody to know he was coming. Seeing people, or being seen, was the last thing on earth he wanted. He was defeated. With the exception of eventually establishing some contact with his boys, he was resigned to living out the rest of his life alone.

## SEVENTEEN

His destination was the Mecklenburg Hotel, a block from the Charlotte bus station. He could walk there and be safely inside in less than two minutes. He didn't know how long he could stay because his social security disability and annuity wouldn't stretch very far.

He remembered it as a nice hotel. His friend and parishioner Bob Hollingsworth had taken him to the restaurant there for beef stroganoff on several occasions in the fifties.

This was the early seventies, and there was no beef stroganoff and no restaurant. Sometime in the ensuing fifteen years, the Mecklenburg Hotel had fallen terminally ill.

To call it a fleabag would be to give fleabag a bad name. The lobby was dirty, littered with torn and faded furniture and four or five broken men who, except for their faces, were mirror images of the hotel's newest tenant.

The room was five dollars a night, cash in advance. At that rate, he knew what it would look like even before he got to see it.

Room 564 measured roughly eight feet by ten. The paint was peeling from the walls and ceiling. The single bed featured a hump in the middle that turned out to be a spring attempting an escape from its dismal surroundings. The room's only chair had a broken arm. There was a telephone on the nightstand but no phone book.

He put down his suitcase and returned to the lobby by way of a rickety elevator. He found a pay phone there and a phone book. He let his fingers do the walking down a list of physicians. They stopped at a name that for some reason or other seemed promising.

He made his way the few blocks to the Square, the intersection of Trade and Tryon streets, the center of town, the connecting point for Charlotte's buses.

It was a short ride, a little over a mile, to the doctor's Freedom Drive office. When he entered, he felt a twinge of nervousness. He hadn't done this in many months. He was out of practice. He might have trouble pulling it off.

His fears proved groundless. By eleven that night, he was lying on his back on the bed reveling in the Dexamyl-and-Doriden high. He didn't feel the broken spring or care about the peeling paint or notice that the air conditioning wasn't working and the room was sweltering.

He awoke the next morning late. He'd have slept longer if he could have, but when the drugs wore off, the heat wore in. With it, through the open window, came the hum of heavy equipment and the clang of steel against steel. A new building was going up directly across the street from the hotel, and he knew that there would be no naps, no beloved sleep here in the afternoons. At least now he had sleep's alternative, Dexamyl. He popped one, dressed quickly, and without bothering to shave, left for the streets of Charlotte. College Street. Church Street. Poplar Street. Third, Fourth, Fifth, and Sixth streets. Trade Street. Tryon Street. On and on he walked. There was nothing else to do. He only hoped that no one he knew would see him.

This became his life, his everyday routine: walking, walking, stopping once in a while to rest on a bench somewhere, and every afternoon at four, eating at the Presto Grill across from the hotel. It was his only meal, and he ate just enough to sustain himself, just enough so that when ten o'clock rolled around, the Doriden would have his stomach to itself and more gaily join the Dexamyl in the dance in his brain. Then came the drowsy high; then came the sleep.

Then came the awakening, the heat, the construction sounds, the morning Dexamyl, the walking, the eating at Presto, the walking again, the Doriden. About all that broke the routine was finding doctors who would service him.

On the days he visited them, he spiffed himself up and looked presentable. Other times, his appearance wasn't a priority. He kept himself clean and did his clothes in a nearby laundromat, but they went unironed and most days he went unshaven.

If he had kept a list of people he didn't want to see on his daily sojourns, Dr. Tom Burnett would have been near the top. It was Dr. Burnett, after all, who had analyzed the pills Gordon left in Arthur Smith's car that night so many years ago. He knew more than most about Gordon's drug problem.

Tom Burnett, of course, was the person Gordon saw outside the Doctors Building on Kings Drive. Gordon had just left it, prescription bag in hand, and was waiting at the curb for a bus when the doctor happened by.

There was no escape. The doctor had seen him. They exchanged brief and friendly hellos. Gordon said, on being asked, that he was doing fine, just fine. Dr. Burnett said he was very pleased to hear that, and then patted him warmly on the shoulder and walked away, leaving an embarrassed Gordon Weekley holding the bag.

A few other people from Providence saw him, too, during that summer. They would honk their horns and pull over to the curb to greet him. He would try to keep walking, to pretend he didn't hear, but invariably he was forced to face them. He knew they were well-intentioned and caring, but he hated those moments more than anything, hated them so much he would have stayed in his room if the room weren't so hot and the construction so loud.

Often he would escape to the serenity of an old cemetery behind First Presbyterian Church, on Fifth Street in the heart of the city. It was a patch of green among the concrete and steel, a favored place of street wanderers, particularly in summer, because the giant oaks gave respite from the sweltering city heat.

He sat on a bench and gazed out over the weathered tombstones. *What a perfect place for me to be spending my life, in Necropolis, the city of the dead.*

He was in his fifties now. It had been almost nineteen years since he stepped behind the pulpit in that little fellowship hall, the only building on the grounds of Providence Baptist Church, a young man looking out over a sea of eager faces, knowing right then that this was going to be a very special church.

How wonderful it would have been, he thought as he looked out over the cemetery, to have grown old with those people, to have shared their lives, been there with them when they laughed and when they cried, watched their children grow up and bring children of their own.

Was it pride that brought him to the city of the dead? It seemed the more successful he became, the more success he wanted: the big house, the invitations to the Billy Graham Crusades, the adulation of hundreds of followers.

"You try to do too much," they had told him. "You work too hard." But even those who told him were quick to call on him for counseling or advice. He always went, and he always wanted to go.

Was it the need for success that drove him to the hospital for the birth of a baby in the middle of the night? Was that what drove him to more committee meetings than he needed to attend?

*No, no, I wanted to be there. I was their pastor. I loved them. Love them still.* But he loved being loved by them, too. He loved their adulation, no doubt about it.

What of his family? If he could do it again, would he spend more time with them? He wanted to think he would have because he had loved them so. But back then, every waking moment had been filled. That wouldn't change. Could he actually turn his back on a phone call from a parishioner in need?

It was too much to think about and there were no answers. It didn't matter now anyway. Besides, it was time to leave Necropolis and eat at the Presto Grill. Then he would return to the Mecklenburg Hotel, where the living dead resided.

On September 28, the phone rang in his room, startling him. Except for an occasional call from one of his boys, the telephone in his room was as silent as the chair with the broken arm.

"There's a man down here to see you," the desk clerk said. "His name's Grady Wilson."

Not Grady Wilson. Not the man closest to Billy Graham, whose encouragement and influence had helped Gordon's star rise so rapidly in those early years. Anybody but Grady Wilson.

He couldn't face him, and he couldn't escape him. Grady knew he was in his room. The desk clerk's call confirmed that. If he didn't go down Grady would come up. Gordon didn't want to be seen, and he wanted his room to be seen even less.

He gritted his teeth, took a deep breath, and rode the elevator down with his head hung like a condemned man. When he stepped into the lobby, he suddenly realized that he hadn't shaved in several days. He knew he looked like hell.

Grady met him at the elevator, shook his hand, and greeted him warmly. He steered him to a corner of the lobby away from the few people who were sitting there.

"Pastor," Grady said, and the sound of the word almost moved the fallen minister to tears. He considered himself no more a pastor than the man in the moon, and yet Grady Wilson, one of the nation's great pastors, was affirming that he indeed still was.

"Pastor," Grady said, "I want you to do something for me. I don't want you to do it for yourself. I want you to do it for me."

Gordon did not answer. He knew whatever it was Grady wanted, he would have to do, but he was hoping against hope that the request would have nothing to do with his addiction.

"I want you to check yourself into the mission."

Gordon felt a sharp stab in his stomach. He could go almost anywhere but there. He had preached there. How would it look now if he went there as one of those he had preached to, those drunks, winos, bums?

"Grady, I..." he stammered, looking away.

"Gordon, you've tried everything else. Nothing's worked. You have to do this. For me. Gordon, look at me."

Gordon looked, and saw what he always saw in Grady's eyes: love, compassion, sincerity.

"Tell me you'll go, Gordon."

To go would be humiliating. To go would be to give up once again the Dexamyl and Doriden. He took a deep breath, then let it out in a long sigh. "I'll need a day or two," he told Grady finally. "I have to get my suit pressed and clean out my room."

Did Grady know he was stalling for just a little more time with his drugs?

"Monday, then," Grady said. "Call Bill Kauffman Monday. I've already talked to him, and he's waiting to hear from you." Gordon knew Rev. Kauffman, the Center director, well from having spoken there so many times in the past.

"Monday's okay," Gordon said, "I'll call him then."

"You can beat this, Gordon. I know you can."

Gordon didn't believe it. If anyone else had asked him to go, he wouldn't have done it.

He wanted the next two days to crawl by, but they flew. Even the euphoria of the late night Dexamyl/Doriden high failed to slow the rapid rotation of the hands on his bedside clock.

He spent most of his remaining fleeting time in his room, staring at the clock, waiting for Monday.

It arrived, ahead of the time in his mind. So did Monday afternoon, and early Monday evening. It was then, with the greatest reluctance, that he leaned across the bed, picked up the phone, and called Kauffman's office.

"I'm sorry, Reverend Kauffman's out of town," the voice said. "He'll be back Thursday."

Joy somersaulted through his heart. "Would you ask him to call me when he gets back?" he said.

Four more days of freedom, and he made the most of them. He increased his daily dosage and ate even less of his normal piddling suppers at the Presto Grill. He got high and stayed there all the way up to and through Thursday. When Kauffman hadn't called by early that evening, he thought he might get yet another day.

He awoke late Friday, took a Dexamyl and started to set out on his walking routine. He got as far as the front desk.

"Weekley," the clerk said, "there's a letter here for you."

He opened it, already knowing by the return address that it was from Rev. Kauffman. He would be very happy to consider Gordon's application to the center and Gordon should call him right away.

Gordon sat several hours in the chair with the broken arm trying to think of any alternative that would seem even remotely plausible to his dear friend Grady Wilson. There were no alternatives. He couldn't afford Appalachian Hall again, and he would never, under any circumstances, return to Broughton.

He could put it off no longer. He took a deep breath, let out a long sigh, and then picked up the phone and called Kauffman. Within the hour, he was sitting in a chair across from the director's desk, dressed in his only suit and trying his best to maintain a sense of dignity.

After a few brief pleasantries, Kauffman launched into a gentle but firm lecture about Gordon's need to get hold of his life. Gordon only heard part of what was being said. He was thinking instead of the times he had preached here, and how driving back to his South Charlotte home, he had commented to himself that he would never be caught dead in a place like the rehab center.

*How could this have possibly happened to me?* He thought of his mother and his father and the great hopes they had for him when he was young, and the great pride they felt in his enormous successes at Boys High School and Furman and Southern Baptist Seminary and in his pastorates.

*If Appalachian Hall and Broughton didn't kill them, this surely will.*

"Did you bring your clothes?" Kauffman asked.

"No, I have to get them laundered, and I have to clean out my room at the hotel. I'll need a couple of days."

"A couple of days, Gordon, no more."

The couple of days passed in a haze of Dexamyl and Doriden, and he made no move toward going to the center.

"Maybe I can get by with just one more day," he thought. "One more."

His thoughts were interrupted by the phone.

"Gordon," Kauffman said from the other end of the line, "you can put this off as long as you want, but sooner or later, you're going to have to face up to the fact that either you get straightened out or you die. I'm going to send one of my men, Bill Wilson, over to get you. Be ready."

"Okay," Gordon said sadly. "I guess I'm ready."

Wilson picked him up and drove him the few blocks to the center. It was located now on West First Street, a half-mile or so west of Trade and Tryon in an old industrial area dotted here and there with small, dilapidated wood frame homes occupied by poor blacks.

It was much larger than the original storefront on College Street and could house more than a hundred men. Built in the 1920s, the three brick buildings had been home to Standard Oil Company until the late '50s. One, a three-story, was divided into apartments for the director and some staff members. Another was rented out to a book distribution company. The third, a large two-story, contained staff offices, the dormitory, the kitchen, and the chapel.

Behind the buildings and occupying the rest of the four-acre tract were three warehouses, one of which served as a bargain store for the sale of used furniture and other goods donated to the center.

It was a far cry from Appalachian Hall, but it was spotlessly clean, and the food was nourishing, and the beds were warm in winter.

Kauffman decided that Gordon, instead of living barracks-style upstairs with most of the men, would be given his own room at the back of the chapel. The chapel was a large open area in the center of the building, which had in its Standard Oil days hummed with the sound of secretaries and typewriters doing the work of the men whose offices lined two of the surrounding four walls. Now the east wall belonged to the mission's staff and the north wall to a few of the men, Gordon Weekley among them. The open space was filled with old theater seats facing an altar and a podium, flanked on each side by an American and a Christian flag. Behind the seats, on the wall that separated his room from the chapel, was a crudely drawn painting of the risen Christ. Jesus was the first person Gordon saw when he stepped from his door every morning on his way to breakfast.

He took his breakfast and every other meal at the staff's table in the dining room. His seat was at Bill Kauffman's left. Kauffman was a close friend of Grady and hunted quail with him often. That and Gordon's being a fellow minister, meant two things: special treatment and special attention.

He appreciated the special treatment. The special attention bothered him. He wanted to get off drugs, but that hadn't stopped him from bringing the last few pills he had into the center with him. He didn't want someone looking over his shoulder.

Kauffman decided that the best therapy for Gordon was work, something to keep him busy. The center offered no classes and no regular counseling sessions. The majority of the men there slept, ate, and attended compulsory chapel services five nights a week. Others either worked in the kitchen, drove trucks to pick up the donated clothing and household goods, or worked in the repair shop or in the store.

Gordon was assigned to the store, but unlike the job at Doug Broadway's furniture store, he did not have to convince people to buy. People came looking for bargains, bought what they needed, and handed him the money.

It was an easy job, and he even found his days there somewhat pleasant. It wasn't the work that sparked his interest, it was a coworker. Jim Lewis was a Catholic who hadn't seen the inside of a church since his days as an acolyte in New York. He had a wife and children who loved him, and he loved them. He was not addicted to booze or to drugs. He was at the center because he needed time and a place to sort out his life, to find meaning in his existence.

From the moment he found out Gordon was a pastor, he besieged him with questions. About the existence of God. About the deity of Christ. About the meanings of Old Testament stories. About baptism. About heaven and hell. About Christian values in a secular world. About rewards and punishment for good and wrongdoing. About contradictions in Biblical texts.

Gordon answered what he could according to his abilities and his beliefs. He did his best to help Lewis find what he was looking for, and he was intrigued by this man's quest. Had he thought about it, he might have been intrigued by his own interest in their many long discussions, because even though he did not know it or even think about it, he was preaching again and counseling.

He was also doing drugs, leaving the center from time to time under the pretense of buying toiletries or visiting someone he knew. He even had a car now, one of the last remnants of his marriage to Norma Lou. Steve had kept it during the years of Gordon's incarcerations and used it to get back and forth from college. Now he was working and had a car of his own, so he returned the '65 Dodge to his dad soon after he entered the center.

The car gave him easy access to his drugs, and his private room gave him the opportunity to hide them and enjoy them.

At the Mecklenburg Hotel, he had had only one personality to deal with, his addictive one. He had taken drugs when he pleased and behaved as he pleased. Here at the center, he lived the double life he had lived so long during the Providence years and later at Appalachian Hall—pretending he was doing well, making the effort, not doing well at all.

He even began going to church again, at Midwood Baptist, but he couldn't decide if he was doing it to throw the hounds off the trail or because he really wanted a spiritual revival. In any event, Gordon's church attendance was his first act of normal social behavior since the days of his job with Broadway.

He attended the mission's nightly chapel services, too, but the "clients," as he and the other men were called, were required to do that. Each service was conducted by a guest minister from a Charlotte church. Gordon knew many of them and was mortified almost daily when they recognized him.

The services were over at eight, and by nine, he would be well into his Doriden, his bliss. Worries about fellow preachers recognizing him would be far, far from his mind.

Gordon was apparently never far from Kauffman's mind.

"Friend," he said on many occasions, "I'm going to break you of those things. I know you're still taking them, and I'm going to help you lick them."

*Nobody else has been able to; I don't know what makes you think you can.*

Whatever plan Bill Kauffman might have had, he didn't implement it. And Gordon didn't stop. In fact, over the months, as he got more comfortable in his surroundings, he increased his dosage. He justified it to himself as the only way to live the drab existence the center offered. He had a near meaningless job, no counseling, and thus no real hopes for a future—leaving him no reason to abstain from drugs. It sounded good. If it hadn't, he'd have thought of something else.

The one thing he truly hated about the center was morning, but he had hated mornings everywhere. They came too soon and brought with them his daily depression, which he had to feel until the first Dexamyl of the day kicked in.

One morning in the sixth month of his stay, he awoke without benefit of his alarm clock. Without bothering to look at it, he rolled to a sitting position on the edge of his bed and lit a cigarette.

*I've never been this groggy. Maybe I took an extra Doriden last night.*

He placed the cigarette on the edge of the ashtray and got to his feet. He fought himself into his robe, then fumbled for a towel on an overhead shelf. *I've got to wake up. I've got to get straight. I don't want Kauffman to see me like this.*

He opened the door, closed it behind him, and padded down the hall to the showers. He tried the cold water first to wake up, but it was too cold to tolerate. He gradually added hot water until he found a mix so comfortable it kept him in his groggy, mildly euphoric state. He stayed there a long time, oblivious to everything except the sound and the soothing feel of the water.

He did not hear the wail of the fire trucks or the shouts of many men or the banging on his bedroom door.

"Gordon, Gordon," he heard Bill Kauffman yelling when he finally turned off the water.

"In here," he called, but Kauffman kept yelling.

*What in the world does he want?* Gordon thought, quickly toweling off and slipping into his robe. *I'd better go see.*

He saw Bill Kauffman emerging from Gordon's smoke-filled room, coughing heavily. He saw five firemen rapidly approaching from the other side of the chapel, axes in hand. He saw smoke pouring out the door.

"Where's Gordon?" Kauffman yelled to no one in particular.

"I'm here, Bill, I'm here," shouted Gordon. When Kauffman turned to look, he looked as if he had seen a ghost.

"Lord, Gordon, I thought you were *in* there. Your door was locked and the room's on fire. I thought you were dead," he said breathlessly.

It took several minutes to put the fire out, and when the smoke cleared, it was obvious that several thousand dollars' damage had been done. Fortunately, the fire had not spread beyond the room itself.

"Gordon, what were you doing up at this hour anyway?" Kauffman asked.

"What hour?"

"One o'clock."

By three o'clock, he was situated in his new home, bed number 38 in the basement dormitory. He looked up and down the rows of sleeping men around him, some snoring loudly, some tossing and turning through twisted dreams. On the brick wall above their heads were cubicles holding their meager worldly possessions. He sighed.

The Doriden was still strong in his veins, and as he lay on the bed, it pushed him rapidly toward sleep—but not before he had a chance to deeply regret what had happened. The damage he had done to the room was bad enough, but the damage he had done to himself was even worse.

The room had given him the appearance of some credibility. It had narrowed the gulf between him and people like Kauffman and Grady Wilson. It had made him seem, at least to himself, more like them and less like the bums in the dormitory. Now he was a bum in the dormitory. The tears welled in his closed eyes as he saw in his mind his car turning off Country Lane, crossing the bridge he had built with his hands, and making its way up the long drive to the house on the hill where Norma Lou and the children were waiting.

## EIGHTEEN

He awoke in the morning deeply embarrassed but resolved to regain whatever he had lost in esteem. He found the going not as difficult as he imagined. Kauffman, to be sure, was put out with him, but he did not lose his job, did not lose his place at the head table, did not lose his freedom to come and go from the center pretty much at will.

He was being given another chance, and he was determined to make the most of it. In the weeks that followed, he cut his Dexamyl intake dramatically, to one a day, and only on days when he felt he absolutely had to have it to fend off the depression. The Doriden, though, was a different story. He stayed off of it for the first few days after the fire, but he truly loved the euphoria it gave him before bedtime and the peaceful sleep that followed. Because he took it only at night after he retired to his bed, he figured no one would know. He also figured that with little or no Dexamyl in his system, Doriden was something he could handle. He would simply have to be more careful with matches.

His next step was to send out signals that he was well on his way to recovery. He believed he was.

"I think," he told Kauffman one morning over breakfast, "that God's leading me back. I feel like I'm starting to function again. Bill, I honestly feel like I'm starting to beat this."

Kauffman seemed to believe him. So did the other staff members. When the burned-out room was repaired, he was permitted to return to it.

He returned also to his physicians when his pills ran low. He even added a new supplier to his list, although this one was not fully a physician. Gordon didn't know exactly what his credentials were. He had simply seen "Dr." in front of the name in the Yellow Pages, and since the address was close to the center, he decided to check it out.

When he got to the office, he went through his usual spiel and concluded by asking for Doriden.

"Doriden," the doctor repeated. Getting up from his desk, he excused himself and disappeared for several minutes.

Gordon was befuddled. This had never happened before. *Maybe he's going to turn me in to someone.* But for the life of him, he couldn't imagine who. He squirmed in his chair and debated whether or not he should get out of there. He couldn't make himself go.

"I'm sorry I took so long," the doctor said, suddenly re-entering the room. "I had to check on something at the pharmacy downstairs. As it turns out, my license doesn't permit me to prescribe Doriden, but I've got something I think will be equally effective. It's called Dalmane. It'll help you with that sleeping problem."

What the doctor failed to tell him was that one of Dalmane's side effects was depression, just what he needed in his already depressed state. But he fought it daily, mostly by announcing to anyone who would listen that he was getting well quickly.

One of the people he told was Bill Albro, when the former Providence parishioner and friend paid a surprise visit at the center.

"I hear you're doing fine," Bill said, sitting across from him in his room that evening.

"I am, Bill, I really am. Coming here was the best thing that could have happened to me. I feel like I have the victory now. I've almost completely beaten this thing."

"Well," said Albro, "it'll be great to see you back in the pulpit again."

"The pulpit?" Gordon said with astonishment. "Bill, my days in the pulpit are over. I can never preach again."

"What do you mean, not preach again?"

"Just what I said. You're looking at an ex-drug addict who also happens to be divorced. Southern Baptists don't want those credentials in a minister."

"Gordon, once you're called, you're called."

"What do you mean?"

"Don't you remember that Bible study week when you taught us the book of Romans? Don't you remember Romans 11:29?"

"Well, of course, I remember. 'For the gifts and calling of God are without repentance.'"

"'The gifts and calling are without repentance,'" Bill repeated.

"Yes, but that doesn't apply to me," Gordon countered.

"Gordon, you taught the lessons, you know full well what it means. When you're called, you're called. You'll preach again. That's what you're in this world to do."

It was something to think about, and in the days that followed, he did, daydreaming, envisioning himself behind the pulpit in a church of his own. When reality came back, he likened those thoughts to a child's fantasy of being an astronaut or a dragon slayer. He couldn't bring himself to believe it could ever happen.

*But maybe,* he said to himself finally, *maybe I could talk to Sunday school classes once in a while, or even Wednesday prayer meetings. And give my testimony. Tell them how God's bringing me back. Maybe someday I could do that.*

He broached the idea with Kauffman. The director bought into it immediately. So did Chaplain Jerry Johnson and his wife, Miriam, who worked in the mission's store. The two had warmed to Gordon from the first moment they met him on the day he arrived at the center. They were missionaries on leave from their post in Vieques, Puerto Rico. Both had outgoing personalities and generous smiles.

The staff's support bolstered his confidence. Still, he felt that even these opportunities would not lead to his ultimate return to the ministry. They would just be something he could do to retrieve a little of what he had lost.

And as it turned out, he didn't have to wait long for an opportunity. After morning services at Midwood one Sunday in the spring of 1974, the pastor, Wendell Davis, asked him if he would consider giving his testimony, not at a Wednesday prayer meeting, or in a Sunday school class, but from the pulpit on a Sunday night. Next Sunday night.

The reality of it hit him hard. This was to be a sermon. He wouldn't be speaking, he would be preaching. He closed his eyes, took a breath, and then said to Davis, "Okay, I'll do it."

He worked on his sermon all week. He wanted it to be as good as any he had ever delivered. He would tell them of his triumphs at Providence, his ultimate fall, and the beginnings of his new journey on the road to victory here at the Christian Rehabilitation Center.

His writing skills came back to him without much difficulty. The hurdle was finding the words to explain that, although he was dealing well with his problem, he had not fully re-emerged as the whole man he had once been. It was important that he say something like that, particularly with Bill and Bettie Kauffman in the audience. It was his loophole, his escape clause, something to keep him from falling completely from their good graces should he be caught in an embarrassing situation with the drugs again. Because if he failed at the rehabilitation center, what was there left for him?

He finished the sermon late that Saturday afternoon. That evening he skipped supper on the chance that he might have to take a Doriden before bedtime. He wanted it to relieve the intensity of the week he had spent writing, and he wanted it for the sleep, for the rest it would afford him. He knew that Sunday night was his big chance to restore some of his credibility. He needed to be as clear-eyed and clear-headed as he could.

He had not taken anything all week, and at ten o'clock that night, he decided he would not take one then. He lay on his bed and listened to music on the radio on his nightstand until he fell asleep sometime after midnight.

He awoke Sunday morning, attended Sunday school and church, and returned to the center for a light lunch and a nap. Late that afternoon, he took a walk. Up Trade Street. Past the Mecklenburg Hotel. On to the Square. North on Tryon. Left on Sixth. Past the old cemetery, Necropolis.

*I'm no longer dead,* he thought. *Not fully alive, but no longer dead.*

At five o'clock, he showered and dressed, then sat at the small desk in his room and read over his sermon for the last time. When he finished, he raised his eyes to the freshly painted ceiling overhead. The fire, one of the lowest points of his last seven years, had taken place only a short time ago, and now here he was, ready to walk out the door and into the pulpit.

At seven, he took his place in a chair beside Reverend Davis. The organ's chords drifted across the half-filled sanctuary, and the worshipers ceased their stirrings and settled.

Gordon felt good. Calm. And he felt even better when, looking over the congregation, he spotted the faces of a half dozen people from his Providence congregation, faithful followers, representative of the many who never gave up on him. Bill and Bettie Kauffman were there, too. He would not let them down.

His mind wandered during the opening prayer and the hymn and the offertory. He thought of the days when all was well with his world, when he was the up-and-coming young pastor with nothing but greatness before him. The greatness, or the chance for it, was gone now, but at least he knew he was still loved by some. Maybe by many. And he was back among them.

He heard Reverend Davis mention his name, and he listened intently as the pastor briefly but glowingly introduced Gordon as a man back from the abyss. Then he was on his feet in front of the microphone, surveying his audience. For the briefest moment, he wondered if he could hold them as he once had, but the self-doubt passed as quickly as it had come. He began to speak.

"Seven years ago, I was pastor of one of the finest churches in this city, some say one of the most challenging opportunities in the Baptist denomination in this state. But my heart had become too attached to a number of things, including being pastor of that nice affluent church. This caused me to lose the main thrust of my calling. I was so busy attending to the administrative needs of that pastorate, and so interested in the construction of a lovely home, that I began to drift away from the close communion I had once had with the Lord. Like Peter, I was beginning to follow him afar off. Ministers can become so interested in washing ecclesiastical pots and pans that they lose the fire of their message and they get less and less done for the Lord where He really needs their witness.

"God had called me long, long ago to His Gospel ministry. But now He was going to have to deal harshly with me in order to bring me back to my main assignment: to preach Christ and Him crucified and to expend the gifts He gave me, winning the lost and dealing with the great needs of men. So God allowed my world to tumble down. He had to strip me of the things that had come to fill up my life, drain me of those things, so that I, being empty, could be filled again with Him. So He took away that beloved church. He took away my wife. He took away my four sons for awhile. He took away my beautiful home. He took away my above-average income as pastors' salaries go. He took away just about everything. I had had no reason to suspect that I was going to be stripped of my all, so in my pained reaction and astonishment, I sought to deaden the pain and restlessness and sleeplessness by using pills. Of course I was to learn that you cannot calm with medication a spirit that God is troubling. But I was not going to learn that for a long time. I plunged deeper and deeper into my desperate effort to get out from under the cloud of depression. I went to an expensive hospital thinking I could get back on my feet. The cost was $260 a week. I emerged eight months later worse off than when I had entered. Nothing but more pills. In fact, I had used them on the sly while in this treatment center.

"I knew I had to find employment, so I drew up a resume outlining my background, my college and seminary degrees, my professional history and began to distribute this resume to scores of companies from "New York to Atlanta. Nothing in the secular world opened.

"Here I was, an able-bodied man with a fairly impressive professional history and two academic degrees who couldn't even get a night watchman's job. God was in control, and He was steering me towards something unbelievably wonderful. That's the kind of a God He is. But He works slowly.

"It has been said the mills of God grind exceedingly slow, but they grind exceedingly fine. So I was to stand on life's sidelines for a while longer. I plunged even deeper into pills and hospitalizations. They were not working. I was restless, despondent, confused. Finally one day I decided to leave yet another hospital where I need not ever have gone in the first place and go to my hometown, there to inhabit an apartment and sit for the rest of my life.

"In a way, this was a form of committing suicide. Finally God was ready to act through my dear friend and former church member, Dr. Grady Wilson. God put me in touch with Reverend Kauffman, who astounded me when he said, I dare you to come work and worship with us for twelve months, and I'll guarantee you will be back in the pulpit preaching, and your witness will be ten times greater ever than before.' I couldn't believe this. It seemed that all doors to employment had been closed. I thought my beloved ministry was especially closed forever. But this was God's challenge to me and God's man delivering the challenge. I accepted the dare.

"I knelt beside my bed in a dingy hotel room and said, 'Lord, I'm flat on my back in life, and the only way I can look is up and so now I look up to you. I've tried everything I know to try. It hasn't worked. I just can't put the pieces of this puzzle together. So, I hereby yield. Please take over. Please come, Lord Jesus, into every compartment of my life. Invade me. Nothing in my hand I bring, simply to Thy cross I cling.'

"So I packed up all my worldly possessions in one suitcase and went to the Rescue Mission. God's reaction has been overwhelming. He's done the following things: One, He gave me peace. Two, He gave me sleep, perhaps one of His most precious gifts, for as I walked the floor at night for years, how insomnia ate upon me. But since that first night at the mission, I've slept like a baby. Three, God also gave me renewed assurance of His need upon my life.

"A night or two after I went to the center, they placed a paper on my dinner plate which read, 'Please be patient with me, God is not through with me yet.' And this has been the unfolding story of my life in the past few months. People were so patient with me. I guess they knew God wasn't through with me yet. And yet for years I had thought He was.

"Four, I was given a lovely room, excellent food, and the companionship of the inspiring staff headed by my two great Christian mentors, Bill and Bettie Kauffman.

"Yes, my witness is ten times greater than it ever was before. Because God let me go into the valley of tribulation with the pills, I can now identify with men who also have walked the road of addiction.

"That is what the payoff for me is. I'm back in alignment with God. I have one room to live in instead of that five-bedroom mansion I once built, and my income now can't begin to compare with what it was then, but I'd rather have the joy of helping lead a man, through Christ, to a glorious new life, than to have all the mansions and the big churches and the nice paychecks in the world. This is the real payoff.

"God has spoken to me as never before in earlier years. He spoke to me one night in our chapel service as the song leader stopped us on the fourth verse of a hymn and said, 'Just let me read this verse; we won't sing it.' And he read these words to my thrilled heart:

*When through fiery trials thy pathway shall lie,*
*My grace, all-sufficient, shall be thy supply:*
*The flame shall not hurt thee;*
*I only design Thy dross to consume, and thy gold to refine.*

"God was speaking loud and clear, just to me. He spoke again one night soon after I went to the center. I awoke from a sound sleep in the night and all that was on my mind was the word 'David.' I took the Bible and began to read about David, how he committed the great sin of adultery and then attempted to cover it up with the sin of murder. And yet after that, he was called a man after God's own heart. I wondered how that could be. And God seemed to say,

'Look further.' So I finally found the fifty-first Psalm, where David, after his great sins, poured out his heart to God in repentance and begged, 'Create in me a clean heart, oh God. Hide Thy face from my sins. Renew a right spirit within me. Restore to me the joy of my salvation. Deliver me from blood guiltiness, oh God: the God of my salvation.'

"As I lay back down on my bed, God seemed to say, 'That's why David was called a man after God's own heart. He repented. He got back in line with me. And if he can commit such sins and repent and then be called a man after God's own heart, I can work the same thing in your life.'

"Yes, God has spoken to me as never before. He has restored to me a renewed place. God is wonderful. And I earnestly ask for the Christian people who hear me this evening to pray that God may continue to abound in my life.

"My life is not perfected, of course. My life is like when you go into a darkroom and are developing a picture. After you put the negative in the chemicals, the picture slowly begins to emerge. It's not clear at first, but as you wait longer and longer, it becomes clearer.

"What God is doing in my life is making all things, good and bad, work together for good for one who loved Him and who still loves Him and is called according to His purpose.

"A man once said that the greatest thing a person could accomplish is to be able to walk away from yesterday. I think that's what I'm trying to do, walk away from yesterday."

Then the service was over. He had done it, had stood again in the pulpit and preached again to the multitudes. And now he was standing in the doorway receiving the compliments and well-wishes of the departing congregation. As he exchanged hugs and handshakes, he felt for the first time in many years the warm glow of reciprocal love between pastor and people.

What he did not feel, indeed, could not feel in his addiction and his denial was remorse for the lies he had just spoken. If Gordon Weekley had been well, he would never have laid the blame for his addiction at the feet of God, but he had done exactly that. If Gordon Weekley had been well, he'd never have said he shouldn't have been hospitalized, but say it he had.

*What value would it be to anyone if I said drugs were the cause of my downfall, not the result of it? If I didn't preach that I was back in God's bosom, what would I preach at all?*

Gordon Weekley was a long way from being well.

## NINETEEN

He felt now that the sermon had helped him clear a huge hurdle on the road back to respectability, and apparently he was not alone in his thinking. A few weeks after that triumphant night, Bill Kauffman sent for him.

"Gordon," Kauffman said, as the two sat facing each other across a desk, "how would you like to be Jerry's assistant?"

He could scarcely believe it. First his own room. Then the sermon. Now assistant chaplain.

Gordon knew Kauffman desperately wanted him to succeed, partly out of compassion and partly because of the director's friendship with Grady Wilson. Grady, after all, had put Gordon in his hands.

Whatever the reasons for the promotion, Gordon readily accepted it. Now he was no longer a client of the center, although he had never truly been treated as one. Clients didn't sit at head tables.

His duties, as Kauffman outlined them, were to be among the men and to talk with them and counsel them when they asked for it. Kauffman also wanted him to give his testimony to whatever audience would hear it. In the months that followed, he repeated his Midwood sermon to a host of attentive and appreciative civic and church audiences, including Carmel Baptist, at the invitation of Jarvis Warren, his former deacon chairman at Providence.

Almost everywhere he went, he encountered someone he knew from Providence or from a previous social circle. Now, he was happy to see them and happy to be seen.

He was seeing more of Steve and Dan, too. Steve by this time had graduated from Wake Forest and was working in an industrial supply company. Dan had moved from hospital work to construction. The two younger boys, still with Norma Lou and her husband, were being educated in military school, and except for an occasional get-together at a neutral site, his contact with them was mostly by phone. He didn't talk with them much because he thought Norma Lou's husband had a deep dislike for him.

Gordon was sorry about that but didn't dwell on it. He dwelt instead on his rediscovered respectability. He particularly enjoyed his equal status with the staff.

His drug problem, when it was mentioned at all, was spoken about in the past tense, and no one seemed to pay any attention to his leaving most of his food untouched.

At the dinner table one evening, he and another former-client-turned-staff-member entranced their audience with recounts of some of their drug binges.

"I remember one night," said the former client, "I was so desperate for a fix, I took a handful of Primatine tablets. They worked, too."

They didn't work well for Gordon. The feeling he got from trying them a few days later was more like an alcohol-induced high than the energizing, euphoric feeling he had gotten from Dexamyl. Luckily, he tried them in the evening in the privacy of his room. When the high faded, he resolved to stay with Dalmane or, preferably, Doriden.

He felt some guilt about his continued use of those drugs, but he also thought he was in good control of them. He had after all abandoned the Dexamyl and was getting through the days without it, although his battle with depression was unceasing. He knew he would lose the battle if it weren't for the beautiful thirty minutes of glow he felt each night when whichever of the sleeping medications he was taking kicked in.

That glow and the one he got from acceptance by friends and peers kept him going. When Jerry and Miriam Johnson announced in mid-1974 that they were returning to Puerto Rico to resume their missionary duties, he felt that his stature improved even more. Kauffman didn't replace Jerry with a head chaplain; he replaced him with a man named Bill Reynolds and made Bill an assistant chaplain, too.

Reynolds was pastor of a small, struggling Methodist church on Mount Holly Road, west of Charlotte. Somehow he and Kauffman had worked it out so he could continue serving that church while also performing his duties at the rehabilitation center.

He insisted on being called "Doctor" and claimed to be a graduate of a seminary, but Gordon had his doubts. Nevertheless, the two got along well and neither seemed to get in the other's way. It was hard for Gordon to dislike anyone, and he tried very hard not to dislike Bill Reynolds.

In fact, in a oblique way, he had Bill Reynolds to thank for Misty. He was guest preaching at Bill's church one evening in December, giving his testimony. When the service was over and all but one of the congregation had left, he picked up his topcoat from a chair in the choir, then said his goodbyes to Bill and made his way toward the door.

The one remaining person, a petite, pretty woman in her mid-forties, was waiting there for him.

I'm Misty DeBruhl," she said, holding out her hand. "I just wanted to tell you how much I enjoyed your sermon."

"Well, thank you," he said. "You seem to have a fine group of people in your church."

"Yes, they do seem to be very nice. I'm just visiting here from out of town. My sister, Lu Ann Harrison, and her husband, Archie, are members."

"I see," said Gordon, noticing now her strawberry blond hair. "Where are you from?" he asked, almost stammering. "Weaverville. It's near Asheville."

"Yes, I know of it. I spent some time in the Asheville area," he said, wishing he could think of something a little more clever, but the only thing that came to mind was Appalachian Hall.

"I'd love to hear you again sometime."

"Yes, yes, that would be nice," he said. "What I mean is, it wouldn't be nice for you to hear me, it would be nice of you." Flushing, he added, "Did that make any sense?"

"Of course it did," she said. "I'll be here for several weeks. Why don't you call me and tell me where your next sermon will be?"

"I'll do that," he promised, and then hastily said goodbye.

He may have been driving a battered old car home that night, but he was riding on cloud nine.

Gordon began to court Misty DeBruhl. He called her the next day for a date and went out with her every night through the remainder of her visit. With his thirty-dollar-a-week assistant chaplain's pay and Social Security disability benefits, he could afford to take her only to an occasional movie and a couple of dinners at inexpensive restaurants. Most of the time, they sat alone together in the Harrison's living room watching television and talking. Misty did most of the talking. She seemed charged with warmth and energy, and it radiated over him like the sun.

It took him only a few days to realize he was in love. He didn't summon the courage to tell her for weeks.

"I'm in love, too," she said, curling up in his arms on the Harrisons' sofa, "and have been since the moment I saw you."

Her words pushed him almost to tears. *She loves me,* he thought, *loves me in spite of everything that's happened in my life.* He had told her everything that had happened, in far greater detail than time would permit in his pulpit testimonials. The only thing he didn't tell her was that he was still doing drugs, but he didn't think that was really necessary, because he was confining himself almost exclusively now to Doriden. He felt he was handling it quite well. The way Gordon saw it, the very fact that he was involved in a romance proved that he was functioning just fine.

Besides, he was speaking almost every Sunday now, and at Wednesday night prayer meetings. He was becoming known again, and accepted, greeted warmly wherever he went. Admiring voices spoke their admiration for him. He had escaped Satan's grasp and returned again to the Lord. He was special.

True, he would never again have the house on the hill. Never again shepherd a flock. But he had love—and respectability. He was on his way to becoming the Gordon Weekley of old, albeit on a smaller scale.

He was also well on his way to becoming a husband. In February, he asked her. Without hesitating, she said yes. Yes, she would marry him. Yes, she would come and live with him in a Spartan apartment that was part of the mission's complex. Yes, it was all right with her if they would never have much, so long as they had each other.

Gordon had told Kauffman of his intention to ask Misty to marry him, and when the director found out that she had accepted, he seemed almost as excited as the groom-to-be. After all, Gordon had been almost a hopeless case when he had come under Bill's wing. Now things were looking up very much indeed, for Gordon and for Bill.

"I want you to marry us, Bill. I want you to officiate."

"I'll be happy to," Bill said. "Where do you want to do it?"

"Providence Baptist Church, if they'll have me."

Providence Baptist was fine with Henry Crouch, the minister who had helped take the church to even greater heights. They were different men, these Providence preachers, with different styles to their pastorates. Gordon had been hands-on, presiding more with his heart than his head. Henry was more corporate in his approach, delegating responsibilities and making certain those responsibilities were carried out. If Gordon was idealistic, Henry was realistic. If Gordon led by serving, Henry served by leading.

Gordon had not set foot in Providence since 1967, and now, on March 15, 1975, he was back—if not in the pulpit, at least at the altar.

He took his vows from Bill Kauffman before a sanctuary filled nearly to capacity with former congregation members.

He had chosen Providence for the wedding because it was home to him, but like a student who's been to college or a young soldier who's gone to war, it was a home he could never fully return to. He could never finally leave it, either. He would always be a part of Providence, and Providence would always be a part of him.

Somewhere on the edge of his consciousness lay another reason he chose to wed there: to announce, by his presence, that he was back. Back from the abyss. Back in the mainstream. Leading a normal life, a credible life, a life very much like the life he had led in those days of his pastorate before drugs brought him to his knees. He believed that.

What was true was the depth of love he felt those few moments at that time and place. He loved the church that had once been his, the people in it, and the person by his side promising to love and cherish him all the days of her life.

They were lovely days in the beginning. After a shoestring honeymoon in New York, the couple moved into one of the apartments at the center. Gordon resumed his duties as chaplain. With Misty by his side, he felt almost whole again. He had no idea where life would take him—maybe no further than where he was now, but that was all right with him. Never again would he have to cross the street to avoid the embarrassment of encountering someone he knew. He could hold his head up, and he did.

What he didn't do was slack off on the Doriden. In fact, with the apartment protecting him from outside eyes, he felt quite comfortable with it. It obviously wasn't affecting his performance because neither Kauffman nor Misty mentioned anything remotely relating to his problem.

But Misty was a traditionalist, a wife who would rarely challenge her husband's attitudes or actions. She had once issued a challenge to her first husband on the subject of alcohol and had found herself on the sidewalk, locked out of his house and his heart. She stayed silent on the subject of Doriden, immersing herself in her new role as chaplain's wife, helping out at the center however she was needed, and providing Gordon with a comfortable and loving place to come home to.

She also enjoyed living in the same town with her sister, Lu Ann. They had always been close, and now they were seeing each other several times a week.

It was Lu Ann who called her one afternoon with exciting news. The television series "Moving On" was scheduled to film an episode in Charlotte, and in an audition for local extras, Lu Ann had been of those selected.

"Moving On" was the story of two truck drivers, one a redneck, the other a college graduate, crisscrossing the country together in their eighteen-wheeler and finding action and adventure along the way. It was a popular program in the seventies, and the filming created a stir in Charlotte.

Gordon and Misty were thrilled for Lu Ann and decided to go watch her scene being filmed. The location was on the northern outskirts of Charlotte, at the Southern 500 restaurant, a popular stopping-off place for truck drivers and stock-car racing fans.

"I have an idea," said Misty. "There's a motel right near there. Let's get a room for the night before, and then we'll just scoot over to the restaurant in the morning."

It sounded like a good idea to Gordon, a chance for a respite from the center.

They checked in around seven and decided to spend the evening relaxing in their comfortable room. Misty relaxed by watching a beauty pageant on television. Gordon relaxed by taking three Doriden.

Before the drug took effect, she had been chatting with him in her bubbly way about this or that contestant, and how well the show was being staged, and how good the talent was. Now she was strangely silent. He wondered if maybe she was getting sleepy. He certainly was.

He awoke the next morning to a half-empty bed. Groggy and still a little high from the Doriden, he stumbled across the floor to the bathroom and washed his face in cold water.

*I wonder where she is,* he thought, as he walked back into the bedroom, patting himself dry with the towel. *Probably getting herself some breakfast.*

That's not what the note on the dresser said.

The note said that she was going on to watch the filming herself. It also said, "...if you can't correct whatever is wrong with you, I think we should discuss a parting of the ways."

What she wrote that morning was all that was said about the matter. She was too timid to confront him or maybe, because of the volatility of her previous marriage, too frightened.

Her note worked—for a while. For a while, he did what he always did when he faced a serious challenge on his drug usage: he quit for several days to prove to himself and his accusers that he was not a slave to the medications. Then gradually, surreptitiously, he began taking small doses every few days until he was convinced the dust had settled.

It settled this time, at least in his mind, in about a week. Then it was back to business as usual. Nothing more on the subject was forthcoming from Misty. If the Kauffmans looked at him with slightly jaundiced eyes now and then, he didn't notice. Besides, they knew nothing about the motel incident.

So Gordon had averted another crisis, and as the trauma of Misty's note faded in the months that followed, he began to realize he was not the same man that drugs had beaten into submission in the late sixties. They no longer controlled him; he controlled them. If he needed evidence to prove that, it was all around him. His relationship with his boys was good. His work at the center was going well. His testimony in the churches and civic clubs brought praise from old friends who knew of his past and from new acquaintances who upon hearing his story were awe-struck at his remarkable comeback.

Virtually everything he had lost he had regained to one degree or another. He no longer had a house on the hill, but he had a place to call home, and it was far removed from Broughton Hospital. He no longer had a church pastorate, but he had a wide audience with his speaking engagements. He no longer had a true congregation, but he had a group of desperate men desperately in need of love. And love was something that Gordon Weekley dispensed freely.

Gordon Weekley was back—back to preaching, to counseling, to working sixteen-hour days, to saying yes to every request anyone made of him. It felt good to be in control of his life again. When depression reared its ugly head, as it did almost daily, he knew night was coming and Doriden was coming with it. That was something to look forward to.

Mornings were also something to look forward too now, because now his days were filled with meaningful tasks, the most meaningful of which was bringing broken men to God.

The other side of that coin, of course, is sending men and women to God, a task that every preacher or chaplain performs with mixed emotions. There is the sorrow of loss and sympathy for the family. There is also the joy of the Promise fulfilled.

But the sorrow is always first. Gordon felt it deeply in September of 1976 when he learned of Jack Groaner's death. Jack had been a client at the center, and over time, he had found his way to God and out of his addiction. Along the way, he had found friends in Gordon Weekley and Bill Kauffman and the other members of the staff.

"I want you to assist me with the service," Kauffman said.

"I'd be happy to," Gordon answered.

And so, on a Thursday morning filled early with the warmth of late summer, in a cemetery in Gastonia, a small town near Charlotte, the friends and family of Jack Groaner gathered around his grave to say goodbye. They sat in folding chairs under the green canopy and looked across the casket at the two men of God who stood facing them.

Kauffman spoke first, offering words of praise for Jack and comfort and reassurance to those who had loved him.

Gordon held an open Bible in his hand, poised to read the words he had read so many times before: *In my Father's house are many mansions. If it were not so, I would have told you. I go to prepare a place for you. And if I go and prepare a place for you, I will come again, and receive you unto myself; that where I am, there ye may be also.*

He did not look down at the text just yet. The words were so familiar there was no need even to glance at them before the time came to read aloud. Instead, he tried to concentrate on what Bill was saying. He found that he could not.

He was tired. The day before had been particularly busy, and although there had been no catastrophes, not much had gone smoothly either. It was one of those days when his mental door had opened wide enough to let more than a small amount of depression slip in. By mid-evening, he had been ready for the blessed relief of the Doriden— not one, but two.

When he had passed through sleep and back into waking, he was wearier than he had been the night before. The heat of this new day was not helping matters. Even the shade of the canopy afforded small respite from it. He would be all right, though. He would get some coffee after the service.

*Poor Jack,* he thought, b*ut he'll find peace there. Eternal happiness.* The tent was so silent. Was Bill finished? Yes. It was his turn. He would read now.

He glanced down at the page, found verse two, and read: "In my Father's housch...'"

*Housch?* he thought to himself. *No, house.*

"In my Father's housch are many massions,'" he continued.

He was so very tired, but he had to get through this. He read on, stumbling and slurring words as he went, going from bad to much worse until it was mercifully over.

*My God,* he thought, the fear rising in his heart, *what's wrong with me?*

"In Jesus' name, amen," he heard Kauffman say, and then everyone was up and walking away from the canopy toward the waiting cars.

*Is it over?* he asked himself. *It must be.*

It was over. The following morning Bill Kauffman called him into his office and fired him.

"I'm sorry, Gordon," he said sadly, "but you're just going to have to leave."

*Leave?* he thought, fear racing through his veins. *How can I leave? There's noplace else to go. This is the last stop.*

He quickly built his case. "Bill," he said, "I know I didn't do well yesterday. I'm sure that's why you feel compelled to let me go. But don't you remember the sermon I preached at Midwood? I said I was like a picture being developed in the darkroom. I'm emerging, slowly, like that picture, but I'm not all the way back yet."

"No, you're not Gordon. You're not even part of the way back. And you're not fooling anybody. Except maybe yourself."

Had Gordon been sent to the mission by someone other than Grady Wilson, a man of great stature in the Christian community, a confrontation might have come much sooner. Now, not even Grady could save Gordon. The kid gloves were off.

Gordon tried one more time. "Bill, you have my solemn word: nothing like this will ever happen again."

The look in Bill Kauffman's eyes told him there would be no reprieve. He was out.

It was November 1967 all over again, the day he resigned his ministry. Only this time, the ministry resigned him. And this time, in a sudden flash, he realized there was no more hope, no more tomorrow-it-will-be-all-right. It would not be all right tomorrow. It would never be all right again.

"I'm sorry," he said quietly to Bill Kauffman, as the tears brimmed his eyes.

"I'm sorry, too," Kauffman replied gently.

There was nothing more to be said, nothing more to do but pack. Misty was there when he got back to the apartment next door. "We have to go," he said. "We have to leave."

"Leave? What do you mean? Leave for where?"

"I wish I knew," he said.

He told her what happened. He had to stand and watch her world collapse, just as he had watched his own only moments before.

"Where will we go?" she asked in a voice so quiet he could barely hear.

"I don't know, maybe your sister's bungalow for a few days. I...I can't think of anywhere else just now."

Then there was a long silence between them. Gordon could hear the motor of an electric clock on the wall above them.

"I'll go on over to the grocery store and get some boxes," he said finally. "I know Bill's not going to be tough on us about leaving, but I think we ought to be out by Sunday, or Monday at the latest."

They spent the rest of that day packing. Misty called her sister Lu Ann and got permission for them to use the bungalow for a while. Gordon was relieved that at least they would have a roof over their heads and crushed by being once again taken in, given shelter, like a stray dog.

If there was any light in this darkest of Gordon Weekley's failures, it was that Misty was packing with him. *Maybe she'll leave me next week, or next month, but she's not leaving me now, though I wouldn't blame her if she did.*

They packed until late into the evening and then climbed into bed exhausted. Gordon did not sleep until the early hours of the morning. He lay looking at the ceiling, watching his life go by. The scene he played over and over again in his mind was the lunch with Dr. Doe.

"I'm having trouble sleeping," he had said. "I wonder if there's anything you can give me?"

That had been eighteen years ago, and the sun had shone on him then as it had on relatively few others. It would not again, certainly not on September 4, 1976, the day just beginning.

It was a day of more packing, more tears in Misty's eyes, more resignation in Gordon's heart.

At ten o'clock that night, the phone rang. He ignored it. He was two rooms away, and he didn't have the energy or the desire to answer it. Whoever it was, it didn't matter. There was nothing to talk about. With anyone.

The ringing stopped and was replaced by the distant sound of Misty's voice. When she didn't call out to him, he assumed it was for her, and he went on packing dishes slowly, methodically, lethargically into the grocery store boxes.

From time to time he could hear her over the clank of the plates and bowls. He didn't know or care who was on the other end of the phone.

After half an hour, she called to him. "Gordon, it's John Hatcher."

He put down a plate and walked quickly to the doorway of the living room. When she looked up, he made X's with both arms, silently waving off the call. When she didn't respond, he whispered harshly, 'I don't want to talk to him."

Hatcher was a member of the mission's board of directors and highly supportive of Gordon's efforts at rehabilitation. Gordon was fond of him but in no mood to hear what were sure to be words of consolation. Consolation would not heal the wound he had suffered. Nothing would heal it. Not now.

"He's coming, John," Misty said into the phone, and Gordon's eyes flashed with anger at her betrayal.

He took the receiver from her hand, steadied himself for a moment, and then spoke.

"Hello, John," he said calmly, warmly, putting on his best face for his unseen sympathizer.

John Hatcher had compassion for him but not sympathy.

"Gordon," he said, "this thing has been going on a very long time. From what you've told me, you've tried everything. Psychiatrists. Hospital treatments. The rehabilitation center. And nothing's worked, has it?"

"No, John, I'm afraid it hasn't," he said softly.

"Well, I think there's one thing you haven't tried. I don't think you've tried God."

"John, I'm sorry, but you're wrong." Gordon was stung. *Of course I've tried God. God's been my life!* "What do you think I've been doing all these years? I've *prayed* about this."

"I'm sure you have, Gordon. But have you really, truly, given this over to Him?"

"I can't tell you how many times I've asked God for help."

"Gordon, maybe you need to give yourself over to Him, along with the problem."

"I committed myself to God a long, long time ago, John." *Why do they think I haven't tried to deal with this? I have. I've tried.*

"Recommit yourself, Gordon. Recommit yourself. Go talk to Him. Pray with me now, please, Gordon, and then give the phone to Misty and go and talk to Him."

John Hatcher prayed for a lost man and asked God to return him to the fold. When the prayer was over, he said, "Go on now, Gordon. Go and talk to Him yourself."

Gordon handed the phone to Misty, then turned and went down the hall and into the darkness of his bedroom. At the side of the bed, he stopped, closed his eyes, and slowly sank to his knees under the weight of his own burdened soul.

He put his elbows on the mattress, intertwined the fingers of his hands, and in the blackness and the silence, sent his heart out through the void in search of its Creator, carrying with it a white flag of surrender.

"God," he prayed, "I can't handle it anymore. I just can't handle it anymore. I've gone as far as I can go. I'm getting ready to lose everything all over again. What ground I've gained, I'm losing all over again. I beg you, God, either take me from this world this night or redeem me from this lie I live. I've been telling everybody I'm getting better. I've been telling myself that for years. But I'm not. I know now that I can't have it both ways. I can't live for me and for You. And if I can't live for You, I don't care much about living at all. Because, God, I can't handle my life. I thought I could. I thought I could handle anything. I thought I could even handle You. That day in the hotel, just before I came to the center, I prayed to You and told You I was yielding my will, but You knew I wasn't yielding and I knew I wasn't yielding. And we both know what's happened since. Whatever happens now is in Your hands, dear God. I'm going to sleep now. Do with me what You will. Thy will be done."

Exhausted, broken, humbled, he rose to his feet, pulled down the covers, climbed into bed with his clothes still on, and fell immediately into sleep, neither knowing nor caring what morning would bring. It was out of his hands.

*Come all ye that are... heavy laden, and I will give you rest.* He had preached those words often to others. Now for the first time in many years, maybe for the first time ever, he had truly taken his burden to the Lord. For this moment, he was not Gordon Weekley, Furman honor graduate, or Gordon Weekley, Providence pastor, or even Gordon Weekley, pastor-turned-addict. He was simply a man, a human being like all other human beings, born into this world with nothing and destined to die in it, either this night or some other, taking nothing with him. If God had a plan for him, so be it. He had neither the strength nor the will to carry out a plan of his own.

How he had acquired his burden in the first place was anybody's guess. Somehow, perhaps, the ingredients that made up the man, both physiological and psychological, had produced a recipe for addiction. There were people in his mother's family who had histories of devastating depression. He had come from a loving but very rigid family, and without neighborhood children to play with, he had spent his early years as a "little man" instead of a little boy. The little man had learned quickly that being good, pleasing people, brought favor. The church

was the major part of his world even as a child, and the church too favored those who were good, those who pleased.

Gordon was a good man, but must a man cast in the role of goodness by those around him live every moment of his life in strict accord with their script for him? Gordon had started smoking at age fourteen, perhaps a small act of rebellion. If it was, it was a rebellion he kept hidden from his parents, just as he kept his drug addiction hidden from his friends and family and even himself.

Maybe drugs had given him relief from carrying the burdens of others. Gordon wasn't just cast in that empathetic role by others. It was who he was.

And he was something else, too: a man who loved his successes, the rapid growth of Providence, his ties to the Billy Graham team, his beloved house on

Country Lane. His major accomplishments came after his addiction was begun, and perhaps his belief in his own abilities made him think he could handle anything, even Doriden and Dexamyl.

Whatever it was, Gordon Weekley needed a miracle. He needed the sun to stand still, the sea to part. He needed Lazarus to rise from the dead or an angel to appear with glad tidings.

Gordon saw no visions that night. He just went to sleep, and in the morning, he woke up. He opened his eyes and saw only the ceiling of his bedroom, badly in need of painting.

Something had changed, though, in the night, in the hours between sleeping and waking. He noticed not what he felt but what he didn't feel. Facing another day of disgrace and humiliation, he felt no anxiety. Facing a day without Dexamyl or Doriden, he felt no desire for them.

He had slept well, deep beyond dreams. He had awakened calm, refreshed, at peace.

It was 6:30 A.M., September 5, 1976. He slipped out of bed quietly so as not to disturb Misty. He showered, shaved, dressed, and made his way to the kitchen for coffee. He sat at the table there and stared out the window overlooking the mission's parking lot and main building. Bill Kauffman would arrive around eight this Sunday morning. Gordon would be there just after him.

He had plenty of time to work out exactly what he would say to his former director, but he didn't use his time for that. He decided he would let his heart speak and not his head. As for right here, right now, he would sit at the table and enjoy a tranquility he had not known for many, many years.

*It's so utterly simple I couldn't see it. I preached it over and over and over, and I didn't see it. How could I have missed it? 'Give yourself over to God, put yourself in God's hands.' How many times have I said that? 'Pride goeth before destruction.' How many times have I said that, too? All these years, the only thing standing between me and God, between me and redemption from this addiction, was me.*

He smiled ruefully and shook his head at his own revelation. *Well, I've got the rest of my life to live. Let's see if I can do something worthwhile with it.*

He finished his coffee, got up, and left the apartment. He decided he would be waiting at the center when Bill Kauffman arrived.

He went down the stairs and walked the fifty paces to the main building. He noticed that the director's car was in the parking lot.

Gordon pushed open the door and smiled a "good morning" to the desk man sitting in a cubicle just inside the entrance. He turned left, mounted a short flight of stairs, and walked straight to Bill's office. The light was on. The door was open. *But I doubt if he's expecting me.*

Kauffman was just getting settled in behind his desk when Gordon greeted him.

"Got a minute, Bill?"

"Sure, Gordon," he said matter-of-factly, waving toward a chair facing the desk, "what can I do for you?"

In virtually every conversation of importance in his life, Gordon had measured his words, making sure he said the right things. It was the nature of the man who always wanted to please others, always wanted to be loved and accepted, never wanted to offend or to anger. Now, in this moment of utmost importance, he was going without a map, letting his feelings and words tumble out to his director.

"Bill," he said, "I need to convince you of something, and I know full well my credibility is not beyond reproach right now."

He paused, waiting for affirmation of that statement from the director. None came.

"We preachers talk about miracles all the time...about the awesome power of God. Well, Bill, last night I was on the receiving end of that power. A miracle happened. Not some Lourdes-type thing, nothing like that, but a miracle all the same.

"I gave it over to God last night...the burden...admitted, finally, that I couldn't handle it. And when I woke up this morning, everything had changed.

"A miracle," he said, wonderment in his voice. "I believe in miracles. Why am I so astounded? Maybe I'm not astounded. Maybe I'm just excited. For the first time since I can remember, for the first time in years, I opened my eyes and faced a morning without worrying about how I was going to get through the day. And look at the day I'm facing—a day when I'm supposed to finish my packing and leave.

"I don't want to leave, Bill. As certainly as I believe in God, I believe I'm here for a reason. I'm here to help other men find the way back. I can't leave. I need this job. I want this job. No, it's not a job, it's what my life has to be about from now on: helping other addicts. My life is His now, Bill, not mine anymore."

The director sat looking at him for a long moment, toying with a pencil he held in his hand. Gordon felt the silence but did not fear it. He had said what his heart had told him to say. That was all he could do.

"Go tell the men that," Bill said finally. "Go into the pulpit tomorrow morning at chapel and tell them what you've told me."

"I'd be happy to. Does this mean you're reinstating me?"

"Go into the pulpit, Gordon. We'll talk after."

The Monday chapel service was scheduled for seven o'clock, leaving Gordon scarcely twenty-four hours to prepare himself for what he was going to say. As he walked back to his apartment, a door in his mind opened and brought back the memory of a similar situation long ago, in 1964: the return from exile in Pennsylvania and the deacons' meeting that lasted until two in the morning and would have gone longer if Arthur Smith hadn't halted the group's debate about Gordon's future by suggesting that he preach one more sermon the following Sunday.

He had had a week to get ready for that sermon, and he had crafted every word like a mason chiseling in stone. It was a masterpiece, a masterpiece of deception and denial. This time there would be no preparation. This time he would speak from his heart to the men just as he had to Bill.

He would speak from his heart from now on, whether to a congregation or simply to the people around him who loved him and hung on to him through all his deceptions and denials. He would speak right now to Misty.

She was up, working her way through a pile of clothes on the bedroom floor deciding which to pack and which to discard.

"Good morning," she sang out with a cheerfulness that Gordon thought did not come as easily to her as it usually did.

"Misty," he said, dropping onto the side of the bed, "Come sit with me. There's something I need to tell you."

"But I've got to sort these...."

"Misty," he said again. She got up and came to him.

"Something's happened," he began, and for the next several minutes he took her on the journey that had begun the night before with John Hatcher and ended that morning with Bill Kauffman.

"Oh, Gordon," she said when he finished, "I don't know whether Bill's going to keep you or not, and I don't care. I mean, I do care, but that's not what's important."

"I know what you mean, dear," he said, "but I want to stay here very much—not because of what people will say if I have to leave, but because I belong here. In any event, we'll know in the morning." With that, he smiled gently and kissed her on the forehead.

"I'm going to take a walk," he said. "I want to think about what happened to me last night, or maybe I just want to enjoy what happened. I'll be back in about an hour. There are some places I want to see."

He wanted to see the Mecklenburg Hotel and the Presto Grill. He wanted to see the old cemetery, Necropolis. He wanted to meet somebody on the street, no one in particular, just somebody he knew from the early days, the golden days. He wanted to look him in the eye and smile and walk over and greet him. He had run away from old acquaintances for years; now, if he had the chance, he would run to them.

The chance didn't come that day, but in a way, it came the next at the seven o'clock roll call and chapel service. He stood at the altar alongside Bill Kauffman and watched the hundred clients of the center shuffle quietly through the door and make their way to their seats.

These were his friends and his acquaintances, and he had let them down with his deception, just as he had let down his Providence pastorate. Letting them down was worse, because they were addicts. The last thing they needed was a chaplain running on drugs.

They liked him, even loved him. He loved them, too. Now, God and Bill Kauffman willing, he might be able to help lead them, or at least some of them, out of their private hells.

"William Anderson," Kauffman called out.

"Here," came a voice from the back.

"John Akers," Kauffman said.

"Present," answered John Akers.

Down the list the director went, through Davis and Hargood and Nance and Williams and the rest. Then it was time for the prayer, and then it was time for Gordon.

"Gentlemen," Kauffman said when the men had settled back into their seats and the rustling had quieted, "I want to present someone to you today. I want to present the new Gordon Weekley."

Gordon stepped forward from where he had been standing and joined Bill Kauffman at the podium. He reached out his right hand and Kauffman took it. He reached out his left arm and drew the director into an embrace.

Then Gordon Weekley turned and faced the world.

Three days later, he would have to face the world inside himself. For Gordon, the third day of abstinence had always been the worst. His mind and body would cry out for Dexamyl and Doriden like a desperate street beggar accosting passersby.

But when he awoke on this third day, he heard in himself no cry for relief or replenishment. He had no withdrawal symptoms at all. The world within Gordon Weekley was at peace. A large part of his heart had told him it would be, but a small part, the part that humanness reserves for itself, had had its doubts. He remembered that Christ's disciples and followers at times had had their doubts, too.

When the withdrawal symptoms didn't come, Gordon admonished himself for even thinking about them. *I have surrendered my will to God. All I have to do is let that will be done. He gave me a miracle. All I have to do is accept it.*

In its own way, addiction is a god, too, and delusion and denial the angels that guard its throne. After eighteen years, Gordon Weekley got past the guards, confronted his adversary, and then did the one thing all addicts must do in the battle with addiction: he admitted he was powerless over it.

Admitting powerlessness is not a defeat. It is the first step toward victory. It opens the door to help from a Power greater than the addict's own, greater than any other. Gordon Weekley saw that open door, and walked in—on his knees.

A little more than a year later, when Bill Kauffman resigned his position to pursue another career, the board of directors offered the executive director's position to an ordained minister with eighteen years of experience in the pastorate and eighteen years of experience with alcohol and drug addiction. The offer was not nearly as lucrative as the one tendered to the same man almost simultaneously by Charlotte's Commonwealth Baptist Church. He had been serving as part-time, interim pastor there for several months while the search committee scoured the Southeast for someone to lead them into the future. The search led right back to the interim pastor, and he was highly honored and sorely tempted. In the end, he declined, choosing instead to accept the post at the mission.

Almost immediately the mission, now named Rebound Christian Rehabilitation Center, began to move away from the "three hots and a cot" approach toward a full program of personal counseling and religious education. In the ensuing years, its reputation as a successful treatment center spread throughout the Christian and secular communities. The director found himself speaking to churches and civic groups in Charlotte and across the nation, giving testimony to God's power. Meanwhile, representatives of other missions flocked to Rebound to study the approaches it used.

In the autumn of his life, the director was enjoying spring. Rising every morning at dawn, he tended the garden that was Rebound, writing thank-you letters to contributors or working on notes for the class he would teach later to the men, until breakfast called him away. Then he'd go back to his office and the little studio next to it, where he'd record five-minute messages of inspiration for radio stations in North Carolina and South Carolina.

Later, he might give a luncheon talk to a civic club or a church circle, followed by a nap at the apartment. By midafternoon, his batteries recharged, he resumed his duties at his desk: counseling a troubled client or two, arranging travel to some distant city where he was to give a talk, meeting with his superb staff to discuss daily operations, receiving guests who were often contributors or potential contributors or the parents or spouses of someone who might need the kind of help Rebound could give them.

When fatigue overcame him, it would be ten or eleven at night. He had a full day every day, and they'd have been fuller still without his coworkers' efforts to pull as much work away from him as they could. He had always been a man who couldn't say no, wouldn't say no to anyone in need, and that would never change. What had changed was the way he handled the many burdens he bore. When he crawled beneath the covers at day's end, he left them on the nightstand. And when he awoke in morning, it was always spring.

It was spring that day in 1987 when just under a thousand worshipers at Providence Baptist Church rose from their seats at the end of the thirty-third anniversary service and followed their pastor, Dr. Henry Crouch, and his guest speaker out the doors into the bright noon sun and across the grounds of the beautiful campus. They walked past dogwoods and azaleas, past the fellowship hall and the old sanctuary, past the new activities center with its gymnasium and indoor track until they came at last to the oldest and smallest building on the grounds.

It was the building where it had all begun for the handful of charter members and their new, young pastor. The building was full of memories—of sermons and suppers, of prayer meetings and revivals, of Sunday school classes and circle meetings, of the then-young children of the then-young members squirming in their folding chairs, twisting their feet on the tile floor, and praying for the benediction to come soon so they could race out into the fields that were now covered by the bricks and mortar of a great church.

The tile floor was covered by a deep carpet. The folding chairs had been replaced by rows of beautiful walnut pews facing an altar and a pulpit and a magnificent work of art, a charcoal icon titled "The Departure of Christ."

The entire interior of the building had undergone a metamorphosis. Where once it had had many purposes, it now had only one. It was a place of respite and peace, a chapel. Some day soon, the children of the children of the charter members would marry here. And some day soon, many of the charter members themselves would be brought here for one last visit on their way to Paradise.

But on this day in May in 1987, the newly refurbished building, this serene little house of worship, was being given a name.

The congregation was gathered twenty deep around the front steps to hear the words of the guest speaker, whose name the chapel would bear, who had risen to great heights here and fallen to great depths, but who through it all had never stopped loving and had never stopped being loved: H. Gordon Weekley, Jr.

EPILOGUE

On a spring afternoon in May, 1990, Gordon Weekley walked to the end of a long hallway and tapped on the locked metal door that was the entrance to Ward C. In a few moments, a nurse's face appeared in the small window cut into the door. She undid the lock and swung the door partly open. "May I help you?"

"I'm Reverend Gordon Weekley. I'm here in Morganton to deliver a sermon, and there's something I've been wanting to do for a long time."

"Uh-huh," she said, not knowing where the conversation was going.

"I used to live here a long time ago. And if you don't mind, I'd just like to stick my foot in the door and take it right back out again."

"No, no, I don't mind. Go right ahead."

Slowly, deliberately, he raised his left foot, placed it inside Ward C, and just as slowly withdrew it.

"Thank you," he said, and turned and walked away. "Reverend Weekley?" she called after him. "Yes," he said, stopping to look back at her. "Congratulations," she said, smiling.

*Lead us not Into Temptation*